EDUCATION IN SOVIET UKRAINE

A Study In Discrimination and Russification

БВГДЕЄЖЗИІ Її КЛМНО

EDUCATION IN SOVIET UKRAINE

John Kolasky

СТУФХЦЧШЩЬЮЯАБВ

PETER MARTIN ASSOCIATES

I wish to thank all those who read the manuscript and made suggestions and recommendations and my stenographer who typed patiently through all of its stages.

LA
853
US
K6

Library of Congress   Catalog Card Number: 68-19628

Peter Martin Associates Limited
17 Inkerman Street, Toronto 5, Ontario

Contents

*Dedicated to every Nation and
national minority fighting to
preserve its language, culture
and national dignity*

ILLUSTRATIONS

TABLES

x

Preface

Although I was born in Canada, Ukraine, the land of my parents, always held a strong fascination for me. Wide reading of Soviet Ukrainian publications convinced me it was a free republic in a voluntary union enjoying the widest freedom for development of its language, culture and customs.

In 1963 came an opportunity I had sought for many years: a chance to study in Ukraine. In August of that year I left for Kiev hoping to become familiar with the land of my ancestors, to acquaint myself with its educational system, superior, I believed, to our own and to pursue my study of the Ukrainian language, literature and history at the famous Shevchenko University in Kiev.

I arrived in Kiev at the beginning of September in high spirits; complications, however, soon began to drain my enthusiasm. An ailment which had developed since I left Canada, became progressively more troublesome and necessitated an operation. Misunderstanding also arose about my course of studies and I was informed that Kiev University did not offer a program that would suit my needs.

Over two weeks passed before I was admitted to a hospital for the operation. When I came out there was still the problem of my course of studies which was finally worked out arbitrarily in a way that was disappointing and unsatisfactory to me. Nearly two months after arrival I settled down to the routine life of a student.

It was not long before various aspects of life in Ukraine began to trouble me deeply, especially the fact that everywhere the Russian language was dominant. The party propaganda, that the non-Russians themselves had initiated this natural process of merging all languages into one, proved unconvincing. Daily observation contradicted the official explanation; everywhere in Kiev there was evidence of pressure to impose the Russian language. In addition there were my personal experiences. Many Russians with whom I came in contact displayed open contempt because I spoke Ukrainian. Occasionally there were even insults. Painfully and slowly the realization came that what I had supported as a paragon of justice was, in reality, the worst type of national oppression. The impact of the truth was disturbing and depressing to the point of illness.

Then slowly, like the bright, warm rays of the rising sun, an awareness of popular but covert opposition to Russification began to penetrate through the darkness of despair. My first encouragement came at a public meeting honouring a famous Ukrainian writer who had been condemned as a bourgeois nationalist* during Stalin's time. Opposition became openly manifest during the question period. All was not harmony and brotherly love; the Ukrainians were not accepting Russification.

I had in the meantime been expressing criticism openly and often with vehemence. This had both a positive and a negative effect. I gained the confidence of many Ukrainians who began speaking frankly to me about Russification. Officials, on the other hand, became embarrassed and annoyed. This produced negative side effects.

It is not accepted practice in the USSR for guests to visit institutions on their own. Arrangements are made through an empowered Soviet agency, one of whose members accompanies the visitor and in whose presence all interviews are made. Because I was opposed to Russification and educational institutions were for the most part Russianized, officials were reluctant to arrange visits and continued to put me off by vague promises. Suffice it to

*See Glossary

say that by the end of my first year I had been taken to only one school in Kiev.

It became clear that if I was to study the school system it had to be done on my own. I proceeded by questioning teachers, graduates, pupils and parents; by a careful examination of textbooks, manuals and books on Soviet education; and finally, by visiting institutions on my own. This had its drawbacks because, without arrangements, it was not possible to meet and speak with officials. However I could mingle and speak with students and discuss courses with them. In the case of general education schools this was not possible, but I met many teachers in my travels and in casual conversation they often provided more information than officials who were always on their guard.

In the meantime Russification troubled me more and more. I often lay awake at nights torn with doubts, conflicts and confusion. How I tried to believe that there was no coercion, that this was a natural and inevitable process to which I would eventually become reconciled. But in the morning I was back on the streets where reality rose up to challenge my wishful thinking. Russians were everywhere with their arrogant overbearing attitude; their contempt, sometimes veiled but often overt, for the Ukrainian language; their open display of a feeling of Russian superiority. It made me wonder why Russians, not Ukrainians, occupied so many positions in Kiev.

Then I decided to delve into this problem thoroughly. Much of my spare time I spent in libraries, sifting through any material that was connected with the subject. I tried to follow every lead, to get confirmation for every statement, to verify every unpublished document and to check and evaluate every source.

My investigations began to reveal a planned discrimination against Ukraine and Ukrainians and a conspiracy against the Ukrainian language. I began collecting any published material that could throw light on the subject and sending it home. Simultaneously my attention was drawn to typewritten manuscripts directed against Russification and clandestinely circulated. These too I collected and secretly channelled to Canada.

Toward the end of my term the authorities became suspicious of my dedicated devotion to academic pursuits. My possession of clippings from Soviet periodicals and newspapers and notes from Soviet sources on the national question was apparently deemed a threat to the security of the Soviet state. However by this time there were cartons of books, newspapers and notes in Canada.

In the meantime my health began to break down. The strain, the tension, the overwork, but above all the great sense of disillusionment over the rank injustice to the Ukrainians was simply too much. I arrived back in Canada in August 1965, ill, confused and uncertain as to what to do. At first I felt that on the basis of the evidence I had collected, it would be possible for Canadians of pro-Soviet sympathies to make a private protest to authorities in the USSR in the hope of stopping, if not reversing, the trend of Russification.

In December, 1965, came a great shock: I received reliable information that after my departure mass detentions and interrogations of people opposed to Russification had begun in Kiev. This was followed by reports in the public press of arrests, convictions and exiles. It became clear that in some respects things had not changed since Tsarist times. Nearly 50 years after Tsarism had been overthrown people were still being persecuted for expressions of honest opinion and nearly 120 years after Shevchenko had been sentenced, Ukrainian intellectuals and writers were still following the well-trodden roads to Siberian exile.

Reports of the new persecution convinced me that private protest to Soviet authorities by a small group was not enough, that it was necessary to expose publicly the policies of Russification. Since the topic is broad I have limited it to education, the field that I as a teacher, who studied the educational system of Ukraine for two years at first hand, know best.

Besides published Soviet sources, many of which are not available here, I have used unpublished materials, information collected from individuals and my personal observations. The reader is naturally interested in how, where, when and from whom this was obtained. The problem is that the KGB is interested in precisely the same questions. In all sincerity I can say that the unpublished material is valid beyond a shadow of a doubt. Information collected from individuals was sifted very carefully. All that did not come first hand or could not be confirmed was rejected. There is a great deal of information at my disposal that could not be used because authorities would immediately know or at least suspect from whom it was obtained.

After I began work on this book other developments took place in Canada in connection with Russification. Many Ukrainian Canadians of pro-Soviet sympathies who had visited the USSR, came back very critical, especially on the national question. In March 1966, at the Twelfth Convention of the Association of United Ukrainian Canadians, which has always supported the Soviet Union, Nicholas Oleniuk, a delegate from Toronto, levelled criticism against the national policy pursued in the USSR and fervently condemned Russification. In April 1967, a delegation representing the Communist Party of Canada and the Association of the United Ukrainian Canadians journeyed to Kiev and Moscow to discuss this problem with state and party leaders. It was led by Tim Buck, long-time leader of the Communist Party in Canada, and made up of William Ross, provincial leader of the party in Manitoba and George Solomon, Tony Bilecki, William Harasym and Peter Krawchuk of the AUUC.

Clearly, I am not alone in my concern over the fate of the Ukrainian language and culture. Evidence showing discrimination against Ukraine and Ukrainians, and the campaign of Russification gives conclusive proof of what many have suspected for so long, exposes the falsity of Soviet proclamations of freedom of national development in the USSR and reveals the plight of Ukraine to the public of the democratic world.

JOHN KOLASKY
Toronto, Canada
October, 1967

1

Lenin
and the national question

In addition to the economic and political grievances in the Russian
Empire at the beginning of the twentieth century there was a
deep-rooted, smouldering problem associated with the presence in
the empire of a myriad variety of large and small non-Russian
nations. The basic cause of discontent among these peoples was
the denial of their national rights, the suppression of their native
tongue and the imposition on them of the Russian language.
Marxists in the empire fully recognized the importance of this
problem and devoted much of their attention to it. As early as the
second congress of the Russian Social Democratic Labour Party[1]
in 1903 they outlined in their program a draft constitution which
would guarantee

> The right of the population to be provided education in its native
> language...[2]

At the party conference in 1913 the position on the national
question was elaborated and restated. The resolution of the
gathering declared in favour of:

> ... full equality of rights for all nations and languages, with the
> absence of a compulsory state language (in this case Russian—
> J.K.) and guaranteeing the population schools with instruction
> in all the local languages and the inclusion in the constitution of
> a fundamental law, which would proclaim as illegal any privileges
> whatsoever to any nation and any breach of the rights of the
> national minorities.[3]

Returning to the problem again on the eve of the Bolshevik revolution, the April Conference of the party adopted a resolution on the national question in which it voiced its support for:

> . . . wide local autonomy, abolition of control from above and abolition of a compulsory state language . . .[4]

The inspiration behind the program and resolutions of the party was V. I. Lenin, the son of a Russian school inspector. He grew up with a strong sensitivity to injustice and became involved in Marxist groups while at university. Endowed with great intelligence and a keen analytical mind, he soon emerged as a leading figure in Marxist circles.

His great erudition, personal contact with European civilization and a thorough understanding of the weaknesses and shortcomings of the Tsarist regime made him fully aware of Russia's great possibilities. These, he was convinced, could only be achieved through the application of Marxist theory to produce a socialist society based on the abolition of exploitation and on equal rights for all citizens. Among the latter was to be included equality of national rights.

With the ardour characteristic of a religious zealot, Lenin carried on several campaigns to defend these rights of the national minorities. A central idea in his doctrine was the right of each nation in the Russian Empire to self-determination. He enunciated this most clearly in his article *Ukraine,* written in June 1917. In it he said:

> Cursed Tsarism made Russians persecutors of the Ukrainian people, in every way fostered in them hatred for those who forbad even the children to speak and study in their native language. Revolutionary democracy in Russia, if it wishes to be really revolutionary, really democratic, should break with this past, should regain for itself, for the workers and peasants of Russia, the fraternal faith of the workers and peasants of Ukraine, among them the right to free separation.[5]

On the question of national languages he was as clear, as emphatic and as explicit. In his article, *Critical Notes on the National Question,* he stated:

He is not a Marxist, he is not even a democrat, who does not recognize and does not defend the equality of rights of nations and languages.[6]

He held up as an example Switzerland, where there were

. . . three state languages, but draft laws for referendums are printed in five languages.[7]

After the Bolsheviks took power, the Second All-Russian Congress of Soviets, at their meeting of November 7-8, 1917, declared in favour of the principle of national self-determination.[8] On November 17, Lenin, as chairman of the Council of Peoples' Commissars, issued the *Declaration of Rights of the Peoples of Russia* in which he declared that the policy of the Soviet government on the national question was based on:

1. Equality and Sovereignty of the Peoples of Russia.
2. The Right of the Peoples of Russia to Free Self-Determination to the Point of Separation and Formation of an Independent Government.   . . . . .
4. Free Development of the National Minorities and Ethnographic Groups Inhabiting the Territory of Russia.[9]

National feelings among non-Russian peoples ran high in the revolutionary period. There sprang up several national movements for independence. After the triumph of the Bolsheviks, non-Russians in the Communist Party took up the fight for implementation of the program on the national question. Many Russians had regarded the resolutions and declarations as mere propaganda devices designed to obtain support in the struggle for power. Now that the party was in power they regarded the national question as solved. Lenin criticized most sharply such points of view. At the Eighth Congress of the party in March 1919, he said of such people:

We have in the Commissariat of Education . . . Communists who say: 'One school, therefore do not dare to teach in any other language except Russian.' In my opinion such a Communist is a Great Russian chauvinist.[10]

In December 2-4 of the same year, the Eighth All-Russian Conference of the party adopted a resolution: *Regarding Soviet*

Policy in Ukraine, composed by Lenin and ratified by the plenum of the CC in November. It outlined clearly the party position on the language question and instructed its members as follows:

> In view of the fact that Ukrainian culture (language, schools, etc.) over a period of centuries was suppressed by Tsarism and the exploiting classes of Russia, the CC of the RCP makes it a duty of all members to assist with all means the elimination of all impediments to the free development of the Ukrainian language and culture... Members of the RCP on the territory of Ukraine should enforce in fact the right of the toiling masses to study and converse in all Soviet institutions in their native tongue, counteracting in every way attempts to push aside by all artificial means the Ukrainian language, and transforming it, on the other hand, into a tool of Communist education of the toiling masses.[11]

This was followed on December 5-9 by the Seventh All-Russian Congress of Soviets. In its resolution, *Concerning the Oppressed Nations,* the congress voiced support for "full abolition of all privileges for any national group whatsoever".[12]

In March 1921, the national question was again discussed at the Tenth Congress of the party. Stalin, then Peoples' Commissar of Nationalities, delivered the main report on this problem; it was met by sharp and severe criticism from delegates of the national republics. Among these were two Ukrainians; V. P. Zatonsky who spoke bitterly of the Russian "colonizing element" in Ukraine with its belief in "one indivisible" Russia, pointing out that the national question was not solved by mere slogans,[13] and M. O. Skrypnyk who stated that in Stalin's report the national question "had not been resolved in the least".[14]

Although Lenin, who had delivered the main political report, did not participate (his health was failing) the resolutions committee, guided by previous decisions and declarations of the party, adopted a document which was designed as a step in the practical solution of the national problem. In sharp, unequivocal terms it condemned the previous practice of the old regime as follows:

> The policy of Tsarism, the policy of landlords and the bourgeoisie in relation to these people (non-Russians—*J.K.*) was to kill among them the beginning of statehood, maim their culture, restrict their language, keep them in ignorance and finally, as far as possible, Russify them.[15]

and emphasized that the duties of the party were to help the non-Russian nations

> ... to develop and strengthen their own operative courts, adminis-
> tration, organs of economy and government in their native
> language, made up of local people, who know the customs and
> psychology of the local inhabitants; to develop their own press,
> schools, theatre, clubs and general cultural and educational
> institutions in the native language; to set up and develop a wide
> network of schools and courses of education both general and
> professional-technical in the native language . . .[16]

In the following year it became evident that there was need of an agreement outlining the permanent relationship between the several Soviet republics. In August the Organizational Bureau of the CC of the RCP set up a committee headed by Stalin to prepare a report.

The latter drew up a project on the basis of which the national republics would give up their status as republics and join the RSFSR as autonomous regions. Lenin, although seriously ill, took a deep interest in the problem, subjected the project to severe criticism and proposed instead that the states form a union of Soviet republics. He particularly stressed the principle of equality:

> We acknowledge ourselves as an equal of the UkrSSR and others;
> together with them and as equals we are forming a new union,
> a new federation . . .[17]

On December 30, 1922, the First Congress of Soviets met in Moscow with delegates from the Russian, Ukrainian, Belorussian and Trans-Caucasian Federated Republics (the latter included Georgia, Azerbaidzhan and Armenia) and announced the formation of the Union of Soviet Socialist Republics which was, according to the declaration of the congress,

> . . . a voluntary union of equal nations with equal rights . . . each
> republic is guaranteed the right to free withdrawal from the
> Union . . .[18]

This right of secession was reaffirmed by both the 1924 constitution of the USSR (article 4) and by the second constitution of 1936 (article 17).

Among the areas of administration designed to come under the jurisdiction of the all-union government were foreign affairs, army and navy, foreign trade, means of communications, post and telegraph, and finance. Lenin seemed to have grave doubts about the advisability of giving the central government control of so many ministries. On December 31, 1922, the day following the formation of the USSR, being too ill to write he dictated several lengthy notes which were later made available to the leaders of the republican delegations to the Twelfth Congress of the party. In one of these he advised that

> . . . it is necessary to introduce the strictest rules regarding the use of the national languages in the national republics which are part of our union, and to check these rules very assiduously. There is no doubt that under the pretext of a single railway service, a single fiscal administration etc. with our present apparatus there will appear very many abuses of a purely Russian character . . . Here will be necessary a detailed code, which can be compiled at all successfully only by the nationals living in the given republic. Besides this, we should under no circumstances rule out in advance the possibility that, as a result of all such work, we may retreat at the following congress of Soviets, that is, leave to the Union of Soviet Socialist Republics only the fields of diplomacy and army, and in all other areas renew full independence of the individual national commissariats.[19]

The Twelfth Congress of the party was held in April 1923. Lenin was unable to attend due to illness; Stalin appeared in the capacity of general secretary, to which post he had been elected at the plenum of the CC in April 1922, following the Eleventh Congress of the party. There were sharp and bitter recriminations that the resolutions on the national question were not carried out, especially from the delegates of Ukraine, Kh. H. Rakovsky, chairman of the Council of Peoples Commissars, and M. O. Skrypnyk.

They had good reason to be bitter. Although the old regime had been overthrown and old property relationships were being rapidly and forcefully altered, the old psychology remained. Russians viewed themselves as a great nation with an advanced culture and a great language.[20] They believed that the imposition of this language on the more backward peoples of the empire would be a step in the interest of civilization. Added to this was the arrogance of the Russian officials, born of arbitrary power and undisputed control. The new Soviet Russian officials were bursting with confidence as a result of the party's victory over all internal opposition and external intervention and glowing with pride at being representatives of the "most revolutionary proletariat", the Russian proletariat.

Under the pressure of non-Russian delegates, the congress, in a resolution on the national question, condemned the attitudes of Russian minorities in the national republics concerning the

> . . . superiority of the Russian culture and the advancing of the thesis about the inevitability of the victory of the higher Russian culture over the more backward peoples (Ukrainian, Azerbaidzhan, Uzbek, Kirkhiz, etc.) as nothing more than an attempt to consolidate the domination of the Russian nationality.[21]

It further expressed regret that

> . . . a significant section of Soviet officials in the centre (Moscow — *J.K.*) and locally, regarded the union of republics not as a coalition of equal state entities set up to guarantee the free development of national republics, but as a step in the liquidation of those republics . . .[22]

The congress recommended to the members of the party that

> . . . organs in the national republics and regions be made up for the most part, of local people who knew the language, conditions of life and manners and customs of the people concerned; special laws be passed, which would guarantee the use of the native tongue in all state organs and departments which serve the local national population and the national minorities—laws, which persecute and punish with revolutionary severity all violaters of national rights and especially rights of national minorities.[23]

The truth of the matter is that Lenin, and through him the Soviet government and the Communist party, made their position on the national and language question quite clear: the USSR was to be a union of equal states with the right of each republic to withdraw if it so chose; there was to be equality of all languages with no compulsory state language; each national culture was to develop freely; education, from elementary to higher, was to be conducted in the native language.

FOOTNOTES

1. In 1918 at its Seventh Congress renamed the Russian Communist Party of Bolsheviks; in 1925 at the Fourteenth Congress renamed the All-Union Communist Party of Bolsheviks; in 1952 at the Nineteenth Congress renamed the Communist Party of the Soviet Union.

2. *Komunistychna Partiya Radyanskoho Soyuzu v rezolyutsiyakh i rishennyakh zyizdiv, konferentsiy i plenumiv Ts K* (Communist Party of the Soviet Union in Resolutions and Decisions of Congresses, Conferences and Plenums of the CC), 1898-1954, I, Kiev, 1954, p. 40.

3. Ibid., p. 291.

4. Ibid., p. 322.

5. *V. I. Lenin pro Ukrayinu* (V. I. Lenin on Ukraine), Kiev, 1957, p. 431.

6. Ibid., p. 312.

7. Ibid., p. 323.

8. Akademiya Nauk SSSR, Institut Prava (Academy of Sciences of the USSR, Institute of Law), *Sezdy Sovetov Soyuza SSR, soyuznykh i avtonomnykh sovetskikh sotsialisticheskikh respublik, 1917-1936 gg* (Congresses of the Soviets of the USSR, Union and Autonomous Soviet Socialist Republics, 1917-1936), I, Moscow, 1959, p. 31.

9. Ministerstvo Kultury Ukrayinskoyi RSR (Ministry of Culture of the Ukrainian SSR), *Kulturne Budivnytstvo v Ukrayinskiy RSR* (Cultural Development in the Ukrainian SSR); *Vazhlyvishi rishennya komunistychnoyi partiyi i radyanskoho uryadu 1917-1959 rr.* (More Important Decisions of the Communist Party and the Soviet Government 1917-1959), Collection of Documents, I, 1917-June 1941, Kiev, 1959, p. 1.

10. *Lenin pro Ukrayinu*, p. 504.

11. Ibid., p. 591.

12. *Sezdy Sovetov*, I, p. 103.

13. *Desyaty sezd RKP(b), Mart 1921 goda* (Tenth Congress of the RCP(b), March, 1921), Stenographic Report, Moscow, 1963, pp. 202, 204.

14. Ibid., p. 210.

15. Ibid., p. 603.

16. Ibid., p. 603-604.

17. *Sezdy Sovetov,* III, Moscow, 1960, p. 11.

18. Ibid., p. 17.

19. V. I. Lenin, *Pro natsionalne i natsionalno-kolonialne pytanniya* (Concerning the National and the National-Colonial Question), Kiev, 1957, p. 534-535.

20. One of the most emotional expressions of this Russian nationalism and one that is most often quoted was made by the writer I. S. Turgenev (1818-1883): "In days of doubts, in days of painful meditation on the fate of my native land, you alone are for me a mainstay and a support, oh great mighty upright and free Russian language! Were it not for you how could I help falling into despair in the sight of everything that is happening at home? But one must not believe that such a language was not given to a great nation!" Quoted in: I. K. Bilodid, *Rosiyska mova—mova mizhnatsionalnoho spilkuvannya narodiv SRSR* (Russian Language—the Language of International Communion of the Peoples of the USSR), Kiev, 1962, p. 12.

21. *Komunistychna partiya,* I, p. 666.

22. Ibid., p. 668.

23. Ibid., p. 669.

2

The national question in ukraine from stalin to khrushchov

Modern Ukraine traces its origins to the Kiev state which flourished from the ninth to the twelfth centuries. After the sacking of Kiev by the Tatars in 1239, it fell under their tutelage. At the beginning of the fourteenth century Ukrainian and Belorussian lands, through dynastic ties, became part of the kingdom of Lithuania which allowed them the Orthodox faith, the use of the native tongue and a wide measure of local autonomy under native administrators. Harassed by the Tatars from the South and the Muscovites from the East, Lithuania was obliged to unite with Poland in 1569.

The Poles began to parcel out large tracts of Ukrainian land to their nobles, who brought with them alien customs, language, religion and administration. These intruders soon came into conflict with the free Ukrainian peasant-warriors called Cossacks, who, under a military leader called a hetman, defended the frontiers against the marauding Tatars.

In 1648 Hetman Bohdan Khmelnitsky led the Cossacks in a war against Poland. After a series of brilliant military victories he became the ruler of a free Ukrainian state. Fear of Poland, however, forced Ukraine into a union with Russia in 1654. *The Pereyaslav Agreement,* negotiated by Khmelnitsky, provided for the more culturally-advanced Ukraine the national and political rights of a sovereign sister state.

It was not long before the Russians were making encroachments. The result was constant friction that led to numerous Cossack revolts. Under Hetman Vyhovsky, who succeeded Khmelnitsky, war broke out and a Russian army of 100,000 was decisively defeated by the Cossacks at Konotop in 1659. In 1709 Hetman Mazeppa formed a military alliance with Charles XII of Sweden who was later defeated by the Russians at Poltava. Despite his temporary victory Vyhovsky, and later Mazeppa, was forced to flee abroad; other hetmen ended their days in Siberian exile; some perished in Russian dungeons.

Slowly Ukraine's rights were forcibly whittled away, the hetmanship was abolished in 1764, her economy was ruined, her manpower depleted through constant recruitment for Russian military campaigns, and the towns and their developing industrial enterprises were completely Russianized by a continuous influx of Russians. Eventually Ukraine became an integral part of the Russian empire, subject to Russian laws and administered by Russian officials in the Russian language.

Ukrainian, which had common roots with other Slav languages but had developed independently and produced its own literature, was not even recognized by the Russians as a separate language. In 1863, P. O. Valuev, the Minister of Internal Affairs, who is famous for his statement "There was not; there is not; there can never be such a thing as the Ukrainian language", issued a circular which forbade the printing of Ukrainian books for schools. Nominally literary works were allowed, but censorship was so restrictive that few were actually published.

National restrictions and harsh economic conditions fostered discontent and the development of the revolutionary movement in Ukraine. This took two paths: there were branches of the RSDLP supported mainly by Russian urban workers, and Ukrainian parties whose support ranged from peasants in the villages to Ukrainian workers and intelligentsia in the cities. The former emphasized economic injustice and regarded Ukraine as an integral part of Russia; the latter placed the main emphasis on the national problem, advocating a socialist federation of all nations comprising the Russian empire, on the basis of equality and local autonomy. With the overthrow of the Tsar in March 1917, Ukrainians organized the Central Rada which advocated autonomy and eventually on January 22, 1918, proclaimed Ukrainian independence.

The members of the RSDLP in Ukraine held a congress in Moscow in July 1918 and formed the Communist Party of Ukraine as a component and integral part of the RCP. The name alone indicates the thinking of the founders on the national question: the parent body was the Russian Communist Party: the new organization was named the Communist Party of Ukraine. A majority of the delegates and the members of the CC were not Ukrainian and the party newspaper was in Russian. In the ensuing civil war the CPU, supported by armies from Russia, established Soviet power in Ukraine.

In the twenties some of the more radical members of the Ukrainian revolutionary parties that had supported the Central Rada, joined the CPU. There were also recruits from among Ukrainians who immigrated from Western Ukraine (a part that remained under Poland) and from the native Ukrainian population. Together with the old guard Ukrainian Communists, such as Petrovsky, Chubar, Zatonsky and Skrypnyk, the Ukrainians became a formidable force in the party. On the basis of decisions of the congresses of the RCP, proclamations of the government of the USSR and the teachings of Lenin, they began, ardently supported by Ukrainian intelligentsia, the Ukrainianization of party and government apparatus and, above all, of the educational system.

However, the majority of members in the party in Ukraine remained Russian till the late 1920's. They and the Russianized non-Ukrainians held many top posts in the party and the government. The attitude of these elements to Ukrainianization ranged from opposition to outright hostility. They buttressed their position with the "theory of the struggle of two cultures", according to which the more advanced Russian culture of the city proletariat would inevitably conquer the backward Ukrainian culture of the peasantry.

This theory was subjected to severe criticism at the Seventh Conference of the CPU, April 4-10 1923.[1] Immediately after the Twelfth Congress of the RCP, the plenum of the CC of the CPU, on June 22 1923, issued a decree which provided for intensified Ukrainianization of state, party and trade union organizations.[2]

This was followed by another decree of the Council of Peoples Commissars of Ukraine on July 27 of the same year, whose purpose was to provide

... the Ukrainian people with education in the native language ...[3]

It instructed the ministry of education to take

... wide measures for the training of new pedagogical personnel, who would be fluent in the Ukrainian language, in order to guarantee both the elementary and higher schools with Ukrainian instructors.
... steps to train in the scientific research institutes new staffs of professors who would know perfectly the Ukrainian language.[4]

The minister of education was O. Ya. Shumsky, a former member of a Ukrainian revolutionary party, who joined the CPU in 1920. He held various posts: member of the CC of the CPU, chief of its Agitation and Propaganda Department and editor of *Chervony Shlyakh (Red Pathway)*, a monthly literary journal. Shumsky advocated rapid and total Ukrainianization of all aspects of life and opposed the directing of non-Ukrainians to fill government and party positions. He came into conflict with Lazar Kaganovich, the general secretary of the CPU, whom he wanted to replace with V. Ya. Chubar, a Ukrainian who had joined the Bolshevik party in 1907. Kaganovich, supported by Stalin and the central party apparatus, began a campaign of vilification against his opponent and Shumsky was forced to resign in March 1927, after which he disappeared from the political scene.[5]

In his place was appointed M. O. Skrypnyk, no less a supporter of the Ukrainianization policy, but a man of greater influence and prestige and considerably more tact. The son of a railroad worker, he became interested in the revolutionary movement while studying in Kharkiv. He joined the RSDLP in 1897 and from then dedicated his life to the party and the revolutionary movement. He was arrested fifteen times, sentenced to a total of thirty-four years imprisonment, exiled seven times and on one occasion sentenced to death. In 1917 Skrypnyk was present at the meeting of the CC which decided on the Bolshevik uprising and he served as a member of the committee that organized it. Shortly after, on Lenin's suggestion, he was directed to Ukraine as the representative of the CC of the party.

Following the civil war in which he actively participated, Skrypnyk at various times held the Ukrainian posts of secretary of Workers'-Peasants' Inspection, Attorney-General, Peoples' Commissar of Internal Affairs, of Justice, of Education, vice-chairman of the Council of Peoples' Commissars and chairman of the State Planning Commission.

He was a member of the CC of the CPU, the CC of the RCP and the Executive Committee of the Communist International, six times delegate to its congresses and leader of the Ukrainian delegation. In the inner party struggles he supported Stalin against the opposition. Among the honours bestowed on him were the Order of the Red Banner and the Order of the Red Banner of Labour.

From his prolific pen flowed many works on art, literature, culture, history of the party, and the national question. In recognition of his contribution in the cultural field, he was made a member of the Communist Academy of the USSR and academician of the Academy of Sciences of the UkrSSR and the Belorussian SSR. There was no doubt that Skrypnyk was the most talented and outstanding Ukrainian in the CPU.

He proceeded quietly, methodically and thoroughly to carry through his policies. On July 3, 1927, the CC of the party in Ukraine issued a decree on the work of Kharkiv University. The clause on Ukrainianization of staff and students is a characteristic description of the procedure followed in higher educational institutions. It reads as follows:

> To hasten the tempo of Ukrainianization of the university. In the first year courses to leave instruction in Russian in only one

group. Russian groups, which, according to plan, are being left
in the second and third year courses, should during the year
master completely the Ukrainian language and in 1928-29 change
over fully to the Ukrainian language. 1928-29 is the deadline for
the Ukrainianization of the lectorial staff . . .[6]

On July 6 there was a major breakthrough in the drive to put
into practice Lenin's maxims on the national question. The All-
Ukrainian Central Executive Committee and the Council of
Peoples' Commissars issued the decree *Concerning the Guaranteeing
of Equal Rights of Languages and the Assisting of the Development
of Ukrainian Culture.* It provided for instruction in the students'
native language in elementary, vocational and higher educational
institutions; and for the teaching of both Ukrainian and Russian
languages in all schools. This meant that for all significant
minorities—Jewish, German, Bulgarian, Belorussian, Moldavian
and Greek, there would be instruction in their native tongue. The
remaining schools would be in Ukrainian. This was a blow to the
hegemony of the Russian language. Of special significance for
education were the following articles:

35. To the post of professor or lecturer in the higher educational
institutions, it is permissible to appoint only individuals who
can lecture in the Ukrainian language.
38. Enrolling in post-graduate studies of individuals who do not
know the Ukrainian language to the extent required by the
Peoples' Commissariat of Education of the UkrSSR is not
permissible.[7]

The process of Ukrainianization of education among the
7,000,000 Ukrainians in the RSFSR had also been proceeding for
several years, but at an abnormally slow pace. There were many
demands for schools in the native tongue for Ukrainian children
in this area. Skrypnyk had placed the question most sharply at the
Twelfth Congress of the RCP in 1923.[8] In October 1927, the Peoples'
Commissar of Education, A. V. Lunacharsky, issued a circular in
which he pointed out that there were only 236 such schools and
outlined plans for the intensification of the process of introduction
of education in the native tongue to Ukrainian children in the
RSFSR.[9] As a result many Ukrainian schools sprang up in various

areas of the RSFSR where Ukrainians lived. In the Kuban area in Northern Caucasus where there lived over two million Ukrainians, descended from Cossacks settled there two centuries before, Ukrainianization took deep roots. Ukrainian became the language of party and Soviet institutions. In Krasnodar there was a Ukrainian pedagogical institute and in Stanitsa Poltavska a pedagogical technicum (teachers' college), which trained Ukrainian teachers for the schools in Kuban.

The application of Skrypnyk's policy in Ukraine seemed to be going well; on November 1 he was able to report to the Tenth Congress of the CPU the following breakdown in percent for language of instruction:

Schools	Ukrainian	Russian
General education	79.1	7.1*
Vocational	51.9	27.6
Technicums	54.0	16.7
Institutes	28.5	45.8[10]

*Instruction in the remaining was probably either mixed, or in the languages of other significant minorities in Ukraine.

This was remarkable progress and the future seemed promising, indeed. The policy of the government of Ukraine however, had been subjected to sharp attacks by the leadership of the Communist Party of Western Ukraine on the grounds that Ukrainianization was protracted and incomplete, and by Russian chauvinistic elements because of the CPU's zealous pursuit of Ukrainianization. The CPU appealed to the Communist International. The latter body replied that

> The Executive Committee of the Communist International fully commends the policy of the CC of the CPU . . .[11]

This approval of the highest Communist authority gave further impetus to the Ukrainianization drive. In May 1929, the Eleventh All-Ukrainian Congress of Soviets fully approved the policy being carried out regarding the national question, recommended that the government intensify this work and noted the following percent achievements in Ukrainianization of education:

Schools	Ukrainian	Russian
General education	81.0	7.1*
Vocational	55.1	11.3
Technicums	54.0	16.7
Institutes	30.0	18.9[12]

*In the case of the first three categories above, the remaining schools were in the language of national minorities; in the case of the institutes, the rest were either mixed or in the languages of national minorities.

This was the high-water mark of Ukrainianization; by this time Ukrainian as the official language was well established, but this fact was never accepted by the Russian minority. Many stories are told of their attitude of open contempt and hostility. Some regarded Ukrainian as a mere dialect, some as an invention of the Germans. One Russian official when spoken to in Ukrainian replied, "Do not speak to me in that non-human tongue." Another, when addressed in Ukrainian, retorted, "Speak to me in a comprehensible language."

Officials who chafed under the regulation that provided for dismissal of those who failed to learn the Ukrainian language often related the following dialogue between two officials:

Is Ukrainian a language or a dialect?
Neither. It is an excuse to dismiss a person from his position.

The author had an interesting but unpleasant experience that illustrates the Russian contempt for the period of Ukrainianization. In a government department in Kiev I addressed a totally strange official who later turned out to be a Russian as so many officials in Ukraine are. My request was made politely in Ukrainian; he replied gruffly in Russian. I then rebuked him very sharply for replying in Russian to a request made in Ukrainian in Kiev, the capital city of Ukraine. He replied just as sharply, "This is not the period of Skrypnyk."

By the end of the 1920's black clouds were already gathering on the Ukrainian horizon. Stalin had overcome all opposition and emerged as undisputed master in the CC. Although undeniably a

man of outstanding ability, singleness of purpose and steadfastness
to a cause, he had been hardened to the point of callousness and
brutality by Tsarist persecution, arrests and exiles. His devotion
to the socialist cause gradually became overshadowed by a thirst
for power and fame arising from a deep sense of inferiority engendered by the hardships and grinding poverty of his childhood.
Eventually he imagined himself as the very embodiment of the
great cause of socialism and viewed an attack on his person as an
attack on the ideal. Each new victorious encounter with an
opponent made him more arbitrary and domineering; each new
success increased his confidence and nourished his arrogance.
Finally he emerged as the infallible prophet marshalling his forces
to usher in a new world order.

He had always exhibited a deep interest in the national
problem and his writings brought him recognition as the foremost
Marxist authority on the subject. In November 1917, he was
elected Peoples' Commissar of Nationalities. Stalin always
appeared to be in the forefront of the fight for national rights
without, apparently, antagonizing Russian nationalistic and
chauvinistic elements. In 1922 he was elected general secretary of
the party, in which post he began quietly, carefully and methodically to appoint to party positions the servile lackeys and henchmen
who would do his bidding. Simultaneously he carefully weeded out
and discredited men whom he could not dominate, men of personal
initiative and independent will.

Before his death Lenin keenly sensed and was deeply disturbed
by the potential danger of a man of Stalin's character in the key
position of general secretary. In January 1923, too ill to write, he
dictated a letter in which he said:

> Stalin is too rude and this defect, although quite tolerable in our
> midst and in dealings among us Communists, becomes intolerable
> in a General Secretary. That is why I suggest that the comrades
> think about a way of removing Stalin from that post and appoint-
> ing somebody else differing in all other respects from Comrade
> Stalin solely in the degree of being more tolerant, more loyal,
> more polite and more considerate to the comrades, less capricious,
> etc.[13]

But Lenin was dying and Stalin was well entrenched. He remained the general secretary.

There is good reason to suspect that a wide discrepancy existed between his professions on the national question and his convictions and future plans of action. He seems to have viewed the development of national cultures and wide local national autonomy in the non-Russian republics as a threat to the centralization he deemed necessary in order for the USSR to survive in a hostile capitalist environment. As early as 1926 he also expressed the fear that:

> . . . in view of the weakness of the independent Communist cadres in Ukraine, this movement, which is very frequently led by non-Communist intellectuals, may here and there assume the character of a struggle to alienate Ukrainian culture and public life from general Soviet culture and public life . . .[14]

In 1929 he began the drive to collectivise the peasantry. The first victims were the middle peasants, the conscious national elements who formed the backbone of the Ukrainian nation. In 1930 he embarked on a campaign to behead the Ukrainian rebirth with the arrest and open trial of forty-five Ukrainian intellectuals, who were accused of being members of a secret anti-Soviet organization, the Union for the Liberation of Ukraine. This was followed by more arrests and secret trials. Eventually all such formalities were dispensed with; people were simply taken away during the night and deported, to vanish without a trace.

The campaign was highlighted in January 1933, by the dispatching to Ukraine from Moscow of nearly 15,000 functionaries of various rank to occupy such positions as chairmen and secretaries in collective farms, district secretaries of the Party, chairmen of district executive committees and secretaries of regional committees of the CPU. In the contingent was V. A. Balitsky, the new Commissar of State Security for Ukraine and P. P. Postyshev, emissary of the CC in Moscow and new first secretary of the Kharkiv Regional Committee and secretary of the CC of the CPU.

The takeover of Ukraine by the central government was complete. Skrypnyk was dismissed as Minister of Education and the drive against "Ukrainian nationalists" began on an unprecedented scale. On November 21, less than ten months after he arrived, Postyshev was able to report the ousting of over 2,000 "nationalist elements" from the Department of Education, over 300 scientific and editorial workers, 200 who occupied positions as managers of departments and sections in eight central organizations and nearly 1,000 from the cooperative and grain procurement agencies.[15] Needless to say people were arrested after their dismissal and shot or exiled to the northern reaches of the great "Motherland" where most of them perished without a trace.

This, however, was but the beginning. Between 1930 and 1935 a total of 15 "conspiracies" against the Soviet government were "uncovered", dragging to their doom thousands of innocent members of the Ukrainian intelligentsia. The climax came in 1937 with the arrest of all the members of the Ukrainian government, all the members of the Politburo of the CPU and nearly all other leading communists in Ukraine. By 1938, through arrest, exile, starvation and firing squad, nearly all Ukrainian intellectuals were eliminated, including writers, historians, artists, philologists, scientists; almost all party and government officials including most of the old Ukrainian Bolsheviks; about a quarter of the peasantry, who starved to death in the famine of 1932-33 which was caused by forced appropriation of all grain; countless numbers of officials, large and small, in all walks of life.

In 1932 began the drive to close all Ukrainian schools in the RSFSR. In some areas this was accompanied by the most summary methods. In the Kuban, an area in Northern Caucasus settled predominantly by Ukrainian Cossacks in the eighteenth, and Ukrainian peasants from the Poltava and Chernihiv regions in the nineteenth centuries, the populace was unable to fulfill their unrealistic grain delivery quotas. In November 1932, the large community of Stanitsa Poltavska was surrounded by detachments of the GPU, all 30,000 inhabitants—men, women and children— were herded together with only their few personal belongings and deported to Siberia. In their place were brought in peasants from Russia. The following day the Krasnodar regional paper announced that the Ukrainian-nationalist-Petlura nest* in Kuban had been liquidated. The settlement was renamed Stanitsa Krasnoarmey-skaya. The Ukrainian language was abolished in the schools of Kuban and the teachers were deported. The whole operation was directed by Molotov and Kaganovich from headquarters in Krasnodar.

Russians were no longer forced to use Ukrainian in state and party institutions. But Ukrainians who remained in official posts attempted to carry on the dogged struggle for Ukrainianization. Even as late as June 1937, on the verge of mass arrests of all top Ukrainian state and party officials, the Thirteenth Congress of the CPU declared in its resolution that

> . . . in the work of a number of organizations of the CPU lately appeared a weakening of attention to the question of the national policy of the party and an underestimation of the importance of this question. This is revealed mainly in the inadequate Ukrain-ianization of party, state and especially trade union and YCL organizations, in the inadequacy of the promotion of Bolshevik Ukrainian personnel to leading party, state, economic and trade union work.[16]

In March 1938, an about-turn was made on the question of Ukrainianization. With the arrests of the leading party and government personnel in Ukraine, a new army of officials arrived from Moscow to take over. It was headed by N. S. Khrushchov. He immediately denounced his predecessors in the vilest language. Speaking to the Fourth Kiev Regional Party Conference he called them

> . . . enemies of the people, bourgeois nationalists, agents of our enemies . . . agents of fascist intelligence . . . mercenaries . . . Polish, German, Japanese spies . . . miserable traitors . . . villians. The Yakirs, Balitskys, Lyubchenkos, Zatonskys[16] and other scum wished to make Ukrainian workers and peasants the slaves of fascism.[17]

After 1937 there was no more talk of Ukrainianization; the emphasis changed to glorification of the Russian language. On

*See Glossary

June 16, 1938, Khrushchov announced at the Fourteenth Congress of the CPU:

> Comrades, now all nations study the Russian language because the Russian workers were the first . . . to raise the banner of revolt . . .[18]

The following day the congress passed a resolution in which it

> . . . underlined with special emphasis the indispensability of liquidating the consequences of the hostile sabotage in the teaching of the Russian language in the elementary and secondary schools and also in the higher educational institutions. Bourgeois nationalists, Trotskyites, Bukharinites acted basely and foully in order to drive out the great Russian language from our schools and higher educational institutions. The efforts of the Trotsky-ites, Bukharinites and bourgeois nationalists were directed toward the alienation of the Ukrainian people from the fraternal friendship with the great Russian people, toward the alienation of Soviet Ukraine from the USSR and the renewal of capitalist slavery.[19]

Russian gradually began to assume again the status of official language, but Ukrainian was still widely used both in the state and party apparatus and in schools. Entrance examinations to higher educational institutions included both the Ukrainian and Russian languages, and institutes advertised courses in both. At the Sixteenth Congress of the all-union party in 1930, Stalin pointed out that not only was there no merging of languages in the USSR, but that it was impolitic to think of promoting such a merger because

> There is a Ukraine which is part of the USSR. But there is also another Ukraine which forms part of other states.[20]

In other words, it was tactically unwise to start a planned campaign to Russify Ukraine while parts of it were under Poland, Romania and Czechoslavakia.

After Poland was attacked by Hitler in 1939 and the Western region of Galicia was added to Ukraine, the Council of the Peoples' Commissars of the UkrSSR on March 4, 1940, passed a decree

> To introduce instruction in the schools of the western regions of Ukraine in the native tongue.[21]

The subsequent war brought many changes: to arouse patriotism there began the glorification of the "Great Russian people" and former Tsarist generals. With the defeat of Nazi Germany the USSR emerged as a great power. The victory was too often attributed to Russia; the other fourteen Soviet republics were forgotten. Russian nationalism and Soviet patriotism became synonymous. After demobilization many Russians settled in Ukraine. New factories were constructed and old ones rebuilt. Many of the specialists to man them came from Russia. Schools and higher educational institutions were reopened. Too often the language of instruction was Russian. Ukraine was now firmly unified under the solid protection of the "elder brother". There was no more need, for tactical reasons, to maintain the Ukrainian language.

The death of Stalin in 1953 gave rise to a new struggle for power between the members of the party hierarchy. Beria, hoping by this manoeuver to gain support of the non-Russians, wrote a memorandum to the CC that the national policy was anti-Leninist and that the national republics should be given more freedom to develop their languages and cultures. There were immediate repercussions in several republics, including Ukraine. A plenum was held of the CC of the CPU at which L. G. Melnikov, the Russian first secretary, was relieved of his post and dropped from the bureau because of his

> ... distortion of the Leninist-Stalinist national policy of our party manifested by the practice of promoting to leading party and government posts in the western regions of Ukraine mainly workers from other regions of the Ukrainian SSR and also in the changing of lecturing in the Western Ukrainian higher educational institutions to the Russian language.[22]

It was apparently deemed unwise to speak the truth and say that many of those promoted to leading party and government posts in Western Ukraine were Russians sent from Russia on the instructions of the central organs in Moscow and that schools and educational institutions in all parts of Ukraine were being Russianized. Nevertheless, it appeared as if Ukraine was on the threshold of a new, more liberal era. Then suddenly Beria was arrested, sentenced and shot. Criticism of Russification was denounced as an attempt to undermine the friendship of the Soviet peoples.

Another contender for the vacant leadership, Khrushchov, used a bolder approach: he denounced his former master and proceeded to rehabilitate the victims, among them those he himself had vilified so enthusiastically in 1937, and promised the national republics that he would work to promote cultures that were "national in form and socialist in content".[23] Millions sighed with relief. By 1957 he was firmly in control and began introducing many changes. On the national question he went a step further along the road paved by his master; Stalin had destroyed the architects and engineers of Ukrainianization; Khrushchov embarked on the policy of destroying the Ukrainian language itself, by undertaking to replace it with the Russian language in the schools of Ukraine.

FOOTNOTES

1. *Komunistychna partiya Ukrayiny v rezolyutsiyakh i rishennyakh zyizdiv i konferentsiy 1918-1956* (The Communist Party of Ukraine in Resolutions and Decisions of Congresses and Conferences 1918-1956), Kiev, 1958, p. 175.

2. *Kulturne budivnytstvo*, I, pp. 229-232.

3. Ibid., p. 239.

4. Ibid., pp. 239-241.

5. In 1936 Shumsky was arrested on a charge of being a member of a conspiratorial anti-Soviet organization. According to a high party official whom I knew, he survived the Siberian prison camps and was released after Stalin's death. The years of exile did not break him or alter his convictions. In prison he wrote a lengthy work in which he attempted to justify his position and after his release he began the long journey to Moscow with it, but died on the way. According to my informant he has not been rehabilitated because in his treatise he expressed nationalist ideas.

6. *Kulturne budivnytstvo*, p. 359.

7. *Visti*, July 22, 1927.

8. *Dvenadtsyaty sezd rosiyskoy kommunisticheskoy partii (bolshevikov)* (The Twelfth Congress of the Communist Party [Bolsheviks]), Stenographic Report, April 17-25, 1923, Moscow, 1923, pp. 522-523.

9. *Visti,* October 25, 1927.

10. *Visti,* November 1, 1927.

11. Quoted in Skrypnyk's speech to the Fifteenth Congress of the All-Union Communist Party. See *Visti,* December 13, 1927.

12. *Kulturne budivnytstvo,* I, pp. 450-451.

13. *Lenin's Last Letters and Articles,* Progress Publishers, Moscow, (no date, probably 1964), p. 8. Lenin's expressed wish was that after his death, the letter be communicated to the regular party congress. Consequently, it was read to the delegates of the Thirteenth Party Congress, May, 1924, but not published until after Khrushchov's revelations of Stalin's crimes at the Twentieth Congress in 1956.

14. J. Stalin, *Works,* VIII, Foreign Language Publishing House, Moscow, 1954, p. 160.

15. P. P. Postyshev, *Borotba za Leninsko-Stalinsku natsionalnu polityku partiyi* (The Struggle for the Lenin-Stalin Nationality Policies of the Party), Kiev, 1935, pp. 64-65.

16. *Komunistychna partiya Ukrayiny,* pp. 586-587.

17. *Visti,* June 8, 1938. Ya. E. Yakir had been a member of the party since 1917. When arrested in 1937 he commanded the Ukrainian Military District. He was shot with Marshal Tukhachevsky and other military leaders in 1937. V. A. Balitsky, chief of the secret police in Ukraine was arrested in 1937, and exiled to Siberia, where he disappeared without a trace. P. P. Lyubchenko joined the party in 1920. From 1934-1937 he was the chairman of the Council of Peoples' Commissars of Ukraine. When the terror began in 1937 he shot himself. V. P. Zatonsky a member of the RSDLP since 1905, was Minister of Education when arrested in 1937. He was called out while attending the theatre with his wife and never heard from again. All except Balitsky have now been rehabilitated.

18. *Visti,* June 16, 1938.

19. *Kulturne budivnytstvo,* I, p. 751.

20. J. Stalin, op. cit., XIII, p. 7.

21. *Kulturne budivnytstvo,* I, p. 808.

22. *Pravda,* July 13, 1953.

23. *XX Sezd Kommunisticheskoy Partii Sovetskogo Soyuza, 14-25 fevralya, 1956* (Twentieth Congress of the Communist Party of the Soviet Union, February 14-25, 1956). Stenographic Report, Moscow, 1956, I, p. 91.

3

Khrushchov's
new law on education

Unprecedented Russification in education was begun shortly after
Khrushchov ousted the so-called "anti-party group" of Molotov,
Malenkov, Kaganovich and others in June 1957 and became
supreme in the CC. Its basis was laid by a number of "theoretical"
propaganda articles, the most important of which appeared in the
organ of the CC of the CPSU under the authorship of a Tadzhik
scholar, director of the Institute of Oriental Studies of the Academy
of Sciences of the USSR and former first secretary of the CP of the
Tadzhik SSR. He criticized "nationalist survivals of the past",
emphasized the growing importance of the Russian language which
had become "the second native language" for non-Russians and
asserted that in a Communist society "the disappearance of
national differences and merging of nations will become inevitable"
with a resulting "development of a single language".[1]

Having laid the theoretical foundations, Khrushchov and the
party leadership began to unfold a plan of reducing the national
cultures and languages of the non-Russian peoples of the USSR
to the common Russian denominator. This was achieved by a bold
scheme to abolish non-Russian schools. On November 16, 1958,
were published the theses of the CC of the CPSU and the Council
of Ministers of the USSR *Regarding the Strengthening of the*

Relationship of School and Life and for the Further Development of the System of Public Education in the USSR, which proposed sweeping changes to improve and expand education, especially technical and vocational. Public interest was centred around clause 19 which reads as follows:

> In the Soviet schools instruction is conducted in the native language. This is one of the more important achievements of the Leninist national policy. At the same time in the union and autonomous republics is also studied the Russian language which is a great means of international communication, of strengthening of friendship among the peoples of the USSR and of introducing them to the treasures of Russian and world cultures.
>
> Nevertheless, we must not fail to take into account that in connection with language study in the union and autonomous republics there is a great overloading of children. As a matter of fact, in the national schools the children study three languages: their native tongue, Russian and a foreign one.
>
> Consideration should be given to the question of delegating to parents the right of deciding to which school, with what language of instruction they wish to send their children. If a child is in a school where instruction is in the language of one of the union or autonomous republics he can, if he wishes, also study the Russian language. And vice versa, a child, attending a Russian school, may, if he wishes, study one of the languages of the union or autonomous republics . . .
>
> Granting the parents the right to choose which language the child must study, appears as the most democratic presentation of the problem, eliminating the resolving of this important question by administrative decree and liquidating excessive burdening of pupils with the study of languages . . .[2]

The clause is a classic example of deceit and hypocrisy. In the first instance it proclaims that instruction is in the native tongue of the pupils and hails this as one of the "achievements of Leninist national policy"; in the second breath it proposes to give parents a "choice" that violates this very principle, after emphasizing that Russian "is a great means of international communication, of strengthening of friendship among the peoples of the USSR". Who could risk undermining such "friendship" or "international communication"?

Furthermore, Russian is the language used in higher educational institutions, in government, industry and commerce. One cannot enter a higher educational institution or obtain worthwhile employment without a knowledge of Russian. The party and government had been proclaiming the great role and importance of the Russian language and the declining role of the others. In addition, people who insisted on perpetuating their national languages and customs were denounced as bourgeois nationalists. How could there be an alternative to the Russian language under such circumstances? There is as much choice as in elections. Soviet citizens have an anecdote based on a bible story to illustrate this. They say that after God created Eve he said to Adam, "Now choose for yourself a wife".

The customary procedure in the USSR was for the party and government to draft decrees which were then hailed by the censored press and "enthusiastically" and "unanimously" approved by legislative bodies and the people. It was anticipated by the hierarchy that such would be the case with the school law. However, Krushchov had opened the dike to criticism by his revelations of the crimes of Stalin, sweeping away the aura of infallibility surrounding party leaders. In addition the political climate had somewhat moderated and people felt more free to speak out.

The result was a growing tendency to question, criticize and oppose unpopular policies. When the new law was proposed for discussion the unexpected and unprecedented happened: a veritable flood of criticism began to sweep down from the national republics. The non-Russians rejected Soviet magnanimity concerning "democratic" procedure in the choice of the language of instruction in schools. They understood very well what was at stake and came out for the status quo on this question. First to publicly criticize article 19 was V. T. Latsis, holder of the honour of National Writer of the Latvian SSR, winner of the State Premium of the USSR, member of the Supreme Soviet of the USSR and CC of the CP of Latvia, and chairman of the Council of Ministers of the Latvian SSR. Latsis had lived in Siberia from 1917 to 1921 when he returned to his native Latvia and worked as fisherman, sailor, stevedore and lumberjack. He joined the Communist Party in 1928 and participated in the Communist underground movement. During the war he was one of the partisan leaders in Latvia. Less than two weeks after the publication of the theses he said:

> It is most expedient to carry on the study of the Latvian language in the Russian schools of Soviet Latvia. To work effectively in a republic a man needs a knowledge of the national language. Abolition of compulsory study of the Russian and Latvian languages in the schools will hardly promote the strengthening of friendship of peoples.[3]

The precedent set by Latsis was followed three days later by V. P. Mzhavanadze, a former lieutenant-colonel in the Red Army, a long-time party functionary, first secretary of the Communist Party of Georgia since 1953, a member of the CC of the CPSU and alternative member of its presidium. Like Latsis he advocated the study of two languages—Russian and Georgian.[4]

At the session of the Supreme Soviet of the USSR in December, representatives of Belorussia, Ukraine, Moldavia, Latvia, Lithuania, Estonia, Georgia, Armenia, Azerbaidzhan and Kirgizia opposed the principle of "choice" and argued for the status quo: compulsory teaching of Russian and the local language in all schools.[5] I. V. Abashidze, a representative from Georgia, criticized those who lived in the national republics but did not learn the local language and fervently added:

> Comrade deputies! We must not set up the Russian and the local indigenous language one against the other by allowing people to choose between them. Both for us are native tongues, both are necessary and both are obligatory . . . Furthermore it seems to us that delegating to the parents the right of deciding to which school, with what language of instruction they wish to send their children, does not conform to the common requirements of Soviet schools.[6]

From many of the speeches it was clear that there was widespread opposition in the republics to article 19. Among those emphasizing this point was A. Ya Pelshe, a corresponding member of the Academy of Sciences of the Latvian SSR and second secretary of the Communist Party of Latvia, who had lived, been educated and held many important party and academic posts in the USSR prior to returning to Latvia after it became an integral part of the USSR in 1940. In his speech he said that the theses had been widely discussed in his country and emphasized that:

> The workers of the republic, especially at parents' meetings, unanimously express the necessity to continue in our republic the teaching of both languages—the Latvian and the Russian.[7]

The Uzbek delegates did not express opposition to article 19 at the session of the Supreme Soviet of the USSR. However, at the Twenty-first Congress of the party the following year, one of Uzbekistan's most prominent sons raised his voice. He was N. A. Mukhitdinov, who at various times had been chairman of the Council of Ministers of the Uzbek SSR; first secretary of the CC of the CP of Uzbekistan; deputy of the Supreme Soviet of the USSR; member of the CC of the CPSU, of its presidium and one of its secretaries; member of government and party delegations to China and Egypt; leader of Soviet delegations to Indonesia, Vietnam and China; representative of the Soviet government at State celebrations in Liberia and holder of many medals and two orders of Lenin. Like opponents of Russification with whom I had become acquainted while living in the USSR, he enlisted the authority of the leader of the Russian revolution. Speaking on behalf of all non-Russians he said:

> ... The great Lenin warned that "nothing will hinder the develop- ment and strengthening of proletarian class solidarity like national injustice and that 'offended' nationals are not as sensi- tive to anything as they are to the feeling of equality and the violation of that equality even though through carelessness or in jest". (Works, Vol. 36, pp. 556-557) Being himself very sensitive and considerate, Lenin sternly condemned the smallest mani- festation of nihilistic, scornful and haughty attitudes to national differences and feelings.
> Every nation is proud of its history, culture and the contri- bution it has made to the development of world civilization. We should in every way support such noble sentiments, remembering at the same time that national cultures are being continually enriched by all the values created by mankind.
> Our country is multinational and consequently multilingual. Each nation lawfully aspires to develop its national language in every way. But every nation of our Fatherland has the highest

love and regard for the Russian language which serves as a great means of communication among them. Everyone knows how great is the gravitation to the study of the Russian language all over the world. The great Russian language has become one of the most widely used and recognized languages by which mankind communicates. Therefore, during the nation-wide discussion of the question of reorganization of the system of national education correct emphasis was placed on the necessity of studying both the local as well as the Russian language in the national schools of the republics. This benevolent aspiration of the Soviet people for the mastery of the local and the Russian languages must be given serious attention.[8]

I have purposely given the backgrounds of some of the critics of article 19 and lengthy quotations from their speeches to show that, even among the most prominent non-Russians who have risen to the highest posts in the Soviet hierarchy, opposition to Russification is very strong.

The Russians regard such expressions as sheer bourgeois nationalism. During my stay in Ukraine I spent periods of time on several occasions with various Russian officials whom I came to know quite well. They would criticize the regime's waste, bungling and burearcracy; voice opposition to it on account of shortages; relate anecdotes by the score poking fun at officials, policies and sacred dogmas; but on the national question they stood as one for the hegemony of Russia and the Russian language. One day I raised the question of the school law. Although often boiling internally because of their naked chauvinism, I always repressed my feeling and they considered me in agreement. I remember so well their characterization of opponents of article 19 as individuals who were stirring up national prejudices.

Many people in Ukraine informed me that the theses on education were widely discussed there. This was confirmed by I. A. Kairov, the former Minister of Education of the RSFSR and president of its Academy of Pedagogical Sciences, speaking to the Supreme Soviet of the USSR. According to him, in Ukraine

> . . . there were more than 90,000 meetings and deliberations at which about 10 million people were present and half a million spoke in discussions.[9]

Although Kairov does not mention it, there was also widespread criticism of article 19, some of which was reported in the press. First was a resolution of condemnation passed by a meeting of the Union of Writers of Ukraine in Kiev, December 1958.[10] This was followed by an appeal in Pravda on December 22 to maintain the status quo in language teaching and was signed by Ukraine's two most outstanding poets—Maxim Rylsky and Mykola Bazhan.[11] The same month the secretary of the Kiev Regional Committee of the Party, P. T. Tronko, wrote an article in the theoretical organ of the CC of the CPU supporting the study of both Russian and Ukrainian in all schools of the republic.[12] Simultaneously Ukraine's representatives were raising the question at the session of the Supreme Soviet in Moscow.

The first to speak was M. S. Hrechukha, member of the presidium of the CC of the CPU and deputy chairman of the Council of Ministers of the UkrSSR, who, speaking on behalf of Ukraine, said:

> We think that the existing plan of studying the Russian language in all national schools . . . should be supported and developed in every way.
> At the same time, it seems to us that the compulsory study of the national language in the national schools should be maintained.[13]

S. V. Chervonenko, secretary of the CC of the CPU in charge of ideological work and a former pedagogue, was more explicit and even more emphatic. He reported that:

> The discussion of problems associated with the study of languages in schools of Ukraine has attracted a great deal of attention. Many years of experience in organization of public education in the republics indicates that compulsory study of both Russian and the national language has been fully justified. Regarding the overburdening of students, we should consider the question of lessening the burden of the students by improving the courses of studies and the programs. But we should retain compulsory study of the Russian and the national languages.[14]

In January Iryna Vilde, a writer from Lviv, Western Ukraine, came out for the study of two languages in a Kiev paper.[15]

In the meantime the Supreme Soviet of the USSR enacted the proposed theses into law on December 24, without the disputed article.[16]

It was left to each national republic to legislate individually on the matter. On April 17, 1959, in spite of wide opposition to it the Supreme Soviet of the UkrSSR passed the new school law unanimously.[17] The article in dispute (no. 9 in the Ukrainian Law) was amended to read as follows:

> Instruction in the schools of the Ukrainian SSR is conducted in the native language of the pupils. Parents decide to which school, with what language of instruction, they wish to send their children. The study of one of the languages of the peoples of the USSR, in which instruction is not conducted in the given school, is realized upon the application of sufficient numbers of the parents and students.[18]

The clause abounds in contradiction and double talk. The first sentence is simple enough: pupils study in their native language, be they Ukrainian or Russian. The following sentence contradicts the first. Parents now have a "choice"; children no longer automatically go to schools where instruction is in their native tongue. This does not apply to Russians; they send their children to Russian schools. Also very significant is the last sentence. What it means is that pupils in a national republic are not compelled to study a second language of the peoples of the USSR. This does not affect the Russian language which was made compulsory from the second grade in 1938[19] and is taught "in all national schools without exception";[20] it applies only to all the other languages of the USSR including Ukrainian. A pupil in Ukraine, in a school with Russian as the language of instruction, need not study Ukrainian as a subject. By Soviet magic the clause begins with instruction in the native tongue and ends up abolishing that very language as a school subject.

This is the subtle two-stage plan for the conversion of education in Ukraine and the other non-Russian republics. The first stage is to change the language of instruction from the native to Russian with the native language as a subject; the second stage is to eliminate the native tongue even as a subject. And lest some may think that the application of the new law will develop on its own, let me quote from an editorial in a Ukrainian language teachers' magazine:

> The achievement of this principle of possibility of choice of the language of instruction . . . can under no circumstances be left to take its own course.[21]

We can best see how the "achievement of this principle" is not "left to take its own course" in the autonomous republics of the RSFSR from where ample evidence is available. Its Supreme Soviet passed the new law on education on April 16. Article 15 reads as follows:

> . . . To grant parents the right to decide to which school with what language of instruction to send their children . . .[22]

The Academy of Pedagogical Sciences and the Ministry of Education, both of the RSFSR, began a campaign in the fifteen autonomous republics of the RSFSR, whose people had been given the right to education in their native languages by a 1918 decree of the People's Commissariat of Education.[23] Schools were selected where experimental teaching was carried on in native classes with Russian as the language of instruction. Periodically conferences were organized on how to teach the Russian language. It was not long before these worthy efforts began to bear fruit as is evident from the following report:

> At the present time in a number of schools of the Russian Federation, in accordance with the wishes of the parents, pupils are changing to instruction in the Russian language. In addition the parents express the desire that the change be made in grade 1.[24]

Among those putting up the greatest resistance to such change are the people who inhabit the Tatar Autonomous Soviet Socialist Republic which lies along the middle Volga with the capital at Kazan. The struggle is uneven. We are informed that in the 1962-63 school year only six percent of Tatar pupils living in the fifteen cities of the republic studied in their native tongue.[25] In Russian-language kindergartens, 35 to 40 percent of the pupils were Tatar children.[26]

Neighbouring the Tatars on the west is the Chuvash ASSR. This nation of more than three quarters of a million descendents of Asians who settled there over one thousand years ago has maintained its language and culture through the centuries. The native language was the medium of school instruction to grade 7 (see appendix xi). Since 1963 all instruction from grade 5 has been in Russian.[27]

East of the Tatars live the three-quarter million Bashkirs. Since 1963 Russian has been the language of instruction from grade 5.[28] Previously the native tongue had been used in all elementary and secondary grades. In some schools Russian is used from grade 1.[29] This is the case in all schools of Ufa, the capital of Bashkiria, according to several reliable informants in the USSR who had personal knowledge of the situation.

One of the national groups living in the Northern Caucasus Mountains is the Ossetians whose population is nearly half a million. They have not been passed over in the drive. A teacher of an Ossetian school reported that in her grade 3 class, which follows a Russian course of studies, there was only one Russian pupil; the rest were native children.[30] This apparently is not the grade in which Russian is introduced as the language of instruction. Another teacher raised the problems associated with "the changing of Ossetian schools to the Russian language of instruction beginning with grade 1.[31] In the 1962-63 school year all teachers of Ossetian schools were given permission to change to Russian as the language of instruction in grade 1. Russian is also used in the local kindergartens.[32]

Also in the Caucasus Mountains, bordering on Georgia, lies the Kabardino-Balkar ASSR with a population equal to that of Ossetia. A report by the Minister of Education of that autonomous republic indicates that:

> In the 1960-61 school year 115 Kabardian and Balkar beginning classes, comprising 50 percent of the pupils of that group, changed to instruction using the Russian language. In those classes all subjects except the native tongue are taught in Russian and the native language is taught as a subject . . .

In the 1964-65 school year in nearly all the first and second grades of non-Russian schools instruction was in Russian; in 1965-66 all beginning non-Russian classes will be changed to the Russian language of instruction.[33]

Further east, between the Volga and Don Rivers on the Caspian Sea, live the Kalmyks. In their schools instruction was through the use of the native tongue to the end of grade 4. Now Russian has replaced the Kalmyk language in grade 4.[34]

South of the Kalmyks, in the Northern Caucasus bordering on the Caspian Sea, is the Dagestan ASSR with a population of over a million. There too is found the same process of Russification. Russian has become the language of instruction from grade 3 and the native tongue is studied as a subject.[35]

In the Chechen-Ingush ASSR, which lies west of Dagestan, the process is complete. According to an official report the indigenous parents "have chosen for their children schools with the Russian language of instruction".[36]

At the foot of the Urals in the east-central part of European Russia lies the Udmurt ASSR with a population of about one and a third millions. The Minister of Education of Udmurtia, N. V. Gorbushchin, reported that the national schools of the Udmurt ASSR are changing to instruction in the Russian language from grade 4.[37] Previously the native tongue was used to the end of grade 7.

Stretching north to the White Sea along the eastern border of Finland lies the Karelian ASSR, with a population of over half a million, of whom about half are Karelians who speak the Finnish language. Since 1958 all instruction in the native schools has been changed to the Russian language[38] in spite of the fact that "Karelian pupils entering school, in the majority of cases, are insufficiently acquainted with the Russian language".[39]

There is no recent data on how far Russification of the schools of the non-Russians of the RSFSR has advanced, but a report in 1963 indicated that the process was going on "in accordance with the wishes of the parents" and that in the 1962-63 school year, of all the pupils of the non-Russian schools, 27 percent in the beginning classes, 53 percent in grades 5-8 and 66 percent in grades 9-11 were instructed through the use of the Russian language.[40]

Such is the fate of the non-Russians of the RSFSR whose constitution in 1925 declared that the national minorities "have the right to receive education in their native tongue" (article 13).[41]

Although not as advanced, the same process is going on in the national republics. But there the change is made quietly, under-handedly, with more care and caution because opposition is strong. Occasionally there is a casual mention or reference which reveals to us what goes on behind the scenes. Pieced together, these give us a fair picture of the process of Russification of schools in the national republics.

In 1960, of a total of about 6,000 in Uzbekistan, 317 schools which were attended by non-Russian pupils conducted instruction in the Russian language.[42] The first secretary of the CC of the CP of Kirgizia boasted in 1964 that in his country there were 317 schools, attended mainly by Kirgiz pupils, where instruction was in Russian and 280 schools with parallel classes in two languages.[43]

How times have changed for the Moslem population in the USSR from November 20, 1917, when the Council of People's Commissars launched an appeal *To all Muslim workers of Russia and the East* which read:

"Your beliefs, your traditions and your national cultural insti-tutions are henceforth declared free and inviolable".[44]

The process goes on relentlessly in all republics. In Armenia the study of Russian before 1924 began in grade 4. Later it was introduced in 3, in 1938 in 2 and in the 1957-58 school year in grade 1.[45]

However, the Russians are not satisfied with introducing the teaching of their language in grade 1. They must reach down lower and get the child before it has fully mastered its mother tongue. We have a rather vivid description of how this is done in the following report:

In Armenia, where the percent of indigenous population is high (90 percent), and where there is a rather insignificant Russian linguistic environment, the study of the Russian language occupies a special place. Even in the pre-school period attempts are made to interest Armenian children in the Russian language and it is taught in kindergartens . . .

During lunch the children are addressed and they answer only in Russian; the conversation during the strolls is in Russian; the Russian language also resounds when they play. All this is important both for those children who after kindergarten will enter Russian schools and especially for those who will study in Armenian schools.

The aspiration to widen the Russian language base is the explanation for the fact that the study of the Russian language is begun in grade 1.[46]

But the pressure of Russification is applied at all levels. At one conference a speaker described how an experiment was introduced in Armenian schools in the teaching of geography in Russian.[47]

Another conference in Ashkhabad in August 1963, decided to try an experiment in teaching a number of subjects in Russian in several schools of the Turkmen SSR.[48]

This of course may be the thin edge of the wedge; next could come "experiments" in teaching other subjects in Russian; to be transformed eventually into permanent practice.

Another republic where Russification is pursued with the most frantic efforts is Moldavia whose people speak a language that differs very little from Romanian. In 1859 Moldavia joined with Wallachia to form the modern, independent Romanian state. This history and relationship the Russians not only ignore but try to obliterate by claiming for Moldavians a different kinship. We read that:

The liberating storm of the great October Socialist revolution came to the national borderlands from Russia—from Petrograd and Moscow. Having freed himself, the Russian brother in his Russian language brought his younger Moldavian brother the first news of peace, land, equality, happiness and a new life.[49]

Since 1958 the language of this "elder brother" has been imposed on Moldavian children from the very first grade.[50] Another means of Russification of education is through the union of two separate Russian and Moldavian schools into one with parallel Moldavian and Russian classes.[51]

How far Russification has advanced is evident from the following table showing the number of schools in that republic for 1964:

Moldavian	1,119
Russian	519
Mixed	149[52]

Moldavian and Russian schools stand in a ratio of almost two to one, but Moldavian and Russian population in 1959 was in a ratio of more than six to one,[53] a clear indication of how far Russification of schools has advanced.

There is also mention of 149 mixed schools. A report two years later (1966) stated that there were "over 150 such schools".[54] Just how many over 150 we do not know, but obviously Russification is not at a standstill in Moldavia.

There is no mention of any Ukrainian schools in Moldavia, although according to the 1959 census there was a Ukrainian population of 420,820.[55] Furthermore, before 1940 when Moldavia was not yet a national but still an autonomous republic within the borders of the UkrSSR, there were both Ukrainian schools and teachers' technicums (teachers' colleges).

Mixed schools are one of the more subtle and insidious methods of Russification. They are being widely used in many republics with local variations and adaptations. Following is an account of this process in Latvia:

> A fruitful form of international education of student youth is the organization in Latvia, on the initiative of the parents, of schools in which pupils study in parallel classes with Russian and Latvian languages of instruction . . . There are already more than 200 such schools.[56]

What is meant by "international education" is clearly revealed in the following report:

> G. A. Zhdanova, head of the Tatar Branch of the Institute of National Schools of the Academy of Pedagogical Sciences of the RSFSR, described the international education of students during the lessons of the Russian language in the national schools . . .
> The better teachers of Tataria strive to make the lessons and extra-curricular activities on the subject of Russian language and literature conform to the basic educational aims.

In the schools of Tataria much is done in this direction. Particular rooms are devoted to Russian language and literature. On display panels are the statements of great men on the significance of the Russian language, their portraits . . .

With the aim of international education are conducted oral discussions and written assignments on the subjects: "Why I love the Russian language" . . . "The Russian language—a giant, clear, beautiful and grand". "The language which Ilich (i.e. Lenin —*J.K.*) loved".[57]

It is quite clear that the "basic aim" of "international education" is to Russify. To be classed as a better teacher one must conform to these aims. The reader can imagine the fate of a native teacher who tried to oppose these "basic aims".

Complete, up-to-date statistics on how far Russification has advanced in the USSR are not available. For the school year 1955-56 the percentage of elementary and secondary general school pupils studying in Russian schools in the USSR was 65 (see table I), but the Russian population in the USSR, according to the 1959 general census, was only 54.7 percent. Thus the percentage of pupils in Russian schools was 10.3 more than the percentage of the Russian population. *For every republic the percent of pupils instructed in Russian was higher than the percent of Russian population in that republic.* It was the highest in the Kazakh, Moldavian, Kirgiz and Belorussian republics.

We can also calculate the percentage of pupils in Russian schools in the USSR for 1958-65 from data for the number of teachers of Russian language and literature in (a) Russian schools and (b) non-Russian schools.

Number of teachers in grades 5-7

	Russian	%	Non-Russian	%
1958 - 59	98,000	67.6	47,000	32.4
1959 - 60	105,000	69.5	46,000	30.5
1960 - 61	114,000	69.5	50,000	30.5
in grades 5-8				
1961 - 62	121,000	69.9	52,000	30.1
1962 - 63	135,000	71.4	54,000	28.6
1963 - 64	139,000	71.6	55,000	28.4
1964 - 65	142,000	71.7	56,000	28.3
1965 - 66	142,000	71.7	56,000	28.3[58]

TABLE I

Percentage of Pupils in Elementary and Secondary Schools
Being Instructed in the Russian and in Other Languages
of the peoples of the USSR, 1955-56

	(1) Percentage instructed in Russian	*(2)* Percentage instructed in other Languages	*(3)* Percentage of Russians in republic	Difference between (1) and (3)
USSR	65	35	54.7	10.3
Russian SFSR	94	6	83.3	10.7
Ukrainian SSR	26	74	16.9	9.1
Belorussian SSR	22	78	8.2	13.8
Uzbek SSR	20	80	13.5	6.5
Kazakh SSR	66	34	42.7	23.3
Georgian SSR	20	80	10.1	9.9
Azerbaidzhan SSR	23	77	13.6	9.4
Lithuanian SSR	11	89	8.5	2.5
Moldavian SSR	33	67	10.2	22.8
Latvian SSR	33	67	26.6	6.4
Kirgiz SSR	49	51	30.2	18.8
Tadzhik SSR	16	84	13.3	2.7
Armenian SSR	9	91	3.2	5.8
Turkmen SSR	21	79	17.3	3.7
Estonian SSR	22	78	20.1	1.9

Source: Tsentralnoe statisticheskoe upravlenie pri Sovete Ministrov SSR (Central Statistical Administration of the Council of Ministers of the USSR). *Kulturnoe Stroitelstvo SSSR (Cultural Development in the USSR). Statistical Handbook,* Moscow 1956, pp. 186-87. For percentage of Russians in each republic: *Itogi vsesouznoy perepisi,* Summary Volume, pp. 184, 202-208.

The percentage of teachers teaching the Russian language and literature in grades 5 to 7 (and grades 5 to 8 from 1961-62) in Russian schools has increased from 67.6 percent in 1958-59 to 71.7 percent in 1965-66, with a corresponding decrease in non-Russian schools from 32.4 to 28.3 percent. Assuming that classes were on the average of the same size in both Russian and non-Russian schools, then in the 1965-66 school year 71.7 percent of the pupils in the USSR were attending Russian schools, whereas the Russian population made up only 54.65 percent of the total population (see appendix I). Conversely, 28.3 percent attended non-Russian schools, while the percentage of the non-Russian population was 45.35. This would mean that 37.6 percent of all non-Russian pupils were attending Russian schools in 1965.

According to this official data there was no increase in Russification of grades 5-8 from 1964-65 to 1965-66. Other statistics seem to contradict this. The number and percent of copies of textbooks published in the USSR for all classes of elementary and secondary schools in Russian and all other languages of the peoples of the USSR for the years 1964-65 and 1965-66 is as follows:

Year	Total number of copies	Copies in Russian	%	Copies in Other Languages	%
1964 - 65	283,305,000	204,500,000	72.2	78,805,000	27.8
1965 - 66	286,899,000	208,502,000	72.7	78,397,000	27.3[59]

For 1964-65 the percentage of textbooks published in Russian (72.2) approximates the percentage of teachers of the Russian language in grades 5-8 of Russian schools; similarly, the percentage published in all non-Russian languages of the peoples of the USSR (27.8) approximates the percentage of teachers of the Russian language in the same grades in non-Russian schools. However, the statistics for 1965-66 show an increase of textbooks in Russian and a decrease in the non-Russian languages of the peoples of the USSR by .5 percent. Of course, the data for schools includes only grades 5-8, whereas the data for textbooks takes in those published for all elementary and secondary general education. But even if there was no increase in grades 5-8, the data on textbooks proves that there was an increase in Russification of non-Russian classes somewhere along the line from 1964-65 to 1965-66.

How far Russification has advanced since 1940 is evident from a comparison of the percentage of the number of copies of textbooks published for general education schools in Russian and in all other languages of the USSR for 1940-41 and 1965-66.

	Percentage of copies in Russian	Percentage of copies in all Other Languages of USSR
1940 - 41	58.2	41.8
1965 - 66	72.7	27.3[60]

The percentage of books published in non-Russian languages in 1940 nearly approximated the percentage of non-Russians in the USSR; by 1965 the percentage had drastically declined. Furthermore, in 1965 books were published in the USSR in 64 languages of the peoples of the USSR,[61] whereas in 1938, when instruction was in the native tongue, school texts were published for 70 nationalities in the RSFSR alone.[62] Apparently some have already lost the right of instruction in their native tongue.

Evidence of increasing Russification is also found in statistics on the number of teachers of the Russian language and literature in Russian and non-Russian schools of the RSFSR for grades 5-8 for three successive years as follows:

	Teachers of Russian in Russian Schools	%	Teachers of Russian in Non-Russian Schools	%
1963	106,900	93.12	7,900	6.88
1964	108,500	93.29	7,800	6.71
1965	108,100	93.59	7,400	6.41[63]

In 1959, 83.3 percent of the population of the RSFSR was Russian and 16.7 percent non-Russian.[64] But in 1965 only 6.41 percent of all teachers of the Russian language and literature were in non-Russian schools. There was a consistent decline each year from 1963. This gives one further reason to suspect the data regarding the number of teachers of Russian in non-Russian schools of the USSR for 1965, which shows no change from 1964. It is unlikely that Russification of national schools in other national republics of the USSR ceased, while it went on unabated in the RSFSR.

The process goes on steadily and relentlessly. Khrushchov's new law on education in 1958 transformed it from a trickle into a flood that is slowly but relentlessly inundating the non-Russian schools and eroding the languages and cultures of the non-Russian nations of the USSR. In spite of this the organ of the CC of the CPSU can declare for all the world to read, that:

> In the Soviet Union there are neither privileged nor under-privileged nations. All nations are equal and enjoy the same rights.[65]

FOOTNOTES

1. B. G. Gafurov, "Uspekhy natsionalnoy politiki KPSS i nekotorye voprosy internatsionalnogo vospitaniya (Successes of the Nationality Policy of the CPSU and Some Problems of Internationalist Education)", *Kommunist,* No. 11, 1958, pp. 18, 23, 17, 16.
2. *KPSS o kulture, prosveshchenii i nauke* (The CPSU on Culture, Education and Science), Collection of Documents, Moscow, 1963, p. 76.
3. *Pravda,* November 29, 1958.
4. Ibid., December 2, 1958.
5. *Zasedaniya Verkhovnogo Soveta SSSR, sosyv 5, sessia 2* (Sessions of the Supreme Soviet of the USSR, 5th convocation, 2nd session), December 22-25, 1958, Stenographic report, Moscow, 1959, pp. 291-440.
6. Ibid., pp. 346-47.
7. Ibid., p. 409.
8. *Izvestiya,* January 31, 1959.
9. *Pravda,* December 24, 1958.
10. This event was reported to the author by participants.
11. *Pravda,* December 22, 1958.

12. "Tsoho vymahaye zhyttya (Life Demands This)", *Komunist Ukrainy*, No. 12, December, 1958, p. 23.
13. *Zasedaniya*, p. 297.
14. Ibid., p. 356.
15. *Pravda Ukrainy*, January 3, 1959.
16. N. K. Goncharov and F. F. Korolev, *Novaya sistema narodnogo obrazovaniya v SSSR* (The New System of Education in the USSR), Moscow, 1960, pp. 55-70.
17. *Radyanska Ukrayina*, April 18, 1959.
18. *Kulturne budivnytstvo*, II, 1961, p. 517.
19. Ibid., I, 1959, pp. 740-44.
20. Editorial, "Sblizhenie natsiy i russky yazyk (The Rapprochement of Nations and the Russian Language)", *Russky Yazyk*, No. 6, 1963, p. 5.
21. Editorial, "Zabezpechyty Neukhylne Provedenya v Zhyttya Zakony pro Shkolu (Guarantee the Steadfast Application of the School Law)", *Ukrainska Mova v Shkoli* (The Ukrainian Language in School), No. 4, 1959, p. 5.
22. N. K. Goncharov and F. F. Korolev, op. cit., p. 79.
23. F. F. Sovetkin, *Natsionalnye shkoly RSFSR za 40 let* (Forty Years of National Schools in the RSFSR), Moscow, 1958, p. 7.
24. M. Baragunov, "Ob obuchenie na russkom yazyke v nachalnykh klassakh (Regarding Instruction in the Russian Language of Beginning Classes)", *Russky Yazyk v Natsionalnoy Shkole*, No. 2, 1963, p. 29.
25. M. Akhiyarova, "Obuchenie na russkom yazyke v selskikh shkolakh (Instruction in the Russian Language in Village Schools)", *Russky Yazyk*, No. 6, 1963, p. 27.
26. A. Gabitov, "Problemny vopros (A Problem Question)", *Russky Yazyk*, No. 3, 1963, p. 80.
27. S. Shamsutginova, "Na seminare v Tsitsu (At the Seminar in Tsitsu)", *Russky Yazyk*, No. 5, 1966, p. 76.
28. V. M. Chistyakov, (editor), *Uchitelyu nachalnykh klassov natsionalnoy shkoly* (For the Teacher of Beginning Classes of the National Schools), Moscow, 1964, p. 6.
29. Ibid.
30. M. Beznusko, "Kak ya dobyvayus praktichekogo ovladeniya russkim yazykom (How I Strive for the Practical Mastery of the Russian Language)", *Russky Yazyk*, No. 3, 1965, p. 52.
31. K. Galkaev, "Ob izuchenii russkoi fonetiki i grammatiki (Regarding the Study of Russian Phonetics and Grammar)", *Russky Yazyk*, No. 1, 1965, p. 20.
32. V. M. Chistyakov, op. cit., p. 22.
33. Sh. Chechenov, "O robote v shkolakh s russkim yazykom obucheniya (Regarding Work in Schools with the Russian Language of Instruction)", *Russky Yazyk*, No. 4, 1965, pp. 45, 47.
34. E. Kotok, "V shkolakh Kalmykii (In the Schools of Kalmykia)", *Russky Yazyk*, No. 4, 1963, p. 74.

35. Yu, Gerbeev, "Nauchno-metodicheskaya konferentsia v Kabar-dino-Balkarii (Scientific-methodological Conference in Kabar-dino-Balkaria)", *Russky Yazyk,* No. 5, 1963, p. 78.

36. M. Umarov and R. Lalaev, "Eshche raz o yazyke obucheniya v natsionalnoi shkole (Once Again Regarding the Language of Instruction in the National School)", *Russky Yazyk,* No. 1, 1966, pp. 40-41.

37. M. Stolyarova, "Konferentsiya v Ufe (Conference in Ufa)", *Russky Yazyk,* No. 5, 1963, p. 85.

38. N. V. Mansvetov, "Sblizhenie natsy i vozniknovenie internat-sionalnoy obshchnosti narodov SSSR (The Rapprochement of Nations and the Emergence of an International Community of the Peoples of the USSR)", *Voprosy Istorii,* No. 5, May, 1964. p. 50.

39. S. Reikhkalainen, "Izuchenie russkogo yazyka v dobukvarny period (Study of the Russian Language in the Pre Primer Period)", *Russky Yazyk,* No. 4, 1964, p. 24.

40. "Sblizhenie natsiy, i russky yazyk (The Rapprochement of Nations and the Russian Language)", *Russky Yazyk,* No. 6, 1963, p. 5.

41. I. P. Tsamerian and S. L. Ronin, *Equality of Rights Between Races and Nationalities in the USSR,* UNESCO, Paris, 1962, p. 28.

42. E. V. Tadevosyan, "Dalneyshee sblizhenie sotsialisticheskikh natsiy v SSSR (Further Rapprochement of the Socialist Nations in the USSR)", *Voprosy Filosofii,* No. 6, June 1963, p. 11.

43. T. Usubaliev, "Ekonomicheskaya i dukhovnaya obshchnost Sovetskikh narodov (Economic and Spiritual Community of the Soviet Nations)", *Kommunist,* No. 2, 1964, p. 19.

44. I. P. Tsamerian and S. L. Ronin, op. cit., p. 26.

45. Z. Makarian, "O nekotorykh voprosakh metodiki russkogo yazyka v armyanskoy sovetskoy shkole (Regarding Some Questions of Methodology of the Russian Language in Soviet Armenian Schools)", *Russky Yazyk,* No. 2, 1966, p. 37.

46. E. Kotok, "Tvorcheski poiski uchiteley Armenii (Creative Practices of the Teachers of Armenia)", *Russky Yazyk,* No. 2, 1966, p. 48.

47. E. Kotok, "Na konferentsii i v shkole (At the Conference and at School)", *Russky Yazyk,* No. 2, 1963, p. 72.

48. "Sblizhenie natsiy i russky yazyk", p. 6.

49. A. Adzhigarey, "V bratskoi Moldavii (In Fraternal Moldavia)", *Russky Yazyk,* No. 6, 1966, p. 25.

50. Ibid., p. 29.

51. Ibid., p. 29.

52. *Russky Yazyk,* No. 6, 1966, p. 35.

53. Number of Moldavians was 1,886,566; number of Russians, 292,930. Tsentralnoe Statisticheshoe Upravlenie pri Sovete Ministrov SSR (Central Statistical Administration of the Council of Ministers of the USSR), *Itogi vsesouznoy perepisi naseleniya 1959 goda* (Totals of the All-Union Population Census, 1959), Summary Volume, USSR, Moscow, 1962, p. 207.

54. A. Adzhigarey, op. cit., p. 29.

55. *Itogi vsesoyuznoy perepisi,* Summary Volume, p. 207.
56. *Pravda,* April 18, 1963.
57. N. Rozyeva, "Voprosy kommunisticheskogo vospitaniya v natsionalnoy shkole (Problems of Communist Education in the National School)", *Russky Yazyk,* No. 1, 1966, p. 81.
58. Tsentralnoe statisticheskoe upravlenie pri Sovete Ministrov SSR (Central Statistical Administration of the Council of Ministers of the USSR), *Narodnoe khozaystvo SSR v 1958 godu* (National Economy in the USSR in 1958), Statistical Annual, Moscow, 1959, p. 819;
    Narodnoe khozaystvo, 1959, p. 734;
    Narodnoe khozaystvo, 1960, p. 758;
    Narodnoe khozaystvo, 1961, p. 682;
    Narodnoe khozaystvo, 1962, p. 556;
    Narodnoe khozaystvo, 1963, p. 560;
    Narodnoe khozaystvo, 1964, p. 672;
    Narodnoe khozaystvo, 1965, p. 683.
59. Gosudarstvenny komitet Soveta Ministrov SSR po pechati (State Committee for Publishing of the Council of Ministers of the USSR), *Pechat SSSR v 1964 godu* (Publishing in the USSR in 1964), Statistical Handbook. Moscow, 1965, p. 64.
60. Ministerstvo kultury SSSR (Ministry of Culture). Glavizdat Vsesoyuznaya Knizhnaya Palata (Glavizdat All-union House of Books). *Pechat SSSR za sorok let 1917-1957* (Forty Years of Publishing in the USSR, 1917-1957), Statistical Handbook, Moscow, 1957, p. 80.
61. *Pechat SSR v 1964 godu,* p. 6.
62. F. F. Sovetkin, op. cit., p. 11.
63. Tsentralnoe statisticheskoe upravlenie pri Sovete ministrov RSFSR (Central Statistical Administration of the Council of Ministers of the RSFSR), *Narodnoe khozaystvo RSFSR v 1963 godu* (The National Economy in the RSFSR in 1963), Statistical Year Book, Moscow, 1965, p. 481;
    Narodnoe khozaystvo RSFSR, 1964, p. 481;
    Narodnoe khozaystvo RSFSR, 1965, p. 465.
    For the school year 1956-57 the percentage of teachers in the RSFSR teaching Russian in grades 5—7 of Russian and non-Russian schools was 92.06 and 7.94 respectively. Tsentralnoe statisticheskoe upravelenie RSFSR (Central Statistical Administration of the RSFSR), *Kulturnoe Stroitelstvo RSFSR* (Cultural Development in the RSFSR), Statistical Handbook, Moscow, 1958, p. 304.
64. *Itogi vsesoyuznoy perepisi,* p. 202.
65. A. Andreev, "Torzhestvo leninskikh idey druzhby narodov (Triumph of Leninist Ideals of Friendship of Peoples)'', *Kommunist,* No. 6, 1960, p. 37.

4

Elementary and
secondary general education

The system of education in Ukraine is a complex structure with a wide division of responsibility and much overlapping of control. There are two ministries of education, one for elementary and general secondary and the other for higher and secondary special. In addition many institutions are under the jurisdiction of other ministries, committees and boards, both republican and all-union.

In Ukraine as in other republics the process of Russification was intensified with the introduction of the new law. In cities parents already had a choice because both Russian and Ukrainian schools were in existence. The introduction of the new law meant that Russian elementary and secondary general education schools were to be extended to the smaller towns where previously there had been only Ukrainian schools. We have confirmation of an increase in the number of Russian schools after the reform from none other than the secretary of the CC of the CPU, who wrote:

> Each year there is an increase . . . in the gravitation to the study of the Russian language . . . In connection with this there is an increase in the number of schools with Russian as the language of instruction.[1]

Almost simultaneously, in identical language, there appeared another article confirming the above.[2]

There is evidence of the extent of this increase of Russian schools in Soviet statistics. These are not always meant to enlighten and it is often difficult to make comparisons for different years, especially as some of the data include only regular day schools and some night, adult and correspondence schools. To compound confusion, we are not advised explicitly as to what types are included. Sometimes the statistics are even contradictory. However, in spite of all this, we can make some comparisons which indicate a definite trend.

In 1960 I. K. Bilodid, the minister of education, who was always very careful about publishing statistics, issued the following incomplete data on the number and language of general education schools of all types:

> Ukrainian—over 30,000 schools
> Russian —nearly 6,000 " [3]

More complete figures for the same schools were published for 1961-62 as follows:

	Number of Schools	%
Ukrainian	33,309	82.11
Russian	6,292	15.51
Moldavian	218	.54
Hungarian	140	.35
Polish	3	.01
Mixed	602	1.48
Total	40,564	100 [4]

It is not possible to make comparisons here as the first figures are not complete. However in the second report, of special interest is the entry "mixed schools". They numbered 602. Another source listed 125 such schools for the year 1956-57.[5] Very significant is their rapid increase between 1956 and 1961, especially as they are one of the means of Russification.

On regular general education day schools there is information from several sources for a number of different years, making possible some interesting and revealing comparisons. The most complete statistics on the number and language of general education day schools and pupils in them was provided by Hryshchenko for the 1953-54 school year as follows:

	Number of Schools	%	Number of Pupils	%
Ukrainian	25,192	85.24	4,460,781	74.91
Russian	4,027	13.63	1,414,551	23.76
Moldavian	173	.59	32,590	.55
Hungarian	98	.33	16,437	.27
Polish	6	.02	2,203	.04
Ukrainian and Russian	52	.18	26,793	.45
Russian and Moldavian	3	.01	1,117	.02
Total	29,551	100	5,954,470	100 [6]

The data indicates that 25,192 Ukrainian schools were attended by 4,460,781 pupils, or by 177 pupils for an average Ukrainian school. But the attendance of an average Russian school was 351, or twice as many as in an average Ukrainian school.

There is also mention of mixed schools—52 Ukrainian and Russian, and three Russian and Moldavian, totalling 55. This is the first indication that such schools existed in the post war years. Hryshchenko further breaks down the statistics for schools as follows:

	Elementary Schools Grades 1-4	Seven year Schools Grades 1-7	Secondary Schools Grades 1-10
Ukrainian	11,185	10,316	3,691
Russian	1,429	1,305	1,293
Moldavian	62	91	20
Hungarian	35	59	4
Polish	2		4
Ukrainian and Russian	1	24	27
Russian and Moldavian		1	2
Total	12,714	11,796	5,041 [7]

It was noted that Russian schools were larger; here the reason becomes clear: 32.11 percent of them are full secondary schools while only 14.65 percent of all Ukrainian schools are in this category.

The following complete report for the school year 1955-56 for the number and language of regular day schools and the number of pupils was published by Cherkashyn:

	Number of Schools	%	Number of Pupils	%
Ukrainian	25,034	85.32	3,845,754	72.79
Russian	4,051	13.81	1,392,270	26.35
Moldavian	159	.54	27,102	.51
Hungarian	93	.32	16,622	.31
Polish	4	.01	1,875	.04
Total	29,341	100	5,283,623	100 [8]

Cherkashyn does not include mixed schools, which makes his total for schools and pupils smaller than Hryshchenko's. Of significance however, is the fact that the number of Russian schools has increased and the number of Ukrainian ones has decreased.

Three years later Bilodid gave a breakdown for general education day schools without any data on the number of pupils:

	Number of Schools	Percentage of Schools
Ukrainian	25,464	84.66
Russian	4,355	14.48
Moldavian	155	.51
Hungarian	100	.34
Polish	3	.01
Total	30,077	100 [9]

Alla Bondar, the minister of education at that time, published the following incomplete statistics on such schools for 1964-65:

	Number	Percentage
Ukrainian	24,485	81.8
Russian	over 4,500	over 15
Total	29,918	[10]

There is careful avoidance of statistics regarding the number of pupils attending each type of school. Since those with Russian as the language of instruction are much larger than the Ukrainian village schools, the 15 percent of schools which are Russian are attended by a greater percentage of pupils. Such statistics would reveal the extent of Russification. This the authorities wish to avoid at all costs.

A comparison of the data from the four sources shows the relative percent of the Ukrainian and Russian schools for the different years:

Report	Year	% Ukrainian	% Russian
Hryshchenko	1953-54	85.24	13.63
Cherkashyn	1955-56	85.32	13.8
Bilodid	1957-58	84.66	14.4
Bondar	1964-65	81.8	over 15

In her report Bondar did not account for over nine hundred schools. Obviously some of them are Moldavian, Hungarian and Polish. Bilodid listed 258 such schools in his 1958 report (see above). If this number is subtracted from 900, there remain 642 schools unaccounted for. These must be the mixed schools where Russian predominates. Their increase is also an indication of the Russifying trend of Ukrainian schools.

Recently Bondar issued new statistics presumably for 1966-67 on schools in Ukraine. But these are not complete making it impossible to compare with her previous data. She reported that in 23,900 or 82 percent of all elementary schools, the language of instruction was Ukrainian.[11] This is approximately the same percentage as she claimed for both elementary and secondary Ukrainian schools in 1963 (see above). Most elementary schools are in villages where Ukrainians predominate. Secondary schools (grades 1 to 10) are for the most part in larger towns and cities and are overwhelmingly Russian (see page 57). Therefore to produce an average percentage of 81.8 in 1963 for all schools there must have been a much higher percentage of Ukrainian elementary schools. Bondar's latest data would indicate that the flood of Russification has also been inundating Ukrainian elementary schools since 1963. But in her report she is in raptures because:

> . . . the working people of Ukraine have acquired the right to develop a culture that is national in form and socialist in content, as well as the right and means to educate their children in their mother tongue.[12]

There is not enough data for periodic comparison of the number of pupils in Ukrainian and Russian schools since the war, but some statistics are available for the pre-war period, making it possible to compare the two periods. According to Cherkashyn (see page 51) 72.8 percent of all pupils attended Ukrainian schools in 1955-56. In 1927, 75.8 percent of the teachers in the schools of Ukraine used Ukrainian as the language of instruction.[13] The percentage of Ukrainian schools for the prewar years was as follows: 1924—66%; 1925—77%; 1926—79.1%; 1927—81%; 1930—85%.[14] Obviously Russification had made considerable strides between 1924 and 1955.

There are also general education night schools with vocational training for working and village youth. These may start from grade 3, although some begin at higher grades. In 1962 the number of pupils in these schools was as follows:

Working Youth	469,000
Village Youth	226,900
Total	695,900[15]

The 1960 catalogue of school publications lists only eight titles of textbooks for such schools. Of these, four make up two identical pairs of language texts, one for Ukrainian schools and one for Russian. The latter editions are larger as the table below indicates:

Author	Grade	Title	Ukrainian Edition	Russian Edition	Percentage in Russian
Horyana	5	*German*	4,600	5,300	53.5
Zvinska	5	*English*	2,600	4,500	63.4[16]

For 1964 the following are listed:

Author	Grade	Title	Ukrainian Edition	Russian Edition	Percentage in Russian
Truby & Yanchuk	7-8	*English*	3,900	11,000	73.8
Horyana & Martiash-villi	7-8	*German*	6,000	11,000	64.7[17]

We see that of the foreign language texts published in Russian and Ukrainian, the edition of the former is larger and its size has increased from 1960 to 1964. However, the number of textbooks published in Ukraine is absolutely inadequate for these schools. The remaining books must come from the RSFSR. They of course will also be in Russian. It follows then, that instruction in these schools will mainly be in Russian. Further evidence of this is supplied by posters announcing opening of registration. All such placards seen by the author in Kiev were in Russian (see figures 1 and 2). If the pupils attending these schools were included in the statistics, the percentage of those instructed in the Russian language would be higher.

There are also pre-school kindergarten classes in which, in Ukraine, in 1964 there were 693,800 children.[18] In the cities these are, for the most part, Russianized. While I lived in Ukraine there was a public outcry against the changing of two of the few remaining Ukrainian kindergartens in Kiev to Russian.

The process is now going on in the smaller towns. A correspondent to a Kiev newspaper reported on the half-Ukrainian, half-Russian jargon spoken by the children in these classes in a small town and blames the teacher.[19] The reporter could not openly and directly criticize Russification, nor the teachers, who in so many cases are the wives of Russian officials sent to Ukraine.

Records of children's songs and games and children's films used in these schools are all in Russian. When the Ukrainian tourist group visited Canada and the United States in 1964, there were many requests for Ukrainian children's films. Emphatic assertions were made by members of the group that these were available and promises were given that some would be sent. Despite many reminders and letters, none have arrived. Several people requested that I procure children's records in Ukrainian for them when I lived in Kiev. Despite many inquiries, even at the ministry of education, I was unable to obtain even one such record because none were available. If the kindergarten children were included in the total, the percentage using Russian language in schools would be still higher.

Figure 1. Poster announcing opening of registration, for 1964-65, for Kiev school number 35 for working youth. The language is Russian, an indication that the school is also Russian. Photo by the author.

Figure 2. **Poster announcing opening of registration, for 1964-65, for Kiev school number 3 for working youth, also in Russian. Photo by the author.**

The extent of Russification of schools in the cities of Ukraine can be seen from the following statistics compiled by officials of the ministry of education of the UkrSSR and never published. They give the number of students attending schools with Russian and Ukrainian language of instruction during the 1958/59 school year in some of the leading cities:

City	Number of Students in Ukrainian Schools	%	Number of Students in Russian Schools	%
Kiev	22,527	26.9	61,247	73.1
Kharkiv	2,913	4.1	68,838	95.9
Odessa	4,687	8.1	52,978	91.9
Dnipropetrovsk	11,056	17.4	52,306	82.6
Donetsk	894	1.2	76,286	98.8
Vinnitsa	4,530	33.0	9,195	67.0
Stanislav	2,693	39.4	4,143	60.6
Sumy	3,800	41.7	5,307	58.3
Zhytomyr	5,134	38.9	8,069	61.1
Khmelnitsky	2,867	43.1	3,786	56.9
Luhansk	1,500	6.5	21,663	93.5
Zaporizhya	8,868	26.6	24,522	73.4 [20]

These statistics reveal an appalling situation: in every city the overwhelming preponderance of students is in Russian schools, although the majority of the population is Ukrainian. Even in such a Western Ukrainian town as Stanislav (now Ivano-Franivsk) less than 40 percent of the pupils attended schools in the native tongue. This was in 1958. Much "progress" in Russification has been made since then. Teachers, party officials and others mentioned many specific cases to the author. The cities of Luhansk and Donetsk no longer had any Ukrainian schools in 1964. In Chernivtsi, out of a total of 40 in 1965, only four were Ukrainian. In Kolomiya, a district centre in Western Ukraine, there were two full middle schools (grades 1-10), both Russian. In every small town, where there were only Ukrainian schools before the war Russian schools now abound, in most cases in a majority.

There is additional information from handbooks for Kharkiv and Odessa for the year 1957, listing various types of schools in both cities and specifying the language of instruction in general education day schools with the exception of eight in Kharkiv. Special institutions such as music, dancing, boarding and night schools are listed, but the language of instruction is not specified. One would surmise that the information is for the school year of 1956-57. Following is the data:

	Number of Schools	Russian	%	Ukrainian	%
Kharkiv	111	73	65.8	38	34.2 [21]
Odessa	79	61	77.2	18	22.8 [22]

Comparing the percentage of Ukrainian schools for 1956-57 in Kharkiv and Odessa with the percentage of Ukrainian pupils for 1958-59, we note that the percentage of Ukrainian schools is higher than that percent of Ukrainian pupils. This is probably due in part to the fact that the statistics for the number of pupils include those attending special schools for which the language of instruction is not specified in the handbooks and which are generally Russian, in part to the fact that Russian schools are larger and in part, no doubt, to the advances in Russification in the two intervening years.

For Lviv there is also some interesting data. In the spring of 1965, the first vice-chairman of the Lviv Regional Executive Committee, T. D. Telyshkovsky, cited to me in a personal interview the following statistics on general education schools in Lviv:

Language of Schools	Number of Schools
Ukrainian	62
Russian	24
Polish	2
Total	88

Half a year later, N. Malanchuk, secretary of the Lviv Regional Committee of the CPU in charge of Agitation and Propaganda, published the following data for the same city:

Language of Schools	Number of Schools
Ukrainian	56
Russian	29
Polish	2
Total	87 [23]

Telyshkovsky's figures are for the 1964-65 school year; Malanchuk's for 1965-66. There has obviously been considerable progress in "internationalizing" education in Lviv. In one year the number of Ukrainian schools declined from 62 to 56 and the number of Russian increased from 24 to 29. Local residents described to the author the Ukrainian schools. Most of them were mixed, with Russian as the dominant language.

Education officials in Kiev would not provide any statistics on the number of Ukrainian and Russian schools in the city. I was simply told that the majority were Ukrainian. While Bilodid was Minister of Education, he was asked at a public meeting of writers how many Ukrainian schools there were in Kiev. His answer was, "I don't know."

The only official available source providing data on the language of schools in Kiev is an atlas which indicates graphically that for the 1958-59 school year half of the seven-year and about two-thirds of the ten-year schools were Russian.[24] This, it must be remembered, was before the introduction of the new school law after which Russification was intensified.

We can further check on the number of pupils attending instruction in Russian and Ukrainian by comparing the number of textbooks published in each language specifically for Ukraine. Following is a comparison of two such books published by the Ukrainian school publishing house, Radyanska Shkola, in 1964:

Author	Grade	Title	Ukrainian Edition	Russian Edition	Percentage in Russian
Dyadichenko, Los and Spitsky	7-8	*History of UkrSSR*	300,000	200,000	40
Dibrova	8	*Geography of UkrSSR*	250,000	200,000	44 [25]

Comparisons of editions for two consecutive years of a text, *Economic Geography of the USSR* by Lyalikov, published for grade 11 of the secondary schools of Ukraine, provides additional confirmation of increased Russification:

Year	Ukrainian Edition	Russian Edition	Percentage in Russian	
1963	220,000	180,000	45	[26]
1964	100,000	130,000	56.5	[27]

Another textbook whose Russian edition increased its percentage of the total is *Electrical Construction* by Andriyevsky, prescribed for grade 8:

Year	Ukrainian Edition	Russian Edition	Percentage in Russian	
1963	200,000	180,000	47.4	[28]
1964	150,000	170,000	53.1	[29]

Among other texts published in Ukraine in 1963, with larger Russian than Ukrainian editions, are the following:

Author	Grade	Title	Ukrainian Edition	Russian Edition	Percentage in Russian	
Tkachenko	5-6	*Wood and Metal Working*	150,000	170,000	53.1	
Chaly	9-10	*Drafting*	170,000	200,000	54.1	
Buryan	9-11	*Lathe Work*	15,000	17,000	53.1	[30]

For some subjects listed in timetables, such as art and physical culture, there is no record of any texts being published in Ukraine. These are brought in from the RSFSR; their language is naturally Russian. For the years 1946-1950 the total number of such books was 60 million copies.[31] This would average out to 12 million per year. Further confirmation that school texts were sent in from the RSFSR was made in a report by Katerina Kolosova, deputy to the Supreme Soviet of the UkrSSR, secretary of the Ukrainian Society for Cultural Relations with Foreign Countries and leader of a group of cultural, political and other personalities to the U.S. and Canada in November-December 1964. In her previous position as

Director of the Department of Education of the CC of the CPU, in which capacity she supervised the work of the ministry of education, Kolosova reported that for the school year 1958-59, 105 titles and 30 million copies of textbooks had been published in Ukraine and over 13 million had been brought in from the RSFSR.[32] A check of the 1958 catalogue of the publishing house of school texts, Radyanska Shkola,[33] confirms her statistics as to the number of titles published for general education schools, excluding night, adult and schools for working and peasant youth. With the exception of Russian language books, no texts were published that year in Russian in Ukraine. The imported Russian books made up about 30 percent of the school texts for general education day schools in Ukraine.

Alla Bondar reported that for the 1963-64 school year 144 titles of textbooks were published in 41 million copies in Ukraine and 17 million were brought in from the RSFSR.[34] The catalogue of Radyanska Shkola publishing house indicates that the above number of books was published in Ukraine for general education day schools only (not including Polish, Moldavian and Hungarian schools).[35] This means that for the day schools in Ukraine in 1963/64, 29.3 percent of the textbooks were imported from Russia and were consequently in Russian, as against 30 percent in 1958/59. It would seem that the proportion of Ukrainian books had increased. However, there is one slight detail that must be taken into account: in 1960, for the first time since the war, there began in Ukraine the publication of school texts in Russian. In 1963-64 they numbered nearly three million copies, not including Russian language texts.[36] Thus the total number of Russian textbooks in Ukraine for the 1963-64 school year for general education day schools amounted to over one third.

Data for 1966 reveals that 34.1 million books for general education schools were published in Ukraine and 15.5 million were imported from the RSFSR.[37] This is an increase in the number of texts from Russia as compared to 1963. These imported books made up 31.3 percent of all texts for general education day schools. There is no data available to the author on how many of the 34.1

million texts published in Ukraine were in Russian, but with increasing Russification it is very unlikely that their number declined since 1963.

Even the textbooks published in Ukrainian are generally translations of Russian editions, except for those that deal with specific Ukrainian subjects written for Ukrainian schools, such as Ukrainian history, geography, language and literature. But even these, although written in Ukrainian, are full of panegyrics to Russia, Russian culture and "the great Russian people". The language is often a dull monotonous jargon with a copious admixture of Russian words, in a style that blatantly defies the rules of grammar and has nothing in common with Ukrainian, either literary or vernacular. Ukrainian school readers are often made up of a large number of translations from Russian. The reader for grade 1 by N. O. Hovyadovska, published in 1964, contained two Ukrainian folk tales, one Ukrainian folk song, 15 selections from Ukrainian classics and 52 translations.[38]

Another glaring example of Russian influence in Ukrainian textbooks is the *Khrestomatiya khorovykh tvoriv* (Anthology of Choir Compositions) published in Kiev in 1965 for teachers of music, students of pedagogical institutes and conductors of amateur choirs for grades 1 to 8, for one to four voices. The size of the edition was 4,500 for a country with over 30,000 general education schools and thousands of amateur choirs. But even this meager edition is unmistakably stamped with the influence of the intruder. Of a total of 90 compositions:

7 are Russian with original text only;
2 are Belorussian in Russian translations;
1 is Belorussian in the original;
31 are Russian with parallel Ukrainian translations ·
19 are Ukrainian folk songs, one of which has a parallel Russian translation;
30 are modern Ukrainian and other songs with parallel Ukrainian and Russian texts.[39]

Obviously this school anthology with its paucity of Ukrainian songs was not meant, as the size of the edition indicates, to be used universally in Ukraine. Teachers are forced to turn to song books published in Russia and teach Russian songs to Ukrainian children. The extent of this practice was brought home to me in Kiev in the autumn of 1964 when I was listening to a festival of Ukrainian school choirs of the Kiev region over the radio. All the songs without exception were Russian.

On June 12-13 1966, the Ukrainians of Czechoslovakia held their eleventh annual folk festival of Ukrainian songs and dances in the town of Svydnyk. Thirty amateur groups from Ukrainian communities participated. There were also two guest ensembles from Soviet Ukraine. The program of the latter two included only one Ukrainian song and one Ukrainian dance.[40]

Even the Ukrainian schools present a picture that is far from Ukrainian. I had an opportunity to visit three in Kiev and one in Chernivtsi; acquaintances described many others. A person walking into such a school, especially in a city or town, will likely find that on the walls hang portraits of Russian writers and leaders of the Communist party and government of the USSR; the slogans, signs and wall newspaper will be in Russian; the janitor will more than likely be Russian; music, art, industrial training and physical education will generally be taught in Russian; the library will be filled with Russian books; most children's and youth magazines will be in Russian. In the senior grades there is technical and industrial training in factories, where pupils go for one whole day each week. Industry is completely Russianized and the instruction is all in Russian.

There are many other evidences of Russification. In Kiev school No. 6 in a French class, I asked for a copy of the textbook. The student handed me a French grammar for a Russian school. In boarding school No. 7 which I visited, also in Kiev, the German textbook was "a translation from the first Russian edition". On the wall of the corridor of the same school was the following sign in Russian:

A procession of ideas, words and deeds of Ilich (Lenin—*J.K.*) is spreading over the whole universe. (Po vsey vselennoy shiritsya shestvie misley slov i del Ilicha).

In school No. 82, also Ukrainian, I was greeted by a Russian principal in Russian. On learning who I was she quickly changed to Ukrainian. Another Canadian student in Kiev described to me her visit to a Ukrainian boarding school; instruction was carried on in Russian; some of the teachers could not even speak Ukrainian.

The Russian language is given increased preference in the school curriculum. The ministry of education published the following timetables for the school year 1956-57:[41]

Number of hours per week for each grade

For full secondary schools with Ukrainian language of instruction.

	Grades									
	1	2	3	4	5	6	7	8	9	10
Ukrainian language	13	10	10	6	7-6*	6-5	5	4-3	3	3
Russian language		3	4	4	5-6	5-6	6	5-4	4	4

*7 hrs. per week in the first term and 6 in the second.

For full secondary schools with Russian language of instruction.

Russian language	13	10	10	6	7-6	6-5	6	5-4	4	4
Ukrainian language		3	4	4	5-6	5-6	5	4-3	3	3

Both languages in grades 1-6 are allotted the same number of hours per week. However, in grades 7-10 Russian is given one hour per week more in both Russian and Ukrainian schools.

The timetables for 1964-65 contained the following changes:[42]

Number of hours per week for each grade

For eight-year and full secondary schools with Ukrainian language of instruction.

	Grades							
	1	2	3	4	5	6	7	8
Ukrainian language	12	8	7-8	6	4-3	4-3	2	2
Russian language		4	5-4	5	3-4	3	2	2

For eight-year and full secondary schools with Russian language of instruction.

Russian language	12	9	9	8	4	4	2	2
Ukrainian language		3	3	3	3	3-2	2	2

Let us now make some further comparisons:

	Grades							
	1	2	3	4	5	6	7	8
Russian language in Russian schools	12	9	9	8	4	4	2	2
Ukrainian language in Ukrainian schools	12	8	7-8	6	4-3	4-3	2	2

In five grades: 2, 3, 4, 5 and 6, the Ukrainian language in Ukrainian schools is allotted less time than the Russian language in Russian schools in the same grades.

Let us proceed with further comparisons:

	Grades							
	1	2	3	4	5	6	7	8
Russian language in Ukrainian schools	0	4	5-4	5	3-4	3	2	2
Ukrainian language in Russian schools	0	3	3	3	3	3-2	2	2

Here we have the same discrimination against Ukrainian in the very same grades. The weekly timetable for literature in senior grades is as follows:

	Grades		
	9	10	11
Ukrainian	3	3	3
Russian	4	3	3

Here again Russian gets preference; in grade 9 it is allotted one hour per week more than Ukrainian. Calculating it on a yearly basis Russian gets 140 hours whereas Ukrainian gets only 105.

There have been many protests against this discrimination toward the Ukrainian language. Some of these have even found their way onto the printed page. At a teachers' convention in Kiev in 1959 there were sharp protests in the section of Ukrainian and

Russian language teachers over the amount of time prescribed for the native tongue, with recommendations for an increase in the number of hours for Ukrainian literature in grades 9-11. In the meeting of directors and deputies of schools for working and rural youth, M. O. Mikhaylenko proposed "an increase of one hour for the study of the native tongue".[43]

In 1965, a Kiev newspaper reported on a conference, held at the Pedagogical Research Institute of that city, concerning problems associated with the teaching of literature in secondary schools. The participants expressed alarm over the continuous decrease in the number of hours for the teaching of Ukrainian literature and pointed to the need to increase them. S. Kryzhanivsky, a Ukrainian poet and critic, who was a member of a Ukrainian tourist group that visited Canada and the United States in November-December 1964, remarked that "even these positions should be held", implying that there was danger of further decreases in the number of hours for the study of Ukrainian literature in secondary schools.[44] He did not name the source of the threat (one does not specify such things in Ukraine) but everyone knew that "the basic principles in the realm of education are laid down by the higher organs of state power of the Soviet Union".[45]

Protests notwithstanding, new measures favouring Russian have been introduced recently. In November 1966, the CC of the Council of Ministers of the USSR passed a decree to improve the work of the secondary general education schools. The number of hours of instruction for grades 1-4 was set at 24 per week and for grades 5-10 at 30. However for non-Russian schools the number is to be increased by two to three to provide time for studying the national language which can only be taken in addition to the full curriculum set for Russian schools. This means an extra examination for children in the national schools. Russian was also given special preference in grades 5-10 of non-Russian village schools where classes over 25 will be divided in two for the study of the Russian language.[46]

There are also many special educational institutions where children are subjected to unrestricted Russification. Among these are pioneer camps where those selected go on week-ends and holidays. The author visited several in Ukraine. In one of these on the island of Khortytsia in the Dnieper River, opposite the industrial town of Zaporizhya, Russian dominated everywhere. Even the camp officials and workers did not know the Ukrainian language. The same was true for the famous pioneer camp—Artek, which stretches for seven miles along the Black Sea, east of Yalta. Even the text of a coloured photo album depicting life in the camp was in Russian with translations in English, German and French.[47]

The cities have pioneer palaces in which children pursue their interests after school and on Saturdays. In the Lviv institution, although Russification was not complete, the Russian influence was strong. Among the group workers were many Ukrainians, but the director was a Russian, T. Martyanova. In the Kiev palace everything was Russianized. In the spring of 1965 an entirely new Pioneer palace was opened. Although foreigners were usually invited to such events, I was not included on this occasion. When an acquaintance who had been at the opening, described the event, the reason became clear; the whole ceremony had been in Russian. How could they invite a foreigner whom they knew to be an implacable enemy of Russification?

In discussing Russian influence we must also mention the Suvorov military and Nakhimov naval schools where children get a general education along with the military arts.[48] Since they are under the all-union jurisdiction, instruction is all in Russian.

This much for the first stage: Russification of Ukrainian schools. Now let us see how the second stage is proceeding—the entire elimination of the Ukrainian language from the schools of Ukraine.

One step in this direction is the elimination of Ukrainian books from school libraries. A correspondent for a Kiev paper reported that in the new school No. 178, there were 1,400 pupils with a library of 3,323 books of which 14 were Ukrainian. In school No. 118, for grades 1-8, comprising 700 pupils, there were 400 Ukrainian books, but for the juniors there was not one.[49] A month later, a group of investigators reported in the same paper that in the

Ukrainian school No. 92, named after Ivan Franko the famous Ukrainian poet, which is rated as one of the finest in the Lenin ward of Kiev, they found very few volumes by Franko and even fewer by other Ukrainian writers. In school No. 47 the only volume by Sosyura, a great Ukrainian lyric poet, was in a Russian translation.[50]

One reason for the lack of Ukrainian books in school libraries is due to the fact that they are simply not available. A teacher from a school in the district town of Yavoriv in Western Ukraine recently complained in the columns of a Kiev newspaper that her school library had a seventeen volume de luxe edition of Emile Zola (presumably in Russian), but did not have and could not obtain the twelve volume edition of Franko or the works of Mykytenko, Dniprovsky, Vukhnal or Kosynka.[51] The winners in a literary contest on Shevchenko could not receive copies of the poets works because these were not available. Instead it was proposed that they be given the works of the German novelist Remarque, also in Russian translation.[52]

In a letter to the Writers Union of Ukraine, the YCL organization of boarding school No. 1 in Uman, a district town in Central Ukraine, complained that the library could not find the works of the Ukrainian authors, among them M. Stelmakh and O. Honchar, the two greatest contemporary Ukrainian novelists.[53]

The absence of Ukrainian books in the libraries of the schools of Ukraine is also the direct result of official policy. A recent list made up of books published in 1965 and authorized by the Ministry of Education of the Ukrainian SSR for school libraries, contained 117 in foreign languages (English, French and German), 111 in Russian and only 99 in Ukrainian. Some books were authorized in the Russian edition although they were also published in Ukrainian. Among these was *The Constitution of the USSR*.[54]

Another list of recommended books for supplementary reading for grades 5-8 were all in Russian. Even the works of leading Ukrainian writers, among them Ivan Franko, are to be read in Russian[55] (See figures 3 and 4).

Children's and youth magazines in school libraries are also

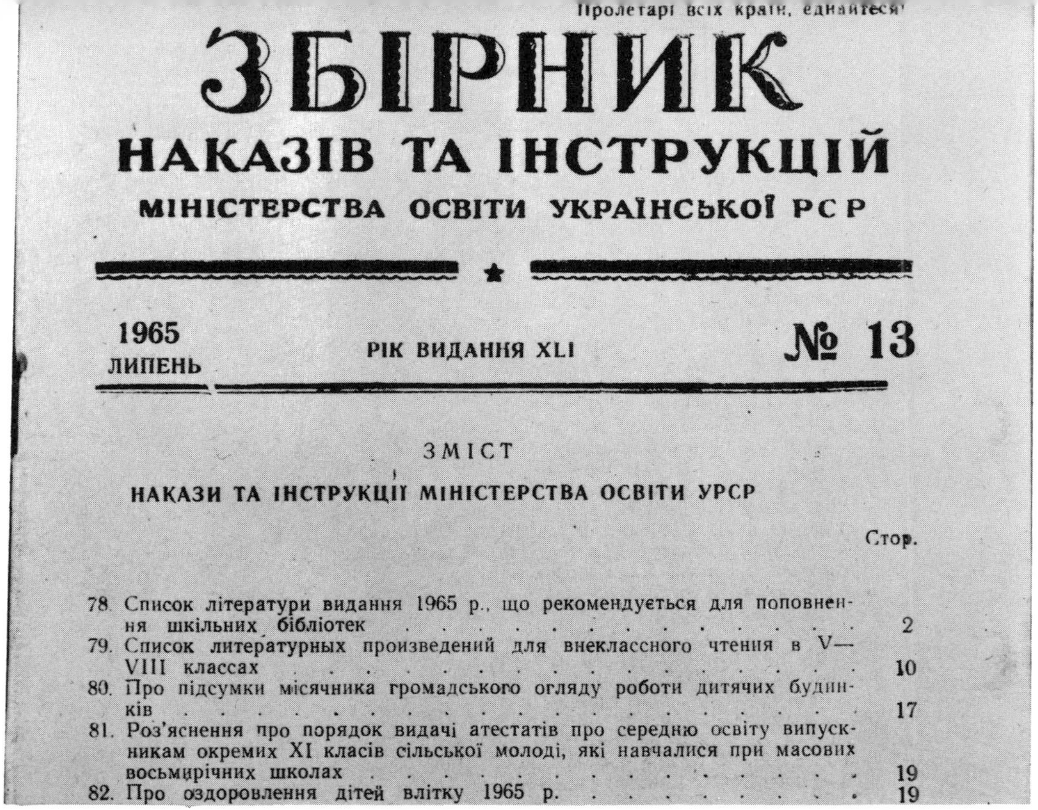

Пролетарі всіх країн, єднайтеся!

ЗБІРНИК
НАКАЗІВ ТА ІНСТРУКЦІЙ
МІНІСТЕРСТВА ОСВІТИ УКРАЇНСЬКОЇ РСР

1965 ЛИПЕНЬ | РІК ВИДАННЯ XLI | № 13

ЗМІСТ

НАКАЗИ ТА ІНСТРУКЦІЇ МІНІСТЕРСТВА ОСВІТИ УРСР

Figure 3. **Title page of a Collection of Directives and Instructions of the Ministry of Education of the Ukrainian SSR, listing books published in 1965 that are authorized for school libraries and books recommended for supplementary reading in grades 5-8.**

Лапин А. Ледовые крылья.
Негримовский А. В школьной мастерской
Орлова А. Школьная агрохимическая лаборатория.
Отрященков Ю. Азбука радиоуправления моделями.
Сворень Р. Усилители и радиоузлы.
Чубенко П. В мире неожиданных загадок.

Детям о здоровье
Гром И. Целебные растения.
Орлов Н. Съедобные и несъедобные грибы.

Спорт — детям
Адуевский В. На прицеле — кольцо.
Васильев В. Здравствуй, ракетка.
Ганчук В. Олимпийский новичок.
Горбунов В. Здоровье — твой клад.
Пашинин В. Богатырская потеха.
Пушкин В. Перед выходом на ринг.
Светов А. Спрашивай — отвечаем.
Соколов Е. Легче воздуха.
Сорокин Ю. Невидимое оружие.
Стариков В. Так начинается спорт.
Филатов Л. Тайны золотой богини.

79. СПИСОК
литературных произведений для внеклассного чтения в V—VIII классах

V класс

В .Смирнова. Герои Эллады.
Сказки народов СССР (в издании для детей и юношества).
Избранные сказки народов стран народной демократии (в издании для детей и юношества) *.
Избранные сказки «1001 ночь» (в изданиях для детей и юношества).
Г. Х. Андерсен. Избранные сказки.
З. Бядуля. Сказки.
А. Бикчетаев. Большой оркестр.
П. Бажов. Уральские сказы. Живое слово.
Ершов. Витя Коробков — пионер-партизан.
Ю. Збанацкий. Среди добрых людей.
А. Гайдар. Судьба барабанщика.
А. Гайдар. Тимур и его команда.
А .Голубева. Мальчик из Уржума.
В. Катаев. Белеет парус одинокий.
Л. Лагин. Старик Хоттабыч.
С. Маршак. Короткая повесть.
А. Мусатов. Стожары.
Ю. Сотник. Невиданная птица.
А. Кононов. Повесть о верном сердце.
Б. Полевой. Наш Ленин.
Е. Стасова. Таким был Владимир Ильич.
О. Ульянова. Младший брат Ленина.
Д. Дефо. Робинзон Крузо.
М. Твен. Приключения Тома Сойера.

* В различных сборниках.

Figure 4. **Page from the Collection of Directives and Instructions of the Ministry of Education of the Ukrainian SSR, listing books authorized for school libraries (upper half of page) and books recommended for supplementary reading for grade 5 (lower half of page). All are in Russian.**

predominantly Russian. A check of the periodical catalogue revealed that 19 titles were published in Russia and only three in Ukraine: *Malyatko, Barvinok* and *Pioneriya*.[56] The last two are published in both Ukrainian and Russian editions. The sizes of these is also significant. For *Barvinok* for 1966 it was as follows:

Total of Magazines Published	Ukrainian	%	Russian	%	
350,000	225,000	64.3	125,000	35.7	57

For *Pioneriya* there was an increase in size of editions from 1966 to 1967 as follows:

	Total of Magazines Published	Ukrainian	%	Russian	%
1966	82,800	57,800	69.8	25,000	30.2
1967	115,000	75,000	65.2	40,000	34.8

Not only is the Russian edition of both magazines high in proportion to the Russian population in Ukraine, but, for the last named it increased in 1967, while the size of the Ukrainian decreased.

The campaign is in full swing to eliminate the Ukrainian language as a subject from non-Ukrainian schools in Ukraine. I. K. Bilodid, the Minister of Education at that time, denied in 1960 that there were Russian schools without Ukrainian language classes, when he said:

> Great attention is given to the Ukrainian language in schools with the Russian language of instruction, where it is studied because of the wishes of the parents.[58]

However Alla Bondar admitted that there are classes without Ukrainian as a subject, but tried to minimize the extent of such cases. She stated that:

> ...in schools with instruction in Russian *there are almost no full classes where Ukrainian is not studied.* (Italics mine—*J.K.*)

She explained that students not studying Ukrainian are children of parents who as a result of their profession are forced constantly to change their place of residence: military personnel, geologists, construction workers and others. But let us ask, Why is Ukrainian not taught in any of the schools of Sevastopol? Or why, in schools where the language of instruction is Moldavian, Hungarian or Polish, Russian is taught as a subject but Ukrainian is not?[60] (See figure 5)

The same process of Russification is going on in other republics. Into Belorussia, whose population in 1959 was 8,030,634,[61] over 34 million copies of textbooks were imported from the RSFSR in nine years (1952-1960). The number of hours of teaching of Russian, which is introduced in Belorussian schools in grade 2, was increased. Belorussian on the other hand is introduced in Russian schools in grade 3, but, whereas all pupils in Belorussian schools study Russian, pupils in Russian schools study Belorussian only "on the basis of choice".[62]

According to reports of Belorussians who visited Kiev when I lived there, Russification in Belorussia has advanced to the stage where there are no schools in Minsk the capital city, with Belorussian as the language of instruction.

Russian is also introduced in grade 1 in the non-Russian schools of Kazakhstan and other "brother republics of our Motherland".[63] The curriculum of the schools of non-Russian minorities in Azerbaidzhan does not include the language of the republic,[64] just as Ukrainian is not included in such schools in Ukraine. Instead they teach Russian and become another means of extending Russification.

Responsible Ukrainian officials informed me that there have lately been ominous moves in the direction of eliminating the Ukrainian language from all Russian schools in Ukraine. The ministry of education of each republic is closely supervised by the section on schools of the Department of Science, Higher Educational Institutions and Schools of the CC of the CPSU. The "instructor", or representative of the latter body to the ministry of education in Ukraine, is a certain Suntsov. On the instructions

УЧЕБНЫЙ ПЛАН

для восьмилетних и средних школ Украинской ССР с венгерским, молдавским или польским языками обучения

№ п/п	Предметы	Недельное количество часов на класс										
		Восьмилетняя школа								Средняя школа		
		I	II	III	IV	V	VI	VII	VIII	IX	X	XI
1.	Родной язык	12	8	7—8	6	4—3	4—3	2	2	—	—	—
2.	Родная литература	—	—	—	—	2	2	2	2	—	—	—
3.	Русский язык	—	4	5—4	5—6	3—4	3	2	2	2	2	3
4.	Русская литература	—	—	—	—	2	2	2	2	1	1	—
5.	Арифметика	6	6	6	6	6	2	—	—	—	—	—
6.	Алгебра	—	—	—	—	—	2	4—3	3—2	3	2—3	2
7.	Геометрия	—	—	—	—	—	2	2—3	2—3	2	3—2	2
8.	Тригонометрия	—	—	—	—	—	—	—	—	—	—	1
9.	Физика	—	—	—	—	—	2	2	3	3	3—4	3
10.	Астрономия	—	—	—	—	—	—	—	—	—	—	1
11.	Химия	—	—	—	—	—	—	2	2	2	2	3
12.	Естествознание	—	—	—	2	—	—	—	—	—	—	—
13.	Биология	—	—	—	—	2	2	2	2	2	—	—
14.	Практические занятия на пришкольном учебно-опытном участке	—	—	—	—	0—1	0—1	0—1	—	—	—	—
15.	География	—	—	—	—	2	2	2	2	—	2—1	2
16.	История	—	—	—	2—1	2	2	3—2	3—4	3	4	2
17.	Обществоведение	—	—	—	—	—	—	—	—	—	—	2
18.	Иностранный язык	—	—	—	—	4—3	3	3	3—2	2	2	2
19.	Труд	2	2	2	2	2	2	2	2	—	—	—
20.	Рисование	1	1	1	1	1	1	—	—	—	—	—
21.	Черчение	—	—	—	—	—	—	1	1	1	1	—
22.	Музыка и пение	1	1	1	1	1	1	1	1	—	—	—
23.	Производственное обучение	—	—	—	—	—	—	—	—	9	9	8
24.	Физическая культура	2	2	2	2	2	2	2	2	2	2	2
25.	Гражданская оборона	—	—	—	—	—	—	—	—	1	—	—
	Всего	24	24	24	27	33	34	34	34	36	36	36
26.	Учебно-производственная практика (часов на год)	—	—	—	—	18	24	48	—	72	108	—
27.	Факультативные занятия (часов в неделю)	—	—	—	—	—	—	—	—	3	3	3

Figure 5. **Timetable for elementary and secondary schools in Ukraine with instruction in Hungarian, Moldavian and Polish. Russian language and literature are included in the curriculum, Ukrainian is not.**

of the CC he has been applying pressure to the Council of Ministers of the UkrSSR to abolish completely the study of the Ukrainian language in Russian schools because "it is too difficult for Russian students to learn both languages". So far the Council of Ministers has been successful in staving off the measure.

Lately a new step was taken to establish greater central control over the republican ministries of general education, which until then had a semblance of independence. The formation of a Union-Republican Ministry of Education of the USSR was announced.[65] Five days later the Presidium of the Supreme Soviet of the UkrSSR passed a decree transforming its ministry of education from republican to union-republican,[66] thus placing it under the jurisdiction of the all-union ministry in Moscow and casting aside the last pretense of autonomy. At the same time the Academy of Pedagogical Sciences of the RSFSR was also given an all-union jurisdiction.[67]

Among the added "blessings" of this new arrangement will be an all-union centre of education located in Russia, directed and staffed by Russians but providing "improved programs of studies, educational plans and textbooks for all schools of the country".[68]

Teachers are subject to the same pressures of Russification. In Ukraine there are only four pedagogical journals; twenty are published in Moscow in Russian.[69] Immediately after the Second World War, however, the following pedagogical journals were published in Kiev in Ukrainian:

Heohrafiya v shkoli (Geography in School)
Istoriya v shkoli (History in School)
Pryrodoznavsto i khimiya v shkoli (Nature Study and Chemistry in School)
Kulturno-osvitnya robota (Cultural-Educational Work)

The first one ceased publication in 1948 and the last three in 1949.[70]

Teacher training institutions in Ukraine have their quotas of Russian students for whom lectures must be in their native tongue, "because they do not understand Ukrainian", and Russian lecturers and professors who use Russian because "they cannot speak Ukrainian". This is particularly true of the 24 regional and two city Institutes for Improving the Qualifications of Teachers. Many of the directors and staff are Russians and they decide whose qualifications are to be improved.

Russification is pursued by many other devious and nefarious means. Draftees are sent away from their native republics for military training. Thus Ukrainians train everywhere but in their own country, while Russians and others are sent to Ukraine. Consequently, Russian-language schools are organized for military personnel. The trainees are encouraged to settle after demobilization in the areas where they trained and more Russian schools are opened to accommodate their children.

Another policy promoting Russification is the directing of Russians to fill leading positions in industry, party and government in the national republics. When a factory is built in Ukraine the personnel to operate it comes mostly from Russia; leading positions in villages are also often filled by Russians. When such bureaucrats arrive they immediately demand Russian schools for their children. One of two things happens: a Ukrainian school becomes a Russian school, or parallel Russian classes are organized in a Ukrainian school and it becomes a "mixed school". This is a first step to a Russian school. Many schools in Lviv, Kiev and other cities are mixed schools. This writer had an opportunity to visit what was supposed to be a Ukrainian school in Kiev—school No. 6. It was in reality a mixed school and Russian predominated everywhere.

Russification is also accompanied by a planned discrimination against education in Ukraine and other republics of the USSR. With 19.68 percent of the total population of the USSR (appendix II), Ukraine had only 16.15 percent of all general education schools (regular day, afternoon and evening for working and rural youth, adult and correspondence) and 17.97 percent of all pupils; the RSFSR, with 54.87 percent of the population had 55.88 percent of the schools and 54.66 percent of the pupils in 1965 (table II). Since education is compulsory in the USSR to the end of grade 8, one can only conclude that many drop out after reaching this level in the UkrSSR and go to work.

TABLE II

Number of General Education Schools of All Types and Number of Pupils Attending in Republics of USSR, 1965

	Number of General Education Schools	%	Number of Pupils	%
USSR	214,290	100	48,255,000	100
Russian SFSR	119,746	55.88	26,374,000	54.66
Ukrainian SSR	34,613	16.15	8,671,000	17.97
Belorussian SSR	13,000	6.07	1,782,000	3.69
Uzbek SSR	8,716	4.07	2,476,000	5.13
Kazakh SSR	10,578	4.94	2,809,000	5.82
Georgian SSR	4,673	2.18	938,000	1.94
Azerbaidzhan SSR	5,491	2.56	1,141,000	2.37
Lithuanian SSR	4,404	2.06	556,000	1.15
Moldavian SSR	2,552	1.19	766,000	1.59
Latvian SSR	1,382	.64	349,000	.72
Kirgiz SSR	2,056	.96	629,000	1.30
Tadzhik SSR	2,834	1.32	583,000	1.21
Armenian SSR	1,574	.73	529,000	1.10
Turkmen SSR	1,603	.75	435,000	.90
Estonian SSR	1,088	.50	217,000	.45

Source: *Narodnoe Khozaystvo 1965*, pp. 684-85.

Education in Ukraine is also discriminated against financially. For 1965 her share of the total budget for all education in the republics of the USSR was 17.39 percent and for general education, 17.42 percent, while Russia's share was 55.98 and 54.22 percent (table III). Worked out on a per capita basis Ukraine received 49.25 roubles for all education and 19.68 for general education; Russia received 56.88 and 21.96 roubles respectively.

It should be pointed out that this discrimination is the result of central planning in Moscow, because there is a single state budget for the USSR from which the central government allots "revenues which go to the union, republican and local budgets".[71]

However the above statistics do not give the complete picture. In addition to the republican budgets, there is a special education budget for the all-union government. This totalled 4,733.5 million roubles for all education and 86.5 million for general education in 1965 (table III). The central government, dominated by Russians, with its centre in Moscow, may use some of this money in the national republics, but the purpose is to extend Russification and central control.

Even the little tots in Ukraine are discriminated against. Crèches and kindergartens are organized to accommodate pre-school children. However, they are not extended in equal measure to all republics. In 1965, of all kindergartens and crèche-kindergartens in the USSR, only 14.38 percent were in Ukraine while 64.27 percent were in Russia. In the former, 15.65 percent of all children were accommodated and in the latter, 63.04 (table IV). The discrimination will fall heaviest on Ukrainian children because Russian children in Ukraine will have preference.

These institutions suffer the same financial discrimination. In 1965 only 14.93 percent of the total budget for all kindergartens in the USSR was allotted to Ukraine, while Russia received 61.73 percent (table V). On a per capita basis this works out to 5.11 roubles for the former and 7.58 for the latter.

School children in Ukraine do not have the same opportunity to attend Pioneer camps as those in Russia. In 1965 Ukraine had only 15.91 percent of all camps in the USSR; Russia had 67.53

TABLE III

Budget for All Education and General Education for the Republics of the USSR, 1965

(In millions of roubles)

	All Education	%	General Education for the Republics	%
Russian SFSR	7,152.9	55.98	2,762.3	54.22
Ukrainian SSR	2,221.4	17.39	887.4	17.42
Belorussian SSR	486.6	3.81	221.4	4.35
Uzbek SSR	512.3	4.01	246.1	4.83
Kazakh SSR	701.6	5.49	267.4	5.25
Georgian SSR	270.9	2.12	120.0	2.36
Azerbaidzhan SSR	256.7	2.01	117.7	2.31
Lithuanian SSR	188.6	1.48	72.9	1.43
Moldavian SSR	169.7	1.33	78.4	1.53
Latvian SSR	150.6	1.18	47.5	.93
Kirgiz SSR	147.1	1.15	62.7	1.23
Tadzhik SSR	144.5	1.13	66.3	1.30
Armenian SSR	166.7	1.30	66.4	1.30
Turkmen SSR	109.6	.86	48.8	.96
Estonian SSR	97.7	.76	29.5	.58
		100		100
Total for republics	12,776.9		5,094.8	
All-union (USSR) budget	4,733.5		86.5	
Total for republics and USSR	17,510.4		5,181.3	

Source: *Ministerstvo finansov SSR, Byudzhetnoe upravlenie* (Ministry of Finances of the USSR, Budgetary Administration). *Gosudarstvenny byudghet SSSR i byudzhety soyznykh respublik* (State Budget of the USSR and the Budgets of the Union Republics). Statistical Handbook, Moscow, 1966, pp. 31, 36.

TABLE IV

Number of Kindergartens and combined Crèche-Kindergartens and
Children in Them in the Republics of the USSR, 1965

	Number of Kindergartens and Crèche-Kindergartens	%	Number of Children in Them	%
USSR	67,537	100	6,207,300	100
Russian SFSR	43,401	64.27	3,913,300	63.04
Ukrainian SSR	9,713	14.38	971,500	15.65
Belorussian SSR	1,525	2.26	168,500	2.72
Uzbek SSR	2,445	3.62	227,400	3.66
Kazakh SSR	4,143	6.13	360,200	5.80
Georgian SSR	997	1.48	83,600	1.35
Azerbaidzhan SSR	943	1.40	76,600	1.23
Lithuanian SSR	544	.80	42,900	.69
Moldavian SSR	618	.91	57,500	.93
Latvian SSR	516	.76	45,900	.74
Kirgiz SSR	547	.81	55,800	.90
Tadzhik SSR	349	.52	47,000	.76
Armenian SSR	666	.99	62,000	1.00
Turkmen SSR	698	1.03	59,800	.96
Estonian SSR	432	.64	35,300	.57

Source: *Narodnoe Khozaystvo 1965*, pp. 686-87.

TABLE V

Budget for Kindergartens for the Republics of the USSR, 1965

(In millions of roubles)		%
Russian SFSR	953.2	61.73
Ukrainian SSR	230.5	14.93
Belorussian SSR	43.8	2.84
Uzbek SSR	66.7	4.32
Kazakh SSR	87.8	5.69
Georgian SSR	19.8	1.28
Azerbaidzhan SSR	20.4	1.32
Lithuanian SSR	15.2	.98
Moldavian SSR	20.5	1.33
Latvian SSR	17.8	1.15
Kirgiz SSR	14.6	.95
Tadzhik SSR	14.5	.94
Armenian SSR	18.5	1.20
Turkmen SSR	11.4	.74
Estonian SSR	9.3	.60
		100
Total for union republics	1,544.0	
All-union (USSR) budget	279.5	
Total for USSR and republics	1,823.5	

Source: *Gosudarstvenny Byudzhet SSSR*, p. 33.

percent. Of all children accommodated, only 15.51 percent were from Ukraine while 69.46 percent were from Russia (table VI).

Another significant aspect of education in Ukraine is that, whereas the UkrSSR obtains a smaller share of the education budget than it rightly deserves, it is not the Russian but the Ukrainian schools that suffer; the former are larger, receive a disproportionate share of the budget and consequently occupy better buildings and are better equipped and better supplied as was often pointed out to the writer while he lived in Ukraine.

This is one inducement for parents to send their children to Russian schools; there are many others. Some parents prefer Russian general education schools because instruction in the higher educational institutions is in Russian; some send their children out of fear and some because of pressure. The program of the party states that:

> Full scale Communist construction constitutes a new stage in the development of national relations in the USSR, in which the nations will draw still closer together until complete unity is achieved.[72]

"Complete unity" is, of course, nothing less than complete Russification.

The new school law gave parents a "choice" of the language in which their children would be instructed. Russians do not "choose"; they remain Russian. But Ukrainians have a choice; they can send their children to Ukrainian or Russian schools. How clever, how magnanimous and how democratic! But the party has decreed that there will be complete unity. No party or government official, who values his position in a country where the passport to security and advancement is unswerving support of policies laid down in Moscow, will risk sending his children to a Ukrainian school. Sycophants and those who wish to get ahead also fall into line. Yes, their children also attend Russian schools; so do the children of cabinet ministers in Ukraine; so did the children of the Minister of Education.[73]

TABLE VI

Number of Out-of-town Pioneer Camps and Number of Children
Accommodated in such Camps in Republics of the USSR, 1965

	Number of Out-of-town Pioneer Camps	%	Number of Children	%
USSR	8776	100	5,073,900	100
Russian SFSR	5926	67.53	3,524,200	69.46
Ukrainian SSR	1396	15.91	787,200	15.51
Belorussian SSR	310	3.53	140,200	2.76
Uzbek SSR	156	1.78	102,400	2.04
Kazakh SSR	385	4.39	195,300	3.85
Georgian SSR	103	1.17	49,800	.98
Azerbaidzhan SSR	104	1.17	46,700	.92
Lithuanian SSR	67	.76	34,700	.68
Moldavian SSR	45	.51	27,200	.53
Latvian SSR	67	.76	34,100	.67
Kirgiz SSR	50	.57	38,100	.75
Tadzhik SSR	27	.31	20,200	.40
Armenian SSR	49	.57	29,500	.58
Turkmen SSR	23	.26	19,000	.37
Estonian SSR	68	.78	25,300	.50

Source: *Narodnoe Khozaystvo 1965*, p. 684.

FOOTNOTES

1. S. Chervonenko, "Tisny zvyazok z zhyttyam—neodminna umova uspikhu ideolohichnoyi roboty (Close Connection With Life is the Indispensible Condition for Success in Ideological Work)", *Komunist Ukrayiny,* No. 7, July, 1959, p. 38.
2. Yu. Shiraev, in *Pravda Ukrainy,* July 25, 1959.
3. *Radyanska Ukrayina,* May 24, 1960.
4. *Ukrayinska Radyanska Entsyklopediya* (Ukrainian Soviet Encyclopedia), IX, Kiev 1962, p. 514. Henceforth referred to as U.R.E.
5. I. E. Kravtsev, in *Pravda Ukrainy,* December 25, 1956.
6. M. S. Hryshchenko, Narysy z istoriyi shkoly v Ukrayinskiy RSR, 1917-1965 (Outline of History of Schools in the Ukrainian SSR, 1917-1965), Kiev, 1966, p. 192.
7. Ibid., p. 190.
8. L. V. Cherkashyn, Zahalne navchannya v Ukrayinskiy RSR (General Education in the Ukrainian SSR), 1917-1957, Kiev 1958, p. 61.
9. *Radyanska Osvita,* February 1, 1958.
10. *Radyanska Ukrayina,* December 5, 1964.
11. *Pravda Ukrainy,* November 3, 1966.
12. Ibid.
13. H. I. Yasnytsky, Rozvytok narodnoyi osvity na Ukrayini 1921-1932 rr. (The Development of Public Education in Ukraine 1921-1932), Kiev, 1965, p. 228.
14. *Bilshovyk Ukrayiny,* No. 3, 1938, p. 7.
15. U.R.E., XVI, Kiev, 1964, p. 341.
16. Ministerstvo Osvity Ukrayinskoyi RSR (Ministry of Education of the Ukrainian SSR), *Tematychny Plan Radyanska Shkola na 1960 rik* (Catalogue of Publications of Radyanska Shkola for 1960), Kiev, 1960, p. 11.
17. Knyzhkova Palata Ukrayinskoyi RSR (House of Books of the Ukrainian SSR), *Litopis knyh* (Annual of Books), Kharkiv, No. 9, September, 1964, pp. 51-52.
18. *Narodnoe khozaystvo,* 1964, p. 677.
19. *Literaturna Ukrayina,* October 6, 1964.
20. They circulate in hand- or typewritten copies in Ukraine. These statistics were quoted in a letter of protest against Russification to the CC of the CPU by a retired teacher. Copies of the letter also circulated.
21. *Kharkov: Sprayvochnaya kniga* (Kharkov: A Guide Book), Kharkov, 1957, pp. 216-20.
22. *Odessa: Spravochnik* (Odessa: A Guide), Odessa, 1957, pp. 155-157.
23. *Pravda,* December 16, 1965.
24. Ministerstvo vyshchoyi i serednoyi spetsialnoyi osvity Ukrayinskoyi RSR (Ministry of Higher and Secondary Special Education of the Ukrainian SSR), *Heohrafiya Kyyivskoyi oblasti: Atlas* (Geography of the Kiev Region: An Atlas), A. S. Kharchenko, (ed.), Kiev, 1962, p. 66.

25. *Litopis knyh,* No. 6, 1964, p. 38; No. 8, 1964, p. 38; No. 9, 1964, p. 51.
26. *Tematychny plan,* 1963, p. 11.
27. *Litopis knyh,* No. 8, 1964, p. 38; No. 9, 1964, p. 51.
28. *Tematychny plan,* 1963, p. 7.
29. *Litopis knyh,* No. 7, 1964, p. 50; No. 8, 1964, p. 37.
30. *Tematchny plan,* 1963, pp. 5, 8, 9.
31. M. S. Hryshchenko, op. cit., p. 208.
32. *Radyanska Ukrayina,* August 31, 1958.
33. *Tematchny plan,* 1958, p. 6.
34. *Radyanska Osvita,* August 21, 1963.
35. *Tematchny plan,* 1963, p. 39.
36. Ibid.
37. *Radyanska Osvita,* May 25, 1966.
38. *Literaturna Ukrayina,* May 21, 1965.
39. P. O. Rudchenko, and V. M. Luzhny, (compilers), *Khrestomatiya khorobykh tvoriv* (Anthology of Choir Compositions), Kiev, 1965.
40. *Zhyttya i Slovo* (Life and Word), Toronto, January 5, 1966, p. 21.
41. *Radyanska Osvita,* August 18, 1956.
42. *Radyanska Osvita,* August 19, 1964.
43. Ministerstvo Osvity URSR (Ministry of Education of the UkrSSR), *Zyizd uchyteliv Ukrayinskoyi RSR, 14-16 zhovtnya, 1959 roku* (Convention of Teachers of the Ukrainian SSR, October 14-16, 1959), Kiev, 1960, pp. 184, 208.
44. *Literaturna Ukrayina,* March 30, 1965.
45. E. P. Pichugina, *Pravo na obrazovanie v SSSR* (The Right to Education in the USSR), Moscow, 1957, p. 24.
46. *Pravda,* November 19, 1966.
47. L. Kondrashchenko, *Respublika krasnykh galstukov* (The Republic of Red Ties), Simferopol, 1964.
48. E. N. Medynsky, *Prosveshchenie v SSSR* (Education in the USSR), Moscow, 1955, p. 20.
49. *Literaturna Ukrayina,* October 23, 1964.
50. Ibid. November 20, 1964.
51. Hryhoriy Kosynka, a talented young writer who was arrested with thirty-six other Ukrainian literary figures in Kiev in December 1934 and charged with "preparation of terrorist acts against employees of the Soviet state" (*Prvda* December 11, 1934). He and twenty-seven others were found guilty and sentenced to be shot. (*Visti,* December 18, 1934). Kosynka was subsequently rehabilitated and a collection of his short stories was published in 1962. During my period in Ukraine I searched for the book in many stores in several cities to satisfy requests of friends in Canada, but found only two copies.
52. *Literaturna Ukrayina,* January 5, 1965.

53. Ibid., May 14, 1965.
54. An edition of 75,000 was published by the Publishers of Political Literature of Ukraine, Kiev, 1965. A copy is in my possession.
55. *Zbirnyk nakaziv ta instruktsiy ministerstva osvity Ukrayinskoyi RSR* (Collection of Directives and Instructions of the Ministry of Education of the Ukrainian SSR), No. 13, July, 1965, pp. 2-17.
56. Mezdunarodnaya Kniga (International Book), *Gazety i zhurnaly SSSR na 1967 god* (Newspapers and Magazines of the USSR for 1967), Moscow, pp. 62-64, 88, 90.
57. The size of editions of Soviet books and magazines is usually given at the back of the publication.
58. *Radyanska Ukrayina,* May 24, 1960.
59. Ibid., December 5, 1964.
60. *Zbirnyk nakaziv ta instruktsiy,* No. 7-8, April, 1964, pp. 26-27.
61. *Itogi vsesoyuznoy perepisi,* Summary Volume, p. 17.
62. I. Ilyushin and S. Umreyko, *Narodnoe obrazovanie v Belorusskoy SSR* (Public Education in the Belorussian SSR), Minsk, 1961, pp. 230, 237, 399.
63. A. I. Sembaev, *Ocherki po istorii Kazakhskoy Sovetskoy shkoly* (Outline of the History of the Kazakh Soviet School), Alma-Ata, 1958, p. 299.
64. M. M. Mekhti-Zade, *Ocherki istorii Sovetskoy shkoly v Azerbaidzhane* (Outline of the History of the Soviet School in Azerbaidzhan), Moscow, 1962, p. 220.
65. *Pravda,* August 4, 1966.
66. *Radyanska Ukrayina,* August 9, 1966. This was followed by the replacement of Alla Bondar as Minister of Education by Petro Platonovych Udovychenko (*Radyanska Ukrayina,* January 22, 1967), a former diplomat and permanent representative of the UkrSSR to the UN from 1958-1961. During my stay in Kiev he was secretary of the Party Organization in Kiev University where he kept himself very busy rooting out student and staff opposition to the policies of Russification. This appointment most likely signalizes a stepped-up campaign of Russification of general elementary and secondary education.
67. *Pravda,* August 24, 1966.
68. Ibid.
69. *Zhurnaly izdalelstva "Prosveshchenie"* (Journals of Prosvshcheniye [Education] Publishing House), Moscow, 1965.
70. Ministerstvo Kultury SSSR (Ministry of Culture of the USSR), Vsesoyuznaya knizhnaya palata (All-Union House of Books), *Piriodicheskaya pechat SSSR 1917-1949* (Periodical Publications 1917-1949), Biblographical Index, Journals, Transactions. Summary Index, Moscow, 1963, pp. 397, 406, 407, 416.
71. Article 14, *Constitution (Fundamental Law) of the Union of Soviet Socialist Republics.*
72. *The Program of the Communist Party of the Soviet Union.* Foreign Languages Publishing House, Moscow, 1961, p. 102.

73. It was a generally-accepted fact in Kiev that children of cabinet ministers usually attended Russian schools. This was confirmed by several responsible officials whom I met in Kiev. Among those mentioned whose children attended Russian schools were B. A. Koval, former Minister of Higher Education and Alla Bondar. P. P. Udovychenko, the new Minister of Education was not mentioned in this connection.

5

Vocational–technical schools and secondary special educational institutions

Schools to train skilled tradesmen for industry, mining, agriculture and other branches of the national economy in each republic are under the supervision of the Central Boards of Vocational-Technical Education of the Councils of Ministers, which in turn are under the direction of the State Committee of Vocational-Technical Education of the Council of Ministers of the USSR. This body, which to July 11 1959, was known as the Central Board of Labour Reserves of the Council of Ministers of the USSR, has wide powers and many functions.

It publishes in Russian the only journal on vocational-technical education in the USSR, *Profesionalno-tekhnicheskoe obrazovanie* (Vocational-Technical Education); under its jurisdiction is the publishing firm Proftekhizdat, which supplies textbooks in Russian for vocational-technical schools in all republics. In addition it operates The Central Scientific Research Centre on Methodology, an all-union enterprise which produces visual aids for vocational-technical schools, The Institute for Improving the

Qualifications and Retraining of Teachers of Vocational-Technical Schools, The Institute for Improving the Qualifications and Retraining of Teachers of Schools for Mechanization of Agriculture, the permanent all-union Exhibition of Technical Inventions of Students and a permanent pavilion at the Exhibition of the Achievements of the National Economy of the USSR.[1]

Vocational-technical schools are attached to a factory or other enterprise and accept pupils who have completed grade 8. There are regular courses for students in full time attendance as well as afternoon and evening courses for those regularly employed. In rural schools instruction is from one to two years; in urban from one to three. In addition there is a wide variety of shorter courses for improving the qualifications of employees, and individual and group training on the job.

The number trained in each institution and their place of employment after graduation is laid down by plans worked out jointly by Gosplan (the State Planning Commission), the State Committee of Vocational-Technical Education of the Council of Ministers of the USSR and the republican ministries. These bodies jointly make recommendations to the Council of Ministers of the USSR (which has jurisdiction over all labour reserves) for transfer of trained personnel from one republic to another and to the far eastern and northern regions.[2]

Pupils for vocational-technical schools may be recruited in one republic, trained in another and directed to work in a third. A reliable informant related to the author the recent case of boys who were sent from the Poltava region in central Ukraine to schools in Russia. On graduation they were directed to construction sites beyond the Urals.

Ukraine is discriminated against in this type of education in comparison to the RSFSR. In 1965 the latter had 63.7 percent of all graduates of vocational-technical schools in the USSR, while Ukraine had 16.36 percent (table VII). But Russia's percentage of the total population of the USSR that year was only 54.87 and Ukraine's was 19.68 (see appendix II). Per 10,000 population Russia had 52 graduates and Ukraine only 38. The same discrimi-

TABLE VII

Number of Graduates of Vocational-Technical Schools in the
Republics of the USSR, 1965

		%
Total in USSR	1,042,200	100
Russian SFSR	663,900	63.70
Ukrainian SSR	170,500	16.36
Belorussian SSR	30,500	2.93
Uzbek SSR	20,000	1.92
Kazakh SSR	86,500	8.30
Georgian SSR	7,700	.74
Azerbaidzhan SSR	8,500	.81
Lithuanian SSR	7,300	.70
Moldavian SSR	9,000	.86
Latvian SSR	8,900	.85
Kirgiz SSR	7,700	.74
Tadzhik SSR	5,800	.56
Armenian SSR	7,900	.76
Turkmen SSR	4,700	.45
Estonian SSR	3,300	.32

Source: *Narodnoe Khozaystvo 1965,* p. 584.

nation existed in all other republics except Kazakhstan where the percentage of graduates exceeded the percentage of population. However, while there is no official data, one can surmise that many of these were not native Kazakhs, but students from the RSFSR and other republics of the USSR.

Personal investigation by the author while in Ukraine revealed that all such schools are conducted in Russian. Confirmation of this Russification exists in various published materials. For example there is *A Handbook for Entrants to City and Vocational-Technical Schools of Dnipropetrovsk Region, Dnipropetrovsk 1964.*[3] This students' handbook is in Russian. Annual statistical handbooks from 1955 to 1964 on publishing in the USSR, show that textbooks for such schools are published in the RSFSR. Books of this type are listed as published in Ukraine only in 1955 (there is no data available before that year); the number of titles was three.[4] The fact that textbooks are in Russian means that the language of instruction is also Russian. This is further confirmed by timetables for such schools for 1957 which list only the Russian language as a subject.[5]

However, in the 1920's and the early 1930's, the language of instruction was the pupil's native tongue. In Ukraine it was either Ukrainian or the language of one of the national minorities: Russian, Jewish, Moldavian, German, etc., where there were large concentrations of such people. Russian was not even taught as a subject in non-Russian schools.[6]

There is a great deal of Soviet propaganda about the numbers studying in the USSR while employed. Among these are workers and employees who improve their academic standing and technical qualifications without losing time from work. Soviet statistics indicate that the workers and employees of Ukraine, for some mysterious reason lag behind those of Russia in this type of education. In 1965, of all those who improved their qualifications in the USSR while employed, 65.67 percent lived in the RSFSR and only 17.94 percent in the UkrSSR (table VIII). Per 10,000 population this works out to 493 in the RSFSR and only 375 in the UkrSSR. In all republics except Russia, Latvia and Estonia, the

TABLE VIII

Number of Workers and Employees who Improved their Qualifications
while Employed in the Republics of the USSR, 1965

		%
Total in USSR	9,445,300	100
Russian SFSR	6,202,900	65.67
Ukrainian SSR	1,694,900	17.94
Belorussian SSR	289,000	3.06
Uzbek SSR	197,300	2.09
Kazakh SSR	396,600	4.20
Georgian SSR	66,100	.70
Azerbaidzhan SSR	84,600	.90
Lithuanian SSR	87,000	.92
Moldavian SSR	66,900	.71
Latvian SSR	111,600	1.18
Kirgiz SSR	52,600	.56
Tadzhik SSR	46,700	.50
Armenian SSR	49,300	.52
Turkmen SSR	31,500	.33
Estonian SSR	68,300	.72

Source: *Narodnoe Khozaystvo 1965,* p. 586.

percentage of such employees was lower than the percentage of the population of these republics.

Semi-professional training is provided by secondary special educational institutions which are governed by regulations of the Council of Ministers of the USSR.[7] Admission rules, entrance examinations and courses of study are authorized by the Ministry of Higher and Secondary Special Education of the USSR. The only journal dealing with problems connected with this type of education, *Srednee spetsialnoe obrazovanie* (Secondary Special Education), is published by the ministry in Russian. There was a total of 714 of these institutions in Ukraine at the beginning of the 1966-67 school year.[8] Among them were regular day, night and correspondence schools. Courses vary from three to five years for graduates of grade 8 and one and a half to three and a half for those who have completed general education secondary schools.

A study of comparative statistics on secondary special education in the USSR reveals the same shocking picture of discrimination against Ukraine in this sphere of education. Of the total number of these institutions in the USSR in 1965, only 18.25 percent were in Ukraine and 58.35 percent in Russia. The proportion of students in those of Russia was even larger—61.74 and in Ukraine smaller—17.65 percent (table IX). The subordinate relationship of Ukraine to Russia is illustrated even more clearly in table X, which gives the number of students per 10,000 population in secondary special educational institutions for the USSR and the republics in the years from 1940 to 1965. The number for Ukraine is consistently lower than the number for the USSR or the RSFSR. If we subtract the number in Ukraine from the number in the RSFSR for each year, we get the comparison of the difference from year to year.

Year	1940	1950	1958	1960	1962	1963	1964	1965
	6	18	14	13	19	25	32	37

Here again we see Ukraine's underprivileged position and the increase of discrimination. A difference of 6 in 1940 has grown to

TABLE IX

Number of Secondary Special Educational Institutions and
Students in them in the Republics of the USSR, 1965

	Secondary Special Educational Institutions	%	Number of Students in these	%
Total in USSR	3,820	100	3,659,300	100
Russian SFSR	2,229	58.35	2,259,300	61.74
Ukrainian SSR	697	18.25	645,900	17.65
Belorussian SSR	122	3.19	122,100	3.34
Uzbek SSR	106	2.77	103,900	2.84
Kazakh SSR	167	4.37	169,900	4.64
Georgian SSR	89	2.33	37,800	1.03
Azerbaidzhan SSR	71	1.86	55,800	1.53
Lithuanian SSR	76	1.99	57,500	1.57
Moldavian SSR	38	.99	33,100	.90
Latvian SSR	52	1.36	38,300	1.05
Kirgiz SSR	36	.94	31,800	.87
Tadzhik SSR	30	.79	23,000	.63
Armenian SSR	45	1.18	31,400	.86
Turkmen SSR	27	.71	21,900	.60
Estonian SSR	35	.92	27,600	.75

Source: *Narodnoe Khozaystvo 1965*, p. 692.

TABLE X

Number of Students in Secondary Special Educational Institutions
of the Republics of the USSR, per 10,000 Population

Year	1940	1950	1958	1960	1962	1963	1964	1965
USSR	50	71	90	95	120	132	145	158
Russian SFSR	53	79	98	105	133	148	164	179
Ukrainian SSR	47	61	84	92	114	123	132	142
Belorussian SSR	39	54	69	76	99	111	127	141
Uzbek SSR	37	62	67	60	77	81	87	98
Kazakh SSR	48	62	82	84	100	111	126	140
Georgian SSR	71	67	66	63	69	75	79	83
Azerbaidzhan SSR	52	69	71	68	87	99	109	120
Lithuanian SSR	22	45	87	115	151	170	184	193
Moldavian SSR	17	54	55	56	69	78	87	98
Latvian SSR	50	91	112	115	139	155	163	169
Kirgiz SSR	38	60	76	77	90	98	106	120
Tadzhik SSR	38	69	61	57	66	70	81	89
Armenian SSR	66	75	80	78	100	112	125	143
Turkmen SSR	57	62	88	76	87	94	103	115
Estonian SSR	20	94	105	126	171	189	203	215

Source: *Narodnoe khozaystvo 1963*, p. 57; *1964*, p. 683.

a difference of 37 per 10,000 population in 1965 between the number of students in secondary special educational institutions in the RSFSR and UkrSSR. In Belorussia the difference was wider:

Year	1940	1950	1958	1960	1962	1963	1964	1965
	14	25	29	29	34	37	37	38

But in Moldavia it was staggering:

Year	1940	1950	1958	1960	1962	1963	1964	1965
	36	25	43	49	64	70	77	81

Apparently not all Soviet republics are advancing to communism at a uniform rate. Some seem to be wallowing in colonial backwardness imposed on them by the "elder brothers" from Moscow.

In 1965 the proportion of specialists with secondary special education was higher in Ukraine, 19.22 percent, and lower in Russia, 60.67 percent, than the percentage of students in the educational institutions of each republic.[9] This was due to the directing of graduates from Russia and other republics to Ukraine. In 1961, for which data is available, only 67.66 percent of the specialists with secondary special education in Ukraine were Ukrainians. Russians comprised 24.34 percent. The remaining eight percent were made up of 38 specified nationalities from all parts of the USSR and 14,106 individuals who were listed under "other nationalities" (see appendix V).

Not only does a youth in Ukraine have less opportunity to enter a technicum in his native land, but he also has less chance of entering such an institution than a Russian in any part of the USSR. The percentage of Russians in the Soviet Union in 1959 was 54.65 and Ukrainians 17.84 (appendix I). But the percentage of Russians in secondary special institutions in 1965 was 64.44 or 206 students per 10,000 of the Russian population in the USSR, Ukrainians only 15 percent or 147 Ukrainian students per 10,000 of the Ukrainian population in the USSR (table XI). Similarly the percentage of Russian specialists with this type of education in the USSR in 1964 was 65.08 and Ukrainians only 15.92 (table XI).

TABLE XI

National Composition of (a) Students of Secondary Special Educational Institutions, 1965 and (b) Specialists with Special Secondary Education Engaged in the National Economy of the USSR, 1964

	(a)	%	(b)	%
Total in USSR	3,659,300	100	6,702,100	100
Russians	2,358,100	64.44	4,361,400	65.08
Ukrainians	548,800	15.00	1,067,100	15.92
Belorussians	127,600	3.49	216,400	3.23
Uzbeks	55,600	1.52	72,900	1.09
Kazakhs	48,300	1.32	57,000	.85
Georgians	31,900	.87	80,700	1.20
Azerbaidzhans	42,900	1.17	68,200	1.02
Lithuanians	49,900	1.36	59,500	.89
Moldavians	19,400	.53	27,600	.41
Latvians	21,000	.57	47,100	.70
Kirgiz	10,100	.28	13,800	.21
Tadzhiks	11,300	.31	16,600	.25
Armenians	43,800	1.20	72,300	1.08
Turkmans	10,700	.29	13,300	.20
Estonians	18,200	.50	36,000	.53
Others*	261,700	7.15	492,200	7.34

Source: *Narodnoe Khozaystvo 1965,* pp. 701, 582.

*Includes 26 other nationalities in each column.

But above all, Ukrainian students are subject to discrimination in admissions to technicums in Ukraine itself as is evident from the following data for the school year 1961-62:

Number of Students in Secondary Special Education Institutions of UkrSSR by Nationality

Total	Ukrainians	%	Russians	%
454,809	314,413	69.1	112,904	24.8[10]

In their native land, Ukrainians, with 76.8 percent of the population made up only 69.1 percent of the students of technicums; Russians with 16.9 percent of the population made up 24.8 percent of the students (see appendix IV). There were 97 Ukrainians per 10,000 of the Ukrainian population and 159 Russians per 10,000 of the Russian population in the secondary special educational institutions of Ukraine in the 1961-62 school year.

It is natural to assume that there is also financial discrimination against the system of secondary special education in Ukraine. Table XII indicates that for 1965 the RSFSR received 60.48 percent of all the money assigned for this type of education for the republics of the USSR, while Ukraine obtained only 17.46 percent. Here again the percentage allotted to Ukraine is lower than the percent of her population. Per capita this amounted to 3.59 roubles for Russia and 2.88 for Ukraine. This same discrimination applied to nine other republics of the USSR.

There was also a special budget of 96,700,000 roubles for secondary special education for the central government in Moscow to further promote its policy of centralization and Russification in this field.

Another area of discrimination in these schools is the Ukrainian language. Careful personal investigation by the author during his two years in Ukraine revealed that the language of instruction in the technicums of transport, construction, production, agriculture, economics, medicine (for training nurses and medical assistants), trade and commerce, forestry, technology and music was Russian. Ukrainian is still used in the cultural-educational and pedagogical schools.

TABLE XII

Budget for Secondary Special Educational Institutions
for Republics of the USSR, 1965

(In millions of roubles)

		%
Russian SFSR	451.3	60.48
Ukrainian SSR	130.3	17.46
Belorussian SSR	25.5	3.42
Uzbek SSR	19.5	2.61
Kazakh SSR	33.5	4.49
Georgian SSR	11.7	1.57
Azerbaidzhan SSR	10.5	1.40
Lithuanian SSR	15.2	2.04
Moldavian SSR	7.6	1.02
Latvian SSR	9.4	1.26
Kirgiz SSR	7.4	.99
Tadzhik SSR	5.7	.76
Armenian SSR	6.7	.90
Turkmen SSR	5.5	.74
Estonian SSR	6.4	.86
		100
Total for union republics	746.2	
All-union (USSR) budget	96.7	
Total for USSR and republics	842.9	

Source: *Gosudarstvenny Byudghet SSSR*, p. 51.

A traveller to the USSR described to me his visit to a technicum in rural Bukovina in Ukraine. The director was away in Moscow on school business; officials whom he met at the school spoke to him in Russian, although he was a Ukrainian; the whole atmosphere at the school—signs, slogans, bulletin boards, books—was also Russian.

A student in a technicum in Kiev who insisted on speaking only Ukrainian was warned several times by officials of the school to speak Russian. Later he was detained by the KGB on suspicion of being a dangerous bourgeois nationalist. The principal then expelled him from the students' dormitory. I asked another student who attended a technicum in Kiev, where most of the pupils were Ukrainian, what would happen if he spoke to the principal in Ukrainian. He replied, "I would not dare."

The fact and extent of Russification of the technicums is confirmed by *The Rules of Admission to the Secondary Special Educational Institutions of the USSR for 1966* in which we read that:

> Entrants to secondary special educational institutions complete entrance examinations of the Russian language for all courses with the exception of individuals who are entering courses where instruction is not in Russian, and who, instead of an examination of the Russian language, complete entrance examinations of the language in which lecturing is conducted in the given course.[11]

The rules also specify the subjects required in entrance examinations. Russian is listed for all courses; Ukrainian is not mentioned.[12] In 1954, however, technicums in Ukraine required entrance examinations in both Russian and Ukrainian.[13] Needless to say the language in which all examinations are conducted is Russian.

The Ukrainian language is taught as a subject in the technicums of Ukraine, but it takes second place to Russian in the number of hours it is alloted. In a bulletin of instructions to directors of secondary special educational institutions dated July 10, 1962 (see figures 6 and 7), the ministry of secondary special education of the USSR laid down the following timetable for the

УРСР

Міністерство вищої і
середньої спеціальної освіти
Української РСР

10 липня 1962 р.

№ 33—858

м. Київ

**НАЧАЛЬНИКАМ УПРАВЛІНЬ
(ВІДДІЛІВ) КАДРІВ І УЧБОВИХ
ЗАКЛАДІВ МІНІСТЕРСТВ, ВІДОМСТВ
І РАДНАРГОСПІВ УКРАЇНСЬКОЇ РСР**

Директорам середніх спеціальних
учбових закладів

В зв'язку з запитаннями директорів середніх спеціальних учбових закладів про введення нових учбових планів і викладання української літератури Міністерство вищої і середньої спеціальної освіти Української РСР р о з'я с н ю є:

1. Учбові плани на базі неповної середньої (8-річної) та середньої (11-річної) школи вводяться на денному, вечірньому та заочному відділах всіх середніх спеціальних учбових закладів Української РСР, починаючи з набору 1962 року (учні, які закінчили семирічну або десятирічну школу, навчаються відповідно за планами для восьмирічної або одинадцятирічної школи).

2. На денних відділах середніх спеціальних учбових закладів на вивчення літератури відводиться 225 годин, з них на російську літературу в учбових закладах Української РСР виділяється 135 годин.

На вивчення української літератури відводиться 120 годин (90 годин за рахунок предмету «Література» і 30 з додаткового учбового матеріалу).

Українська література вивчається на I і II курсах за програмою, затвердженою Міністерством вищої і середньої спеціальної освіти Української РСР, з проведенням екзамену в IV семестрі — письмово—твір (крім педагогічних і культосвітніх училищ, які працюють за окремою програмою).

3. У вечірніх середніх спеціальних учбових закладах і відділах на вивчення літератури відводиться 210 годин, з них на російську літературу — 120 і українську — 90 годин. Українська література вивчається на I і II курсах без проведення екзаменів.

4. У заочних середніх спеціальних учбових закладах і відділах вивчається російська і українська література.

Figure 6. **Instructions to principals of secondary special educational institutions allotting 135 hours per year to Russian literature and 120 to Ukrainian in day schools and 120 and 90 respectively in night schools.**

З російської літератури виконуються дві контрольні роботи і проводяться екзамени на першому і другому курсах.

З української літератури виконуються дві контрольні роботи (на I і II курсі) і проводиться екзамен на другому курсі.

5. Учням денних, вечірніх та заочних відділів, які не вивчали української мови та літератури в загальноосвітній школі, рекомендується самостійно вивчати додаткові розділи російської літератури в обсязі 90 годин, тобто в повному об'ємі годин, відведених відповідно учбовими планами на вивчення літератури.

Заступник Міністра   **І. ДЗЮБКО**

БФ 17121   Підписано до друку 10.VII-1962 р.   Зам. 3569—1500

Друк. УУБ м. Київ, вул. Кірова, 12/2

Figure 7. **Instructions (continued) specifying that students, who had not studied the Ukrainian language and literature previously, are not required to take it in secondary special educational institutions.**

study of literature with the number of hours allotted to each per year:

Russian in day schools—135
Ukrainian in day schools—120
Russian in night schools—120
Ukrainian in night schools—90

There is no mention of examinations in Russian literature and we assume that these are held, but it is specifically stated that there are no examinations in night schools in Ukrainian literature. In correspondence schools there are to be two examinations in Russian literature and only one in Ukrainian. Students entering technicums who had never studied the Ukrainian language are not required to take it.

This atmosphere in which Ukrainian is relegated to second place, encourages Russian students to show their disregard and even contempt for the Ukrainian language. Several incidents were related to the writer by educators. In the Odessa cooperative technicum, when she entered the classroom, the teacher of Ukrainian often found insults written on the blackboard, such as the following: "Now begins the lesson of the donkey language".

In the Odessa theatrical technicum, Russian students announced at the beginning of the 1964-65 school year to the teacher of Ukrainian that:

We have no intention of working on the Ukrainian stage, we spit on the Ukrainian stage (nam naplevat na Ukrainsku stsenu), and, therefore, will not participate in your lectures.

They then walked out and stayed out. The director took no disciplinary measures.

Authorities not only do not punish such demonstrations of scorn and contempt for the Ukrainian language, but covertly encourage and then hold them up as manifestations of popular will and use them as pretexts for further Russification.

Several cases were related to this writer of Russian teachers in technicums, who waged persistent campaigns against the Ukrainian language. In the Odessa cultural-educational school which trains librarians and cultural workers for villages, a Russian teacher of history proclaimed that: "The Ukrainian is a dying language. We have a universal language—Russian. We should stick to it and cultivate it". Similar ideas were as emphatically expressed by Russian teachers in the Odessa technicum of food industry. On the other hand, should a Ukrainian speak up in defense of the Ukrainian language, he would immediately be branded as a bourgeois nationalist and terrorized into silence.

How far Russification has advanced in technical secondary special educational institutions is revealed in a teachers' handbook on methodology, written by the principal of a construction technicum in Kharkiv, Ukraine. There is no mention of the language of instruction, but the book is in Russian, all references are Russian and the author according to name, also appears to be a Russian. In the chapter on the use of video he mentions the names of films; all are in Russian. In a bibliography on the use of films he lists books and catalogues; these are also all Russian. At the end of the book is a timetable with a list of subjects and teachers. Of these, 48 percent have typical Russian names and only 32 percent Ukrainian ones.[14]

In addition to their theoretical studies students undergo practical training. In the case of those who attend industrial technicums it will be in factories or on construction sites. There too all instruction is in Russian. While he is attending school, each is given a student's card and a record booklet in which periodically his progress is noted.[15] Both are of a standard form for all students of technicums in the USSR and both are in Russian.

We can gauge the extent of Russification of the technicums of Ukraine by analyzing the data on textbooks published in the republics of the USSR for these schools. Unfortunately statistics are available only for 1955. The number of titles and copies for that year was as follows:

	USSR	RSFSR	%	UkrSSR	%	Other republics	%
Titles	334,000	254,000	76.00	19,000	6.00	61,000	18.00
Copies	6,393,000	6,042,000	94.51	187,000	2.93	164,000	2.56[16]

The RSFSR with 56.3 percent of the population published 76 percent of the titles and 94.51 percent of the number of copies. We do not know the language of the 2.93 percent of the copies published in Ukraine, but none of those published in Russia was in Ukrainian.

In the years from 1955 to 1965 there are no listings of textbooks for technicums under the national republics in this source, but the following data on the number of titles of textbooks for secondary special and vocational-technical schools in the USSR written in Russian and in all other languages of the peoples of the USSR is even more revealing:

Year	Total for USSR	Russian	%	All other languages of USSR	%	In other language*	%
1962	1,524	1,196	78.50	311	20.40	17	1.10
1963	1,482	1,143	77.10	319	21.50	20	1.40
1964	1,723	1,353	78.53	311	18.05	59	3.42
1965	1,977	1,605	81.18	269	13.61	103	5.21[17]

*These are probably for foreign language courses.

Here we find that in all the non-Russian languages of the USSR, which are the native tongues of 45.35 percent of the population (see appendix I), the number of titles published in 1965 was only 13.61 percent of all the textbooks for technicums in the USSR. This was a decline of 6.79 from 1962.

The number of copies of these books in thousands for the same years was as follows:

Year	Total for USSR	Russian	%	All other languages of USSR	%	Foreign language	%
1962	14,181	13,110	92.4	730	5.1	341	2.5
1963	19,296	17,903	92.8	1,177	6.1	216	1.1
1964	18,136	16,766	92.4	1,072	5.9	298	1.7
1965	19,875	18,388	92.5	920	4.6	567	2.9[18]

From this it is evident that the percentage of copies of books for secondary special educational institutions in the USSR in all non-Russian languages was even smaller than the number of titles. In

1965 the latter made up 13.61 percent of the total, while the former was only 4.6 percent.

A special catalogue of all technical books published in the UkrSSR for 1965 lists eleven textbooks for technicums. Of these, ten are in Russian with editions up to 40,000 and one in Ukrainian with an edition of 4,000.[19] (see figure 8)

The Ukrainian monthly journal of books lists the following three handbooks for students of technicums (all in Russian):

> *Donetsk City School of Artists—Decorators of Graphic Propaganda, Regulations and Course of Studies.* Donetsk, 1963.[20]
>
> *Donetsk Agricultural Technicum (Handbook for Entrants).* Donetsk, 1964.[21]
>
> *Lviv Medical School No. 2. (Handbook for Entrants).* Lviv, 1964.[22]

It is significant that even the handbook for the school in Lviv (a city where there were virtually no Russians before 1939) should be in Russian.

Significant also is another fact: the technicums are not all under one authority. Some belong under the direct administrative jurisdiction of the Ministry of Higher and Secondary Special Education of the republic; others come under various other ministries, committees and agencies. But strange as it may seem, many of these are agencies of the USSR. Thus in Ukraine in 1964, of 659 technicums, 42 came under the jursidiction of such agencies. Among these were the following:[23]

Number	Type of Technicum	Agency which has jurisdiction
4	communications	Ministry of Communications of the USSR
5	hydro power	State Committee of Energetics & Electrification of the USSR
7	construction	State Production Committee of Transport Construction of the USSR
15	railway transport	Ministry of Means of Communication of the USSR

There are those who applaud the new rulers Brezhnev and Kosygin as heralds of a new era in the USSR. Certainly they have

ных для расчета. К каждой лабораторной работе дана методика расчетов и необходимый справочный материал.

Книга составлена применительно к универсальным лабораторным макетам, разработанным в Харьковском политехническом институте им. В. И. Ленина, и является учебным пособием по курсу «Электропитание радиоустройств».

Заказано . . . . экз.

2. Для технікумів

135. КОЛПАКОВ Ю. Г., инж.— **Электрооборудование коксохимических заводов.**

Издательство «Техніка», язык русский, 18 печ. лист. Цена 90 коп. Тираж 2000.

Выход в свет в I кв. 1965 г.

В книге описано электрооборудование коксохимических заводов, кратко изложены теория электрического привода, схемы ручного и автоматического дистанционного пуска и управления электроприводами.

Книга предназначается для учащихся техникумов, изучающих электрооборудование и электропривод и в коксохимическом производстве по сокращенной программе.

Темплан 1964 г., № 129.

Заказано . . . . экз.

136. ИВАНОВА Н. И., канд. техн. наук, и др.— **Задачи и расчеты по электротехнике** (изд. II).

Издательство «Техніка», язык русский, 15 печ. лист. Цена 70 коп. Тираж 8000.

Выход в свет во II кв. 1965 г.

В книге помещены задачи и формулы для расчетов по основным разделам электротехники: электрическое поле, электрическая цепь постоянного и переменного токов, электромагнетизм, электрические измерения, электрические машины, трансформаторы, преобразователи и выпрямители тока, электропривод, электрическое освещение, электрические сети. Для облегчения усвоения материала некоторые задачи даются с решением.

Книга составлена в соответствии с программой курса «Общая электротехника» для средних специальных учебных заведений неэлектрических специальностей и предназначена в качестве учебного пособия для учащихся стационарных, вечерних и заочных отделений техникумов.

Заказано . . . . экз.

137. ВОЕВОДСКИЙ С. А. инж., **ХАСКИН А. Н., КРАСНИЦ З. Я.**— **Курс черчения.** (Часть II).

Издательство «Техніка», язык русский, 17 печ. лист. Цена 70 коп. Тираж 30 000.

Выход в свет во II кв. 1965 г.

Учебное пособие состоит из двух частей и содержит методические указания, программный материал, вопросы для самопровер-

Figure 8. A page from a catalogue of all technical books published in the UkrSSR for 1965, listing books for technicums. They are in Russian.

made some changes. Krushchov had divided the republics into economic regions; over each was a Council of the National Economy which had jurisdiction over all the means of production in the region. Many technicums in Ukraine were also under these local bodies. In 1966 the councils were reorganized into ministries. This affected the jurisdiction over technicums in Ukraine. All those that had been under the Councils of the National Economy of the UkrSSR, after the reorganization came under the ministries of the USSR. Among those were the following technicums[24] (see figures 9 and 10):

4	automation
4	industry of food supplies
5	mechanical
7	chemical industry
11	light industry
15	mining
22	machine building

Consequently in 1966, out of a total of 673 technicums in the UkrSSR, 140 or 20.8 percent were under the jurisdiction of agencies and ministries of the USSR—an increase of 98 from 1964. Moreover, these institutions and their affiliates are "opened, reorganized and closed by the ministries and agencies of the USSR in agreement with the Ministry of Higher and Secondary Special Education of the USSR and the Ministry of Finances of the USSR".[25]

Further changes have been made for the 1966-67 school year. The following additional four secondary special educational institutions were transferred from republican (UkrSSR) to union (USSR) jurisdiction:

The Kiev Technicum of Instrument Making for Semi-Conductors
The Dniproderzhynsk Chemico-Technological Correspondence
   Technicum
Technicums of Credit Accounting (Lviv and Kharkiv)[26]

The technicums in Ukraine, with few exceptions, have become islands of foreign culture with discrimination against both the Ukrainian language and Ukrainian students. The Ministry of

3. ДНІПРОПЕТРОВСЬКИЙ МАШИНОБУДІВНИЙ ТЕХНІКУМ

(Придніпровський раднаргосп)

м. Дніпропетровськ, вул. Державіна, 74

Спеціальності: 1) металургійне машинобудування, 2) ковальсько-пресове машинобудування.

Приймаються особи, які закінчили неповну середню школу.

У технікумі є вечірній відділ із спеціальностей: обробка металів різанням, металургійне машинобудування, монтаж і ремонт металообробних і автоматичних ліній, ковальсько-пресове машинобудування. Приймаються особи, які закінчили неповну середню школу.

4. ДРУЖКІВСЬКИЙ МАШИНОБУДІВНИЙ ТЕХНІКУМ

(Донецький раднаргосп)

м. Дружківка, Донецької області, вул. Леніна, 32

Спеціальності: 1) гірниче машинобудування, 2) гірнича електромеханіка, 3) зварювальне виробництво, 4) експлуатація автоматичних пристроїв у машинобудуванні.

На першу спеціальність приймаються особи, які закінчили неповну середню або середню школу, на інші — особи, які закінчили неповну середню школу.

У технікумі є вечірній відділ із спеціальності гірниче машинобудування. Приймаються особи, які закінчили неповну середню школу.

5. КИЇВСЬКИЙ ВЕЧІРНІЙ МАШИНОБУДІВНИЙ ТЕХНІКУМ

(Київський раднаргосп)

м. Київ, вул. Індустріальна, 9/11

Спеціальності: 1) машинобудування харчової промисловості, 2) автотракторобудування, 3) обробка металів різанням, 4) монтаж і ремонт металообробних верстатів і автоматичних ліній, 5) хімічне машинобудування.

На першу спеціальність приймаються особи, які закінчили неповну середню школу, на інші — особи, які закінчили неповну середню школу.

6. КИЇВСЬКИЙ ВЕЧІРНІЙ МАШИНОБУДІВНИЙ ТЕХНІКУМ

(Київський раднаргосп)

м. Київ, Брест-Литовське шосе, 111/2

Спеціальність — обробка металів різанням.

Приймаються особи, які закінчили неповну середню або середню школу.

У технікумі є заочний відділ із спеціальності ливарне виробництво чорних металів. Приймаються особи, які закінчили неповну середню школу.

7. КІРОВОГРАДСЬКИЙ ТЕХНІКУМ СІЛЬСЬКОГОСПОДАРСЬКОГО МАШИНОБУДУВАННЯ

(Придніпровський раднаргосп)

м. Кіровоград, вул. Фрунзе, 6

Спеціальності: 1) обробка металів різанням, 2) ковальсько-штампувальне виробництво, 3) сільськогосподарське машинобудування, 4) ливарне виробництво чорних металів.

На першу спеціальність приймаються особи, які закінчили неповну середню або середню школу, на інші — особи, які закінчили неповну середню школу.

У технікумі є вечірній відділ із спеціальностей обробка металів різанням, ковальсько-штампувальне виробництво, сільськогосподарське машинобудування, ливарне виробництво чорних металів. Приймаються особи, які закінчили неповну середню або середню школу, на інші — особи, які закінчили неповну середню школу.

8. КРАМАТОРСЬКИЙ МАШИНОБУДІВНИЙ ТЕХНІКУМ

(Донецький раднаргосп)

м. Краматорськ, Донецької області, вул. Велика Садова, 76

Спеціальності: 1) обробка металів різанням, 2) ливарне виробництво чорних металів, 3) металургійне машинобудування.

На першу спеціальність приймаються особи, які закінчили неповну середню або середню школу, на інші — особи, які закінчили неповну середню школу.

У технікумі є вечірній відділ із спеціальностей обробка металів різанням, ливарне виробництво чорних металів. Приймаються особи, які закінчили неповну середню школу.

У технікумі є заочний відділ із спеціальностей обробка металів різанням, ливарне виробництво чорних металів, металургійне машинобудування. Приймаються особи, які закінчили неповну середню школу.

9. КРЮКІВСЬКИЙ МАШИНОБУДІВНИЙ ТЕХНІКУМ

(Харківський раднаргосп)

м. Крюків-на-Дніпрі, Полтавської області, вул. К. Лібкнехта, 13/5

Спеціальності: 1) обробка металів різанням, 2) зварювальне виробництво.

Приймаються особи, які закінчили неповну середню школу.

У технікумі є вечірній відділ із таких самих спеціальностей. Приймаються особи, які закінчили середню школу.

Figure 9. Pages from a student's handbook for 1964, listing the machine building technicums. They are under the jurisdiction of the Regional Councils of the National Economy of Ukraine.

6. КИЇВСЬКИЙ ВЕЧІРНІЙ МАШИНОБУДІВНИЙ ТЕХНІКУМ
(Міністерство харчового і нафтового машинобудування СРСР)
м. Київ, Брест-Литовський проспект, 59

Спеціальності: 1) машини і устаткування підприємств хлібопекарської, макаронної та кондитерської промисловості, 2) обробка металів різанням, 3) монтаж і експлуатація металообробних верстатів і автоматичних ліній, 4) хімічне машинобудування; 5) монтаж і автоматизація.

На першу спеціальність приймаються особи, які закінчили середню школу, на інші — особи, які закінчили неповну середню або середню школу.

7. КИЇВСЬКИЙ ВЕЧІРНІЙ МАШИНОБУДІВНИЙ ТЕХНІКУМ
(Міністерство будівельного, дорожного і комунального машинобудування СРСР)
м. Київ-62, Брест-Литовський проспект, 111/2

Спеціальності: 1) обробка металів різанням, 2) ливарне виробництво чорних металів.

На першу спеціальність приймаються особи, які закінчили неповну середню або середню школу, на другу — особи, які закінчили неповну середню школу.

8. КІРОВОГРАДСЬКИЙ ТЕХНІКУМ СІЛЬСЬКОГОСПОДАРСЬКОГО МАШИНОБУДУВАННЯ
(Міністерство тракторного і сільськогосподарського машинобудування СРСР)
м. Кіровоград, вул. Фрунзе, 6

Спеціальності: 1) обробка металів різанням, 2) ковальсько-штампувальне виробництво, 3) сільськогосподарські машини, 4) ливарне виробництво чорних металів.

На першу спеціальність приймаються особи, які закінчили неповну середню або інші — особи, які закінчили неповну середню школу.

9. КРАМАТОРСЬКИЙ МАШИНОБУДІВНИЙ ТЕХНІКУМ
(Міністерство важкого, енергетичного і транспортного машинобудування СРСР)
м. Краматорськ, Донецької області, Велика Садова вул., 101

Спеціальності: 1) ливарне виробництво чорних металів, 2) металознавство і термічна обробка металів, 3) ковальсько-штампувальне виробництво, 4) обробка металів різанням, 5) інструмен-

тальне виробництво, 6) прокатні і волочильні стани та устаткування, 7) планування на підприємствах машинобудівної промисловості.

Приймаються особи, які закінчили неповну середню школу.

У технікумі є вечірній відділ із спеціальностями: ливарне виробництво чорних металів, металознавство і термічна обробка металів, обробка металів різанням, бухгалтерський облік. Приймаються особи, які закінчили неповну середню школу.

У технікумі є заочний відділ із спеціальностями: ливарне виробництво чорних металів, металознавство і термічна обробка металів, монтаж і експлуатація металообробних верстатів і автоматичних ліній, обробка металів різанням, інструментальне виробництво, планування на підприємствах машинобудівної промисловості. Приймаються особи, які закінчили неповну середню школу.

10. КРЮКІВСЬКИЙ МАШИНОБУДІВНИЙ ТЕХНІКУМ
(Міністерство важкого, енергетичного і транспортного машинобудування СРСР)
м. Крюків-на-Дніпрі, Полтавської області, вул. К. Лібкнехта, 13/5

Спеціальності: 1) обробка металів різанням, 2) технологія зварювального виробництва.

Приймаються особи, які закінчили неповну середню школу.

У технікумі є вечірній відділ з такими самими спеціальностями. Приймаються особи, які закінчили неповну середню школу.

11. КРИВОРІЗЬКИЙ МАШИНОБУДІВНИЙ ТЕХНІКУМ
(Міністерство чорної металургії УРСР)
м. Кривий Ріг, Дніпропетровської області, вул. Мусоргського, 10

Спеціальності: 1) технологія зварювального виробництва, 2) інструментальне виробництво.

На першу спеціальність приймаються особи, які закінчили неповну середню або другу — особи, які закінчили середню школу.

У технікумі є вечірній і заочний відділи з такими самими спеціальностями. Приймаються особи, які закінчили неповну середню або середню школу.

12. ЛУГАНСЬКИЙ МАШИНОБУДІВНИЙ ТЕХНІКУМ
(Міністерство важкого, енергетичного і транспортного машинобудування СРСР)
м. Луганськ, вул. Фрунзе, 110

Спеціальності: 1) обробка металів різанням, 2) ливарне виробництво чорних металів, 3) локомотивобудування, 4) електромашинобудування.

На першу спеціальність приймаються особи, які закінчили неповну середню школу, на інші — особи, які закінчили неповну середню школу.

У технікумі є вечірній і заочний відділи із спеціальностями: електроустаткування промислових підприємств і установок, обробка мета-

Figure 10. Pages from a student's handbook for 1966, listing the machine building technicums. They are under the jurisdiction of ministries of the USSR.

Higher and Secondary Special Education of the Ukrainian SSR, whose role has been that of administrative agent acting on orders of the all-union ministry in Moscow, has even been losing that tenuous jurisdiction. In the face of this, shamelessly and hypocritically, the hierarchy in the Kremlin announced to the world that it is:

> . . . promoting the free development of the languages of the peoples of the USSR and the complete freedom of every citizen of the USSR to speak, and to bring up and educate his children, in any language, ruling out all privileges, restrictions or compulsions in the use of this or that language. By virtue of the fraternal friendship and mutual trust of peoples, national languages are developing on a basis of equality and mutual enrichment.[27]

FOOTNOTES

1. *Na blago i schaste naroda* (For the Welfare and Happiness of the People). A collection of Documents, Moscow, 1961, pp. 70-71.

2. N. N. Zabelin and others, *Planirovanie podgotovki i raspredeleniya rabochykh kadrov v SSSR* (The Planning of Training and Distribution of Labour Cadres in the USSR), Moscow 1960, Chap. IV; *Na blago i schaste naroda,* p. 41; L. A. Komarov, *Planirovanie podgotovki i raspredeleniya spetsialistov v SSSR* (The Planning of Training and Distribution of Specialists in the USSR), Moscow, 1961, p. 60; *Sbornik zakonov SSSR i ukazov presidiuma Verkhovnogo Soveta SSSR 1938-1958* (Collection of Laws of the USSR and Decrees of the Presidium of the Supreme Soviet of the USSR 1938-1958), Moscow, 1959, p. 418.

3. *Litopis knyh,* No. 9, 1964, p. 53.

4. Gosudarstvenny komitet Soveta Ministrov SSR po pechati (State Committee for Publishing of the Council of Ministers of the USSR), *Pechat SSSR v 1955 godu* (Publishing in the USSR in 1955), Statistical Handbook, Moscow 1956, p. 106.

5. A. N. Veselov, *Profesionalno-tekhnicheskoe obrazovanie v SSSR* (Vocational-Technical Training in the USSR), Moscow, 1961, p. 389.

6. Ibid., p. 314.

7. "Zakon 'Ob ukreplenie svyazi shkoly s zhiznu i o dalneyshem razvitii sistemy narodnogo obrazovaniya v SSSR' ot 2 dekabrya, 1958 goda (The Law 'Regarding the Strengthening of School and Life and for the Further Development of the System of Public Education in the USSR', December 24, 1958)", *O kommunisticheskom vospitanii i ukreplenii svyazi shkoly s zhiznu* (Regarding Communist Education and the Strengthening of Relationships of school and Life), A Collection of Documents, Moscow, 1964, p. 77.

8. *Dovidnyk dlya vstupnykiv do serednikh spetsialnykh uchbovykh zakladiv Ukrayinskoyi RSR na 1966 rik* (Handbook for Entrants of Secondary Special Educational Institutions of the Ukrainian SSR 1966), Kharkiv State University, Kharkiv, 1966, pp. 5, 18, 227-254.

9. *Narodnoe khozaystvo 1965*, pp. 578-79.

10. Tsentralnoe statisticheskoe upravlenie pri Sovete Ministrov SSR (Central Statistical Administration of the Council of Ministers of the USSR *Srednee spetsialnoe obrazovanie v SSSR* (Secondary Special Education in the USSR), Statistical Handbook, Moscow, 1962, p. 75.

11. *Dovidnyk dlya vstupnykiv do serednikh spetsialnykh uchbovykh zakladiv na 1966 rik*, p. 9.

12. Ibid., pp. 9-10.

13. *Radyanska Ukrayina*, July 4 and 10, 1954. See back page for announcements of opening of registration.

14. V. G. Putilin, *Organizatsiya uchebnoy i vospitatelnoy raboty v tekhnikume* (Organization of the Work of Education and Training in a Technicum), second edition, Kharkov, 1959.

15. "Polozhenie o srednykh spetsialnykh uchebnykh zavedeniyakh SSSR (Regulations Governing Secondary Special Educational Institutions of the USSR)", *O kommunisticheskom vospitanii*, p. 284.

16. *Pechat SSSR v 1955 godu*, pp. 100, 104, 105.

17. *Pechat SSSR v 1962 godu*, p. 52.
    Pechat SSSR v 1963 godu, p. 50.
    Pechat SSSR v 1964 godu, p. 64.
    Pechat SSSR v 1965 godu, p. 50.

18. Ibid.

19. Derzhavny kominet rady ministriv Ukrayinskoyi RSR po presi (State Committee for Publishing of the Ukrainian SSR), *Zvedeny tematychny plan vypusku literatury vudavnytstv Ukrayiny na 1965 rik: Tekhnika, Khimiya, Budivnytstvo, Arkhitektura, Komunalne Hospodarstvo* (Summary of Publications of Literature of Publishers of Ukraine for 1965: Technology, Chemistry, Construction, Architecture, Communal Economy), Kiev, 1964, pp. 47-50.

20. *Litopis knyh*, No. 1, 1964, p. 40.

21. Ibid., No. 7, 1964, p. 50.

22. Ibid., No. 9, 1964, p. 53.

23. *Dovidnyk, dlya vstupnykiv do serednikh spetsialnykh uchbovykh zakladiv, na 1964 rik*, pp. 5-171.

24. *Dovidnyk, dlya vstupnykiv do serednikh spetsialnykh uchbovykh zakladiv, na 1966 rik*, pp. 58-226.

25. Polozhenie, *O kommunisticheskom vospitanii*, p. 283-84.

26. *Dovidnyk dlya vstupnykiv do serednikh spetsialnykh uchbovykh zakladiv, na 1967 rik*, pp. 103, 106 and 192.

27. *The Program of the Communist Party of the Soviet Union*, pp. 104-105.

6

Higher education

Policies on higher as well as all other education are formulated by the Council of Ministers of the USSR and the CC of the CPSU. All higher education is under the direct guidance of the Ministry of Higher and Secondary Special Education of the USSR or through various agencies and ministries.[1] It has full powers to regulate all aspects of the work of these institutions, from setting up unified courses of study to regulations governing internal management such as the hiring of personnel, the hours of work, measures to be taken in case of infraction of rules by faculty members and where to keep the keys for the auditorium, laboratories and lecture rooms.[2]

The discrimination against Ukraine, its students and language, is even more marked in higher education than in the elementary and secondary field. She also receives a smaller percentage of the total budget of the USSR for higher education than her percent of the population, while Russia receives a higher percentage. In 1965 Ukraine's share was 16.79 percent and Russia's, 62.14 (table XIII). Calculating it on a per capita basis, the latter obtained 6.71 and the former only 5.06 roubles. Belorussia received 4.91 and Moldavia only 3.90 or slightly more than half of Russia's amount.

The same discrimination against Ukraine prevails as regards the number of higher educational institutions which, with the

TABLE XIII

Budget for Higher Educational Institutions in Republics
of the USSR, 1965

(in millions of roubles)

		%
Russian SFSR	844.2	62.14
Ukrainian SSR	228.2	16.79
Belorussian SSR	41.9	3.08
Uzbek SSR	48.0	3.53
Kazakh SSR	49.0	3.61
Georgian SSR	25.4	1.87
Azerbaidzhan SSR	23.3	1.72
Lithuanian SSR	18.8	1.38
Moldavian SSR	13.0	.96
Latvian SSR	11.5	.85
Kirgiz SSR	10.8	.79
Tadzhik SSR	10.3	.76
Armenian SSR	17.8	1.31
Turkmen SSR	6.5	.48
Estonian SSR	9.9	.73
		100
Total for union republics	1,358.6	
All-union (USSR) budget	235.2	
Total for USSR and republics	1,593.8	

Source: *Gosudarstvenny Budghet SSSR*, p. 50.

TABLE XIV

Number of (a) Higher Educational Institutions and (b) Students
in Them in the Republics of the USSR, 1965

	(a)	%	(b)	%
Total in USSR	756	100	3,860,500	100
Russian SFSR	432	57.14	2,353,900	60.97
Ukrainian SSR	132	17.46	690,000	17.87
Belorussian SSR	27	3.57	104,000	2.69
Uzbek SSR	32	4.23	165,800	4.30
Kazakh SSR	39	5.15	144,700	3.75
Georgian SSR	18	2.38	76,600	1.98
Azerbaidzhan SSR	11	1.46	67,000	1.74
Lithuanian SSR	11	1.46	46,400	1.20
Moldavian SSR	7	.93	36,300	.94
Latvian SSR	10	1.32	33,100	.86
Kirgiz SSR	8	1.06	32,200	.83
Tadzhik SSR	7	.93	30,400	.79
Armenian SSR	11	1.46	38,900	1.01
Turkmen SSR	5	.66	19,900	.52
Estonian SSR	6	.79	21,400	.55

Source: *Narodnoe Khozaystvo 1965*, p. 691.

exception of pedagogical institutes, "are organized, reorganized and liquidated by the Council of Ministers of the USSR".[3] In 1965 Russia had 57.14 percent and Ukraine only 17.46 of these academic establishments in the USSR (table XIV). Furthermore, Ukraine's percentage has consistently declined from 1940 as indicated by the following data:

Comparison of number of Higher Educational Institutions in RSFSR and UkrSSR

	1940-41	1950-51	1958-59	1962-63	1963-64	1964-65	1965-66
USSR	817	880	766	738	742	754	756
RSFSR	481	516	441	426	427	432	432
Percentage of total	58.9	58.6	57.6	57.7	57.5	57.3	57.1
UkrSSR	173	160	140	133	131	132	132
Percentage of total	21.0	18.2	18.3	18.0	17.7	17.5	17.5 [4]

There is also unfair distribution of professorial staff whose members are assigned by the Ministry of Higher and Secondary Special Education of the USSR.[5] There are no recent statistics available to this author, but for the years 1951-55 Ukrainian institutions had 10.4 percent of the doctors, 8.7 percent of the professors and 13 percent of the associate professors, while Russia had 76, 79 and 72.2 percent respectively (table XV).

The percentage of all students in the USSR in these institutions in 1965 was 60.97 in Russia and only 17.87 in Ukraine (table XIV). It is also interesting to note Ukraine's percentage of the total number of students in the higher educational institutions of the USSR (Russian Empire in 1914-15) in previous years:

1914-15	1927-28	1933-34	1940-41
(present boundaries)			
27.6	17.3	21.0	24.2 [6]

It is quite obvious that Ukraine's standing in higher education in relation to Russia has declined under the Soviet regime.

This subordinate relationship can also be illustrated by comparing the number of students per 10,000 population in the higher

TABLE XV

Number of (a) Doctors, (b) Professors and (c) Associate Professors in the Higher Educational Institutions of the Republics of the USSR, 1951-55

	(a)	%	(b)	%	(c)	%
Total in USSR	2,857	100	2,290	100	11,843	100
Russian SFSR	2,182	76.0	1,790	79.0	8,517	72.2
Ukrainian SSR	297	10.4	202	8.7	1,536	13.0
Belorussian SSR	27	.9	26	1.1	216	1.8
Uzbek SSR	54	1.9	59	2.6	261	2.2
Kazakh SSR	47	1.6	31	1.3	210	1.8
Georgian SSR	95	3.3	71	3.1	291	2.5
Azerbaidzhan SSR	41	1.4	32	1.4	238	2.0
Lithuanian SSR	5	.02	7	.03	62	.5
Moldavian SSR	5	.02	8	.04	68	.6
Latvian SSR	4	.01	8	.04	81	.7
Kirgiz SSR	13	.44	18	.8	70	.6
Tadzhik SSR	9	.03	7	.03	47	.4
Armenian SSR	51	1.6	26	1.1	186	1.6
Turkmen SSR	14	.5	4	.02	26	.2
Estonian SSR	13	.4	11	.6	34	.3

Source: K. T. Galkin, *Vysshee obrazovanie i podgotovka nauchnykh kadrov v SSSR,* Moscow, 1958, p. 165. The percent calculations are as given in the original.

educational institutions of each republic for the years for which data is available. Table XVI indicates that the number in the RSFSR was higher than the average for the USSR for every year since 1950; the number in Ukraine on the other hand is lower than either the number for the RSFSR or the USSR for every year since 1940 when it was higher. The number in the RSFSR was also higher than for any other republic in 1963, 1964 and 1965. A comparison of the difference between the number in Russia and in Ukraine for the years from 1950 is also significant:

1950	1958	1960	1963	1964	1965
23	25	27	40	33	34

The difference between the number in Russia and Belorussia is even greater:

1950	1958	1960	1963	1964	1965
36	45	52	59	63	66

The difference between the number in Russia and Moldavia defies comprehension:

1950	1958	1960	1963	1964	1965
41	60	61	72	75	78

With one exception (Ukraine 1964) the difference had been increasing annually for all three countries.

Many students in the USSR receive aid in the form of monthly stipends. Wages for workers and employees for 1964 were, on the average, 90 roubles per month[7] which would make it impossible for the son or daughter of the average citizen to attend a higher educational institution without a stipend. The number receiving this assistance is shown in table XVII. Of the total in the USSR in 1960, 60.73 percent of the stipends were distributed in the RSFSR and only 17.66 percent in the UkrSSR. In several other republics, among them Belorussia and Moldavia, the percentage of stipends was even smaller as compared to the republic's percentage of the population.

TABLE XVI

Number of Students per 10,000 Population in Higher Educational
Institutions of the Republics of the USSR

	1940	1950	1958	1960	1963	1964	1965
USSR	41	69	104	111	144	157	166
Russian SFSR	43	77	116	124	161	176	186
Ukrainian SSR	47	54	91	97	121	143	152
Belorussian SSR	24	41	71	72	102	113	120
Uzbek SSR	28	65	107	115	142	152	157
Kazakh SSR	16	46	71	76	98	111	119
Georgian SSR	77	98	119	134	158	167	168
Azerbaidzhan SSR	44	98	97	91	121	130	144
Lithuanian SSR	20	45	90	95	130	145	155
Moldavian SSR	10	36	56	63	89	101	108
Latvian SSR	52	73	88	101	132	140	146
Kirgiz SSR	19	49	77	78	101	113	122
Tadzhik SSR	15	46	92	95	101	108	118
Armenian SSR	82	111	111	107	141	158	177
Turkmen SSR	22	54	85	81	94	99	104
Estonian SSR	45	80	101	111	142	156	166

Source: *Narodnoe khozaystvo 1964*, p. 683.

TABLE XVII

Number of Students in Higher Educational Institutions of the
Republics of the USSR Receiving Stipends, 1960

		%
USSR	847,031	100
Russian SFSR	514,374	60.73
Ukrainian SSR	149,580	17.66
Belorussian SSR	24,904	2.94
Uzbek SSR	34,138	4.03
Kazakh SSR	28,988	3.42
Georgian SSR	16,317	1.93
Azerbaidzhan SSR	13,317	1.57
Lithuanian SSR	11,829	1.40
Moldavian SSR	8,239	.97
Latvian SSR	9,551	1.13
Kirgiz SSR	7,685	.91
Tadzhik SSR	8,711	1.03
Armenian SSR	7,569	.89
Turkmen SSR	6,376	.75
Estonian SSR	5,453	.64

Source: *Vysshee obrazovanie*, p. 161.

The whole policy of discrimination is also reflected in the number of graduates in the republics. In 1959 the number per 1000 of the population in the USSR was 18, in the RSFSR 19 and in UkrSSR only 17. For some of the other republics the figure was lower. However in 1939 the number for both Russia and Ukraine was the same: seven per 1000 population (table XVIII). Here too the responsibility lies at the door of the central authorities because "the quota of students in educational institutions is also determined by the Ministry of Higher Education of the USSR in accordance with the state economic plan".[8]

With some exceptions, students in the USSR are required to go to work for at least two years after graduating from secondary school before being eligible for admission to a higher educational institution. However, these exceptions do not apply in the same measure to students of all republics. In the RSFSR 43 percent of those admitted in 1960-61 were exempt; in Ukraine only 25 percent. Stating this in reverse; only 57 percent of the students in the RSFSR had worked before being admitted; whereas in Ukraine 75 percent had such experience.[9]

But the discrimination against students in Ukraine is felt mainly by the Ukrainians. It is much easier for an urban than for a rural youth to gain admittance to a higher educational institution. The reasons for this are many: city schools are better equipped and provide better instruction; intellectual stimulation is greater in a city environment; the language of instruction in city schools is, for the most part, in Russian, which is also the language used in the higher educational institutions and the language in which entrance examinations are written. Russian youths are consequently favoured because most of them live in the cities.[10]

They are also favoured because Russians occupy a disproportionate number of leading positions in the republic. An influential parent can mean more in terms of educational advancement in the USSR than sheer mental ability and high academic achievement. Krushchov admitted at the Thirteenth All-union Congress of the Komsomol that the children of party members went on to higher education while the others went to work after

TABLE XVIII

Number of Graduates of Higher Educational Institutions
per 1,000 Population in Republics of the USSR in 1939 and 1959

	1939	1959
USSR	6	18
Russian SFSR	7	19
Ukrainian SSR	7	17
Belorussian SSR	4	12
Uzbek SSR	3	13
Kazakh SSR	5	12
Georgian SSR	11	38
Azerbaidzhan SSR	7	21
Lithuanian SSR	2	13
Moldavian SSR	3	10
Latvian SSR	7	21
Kirgiz SSR	2	13
Tadzhik SSR	2	10
Armenian SSR	6	28
Turkmen SSR	3	13
Estonian SSR	8	21

Source: *Vysshee obrazovanie*, pp. 30-31.

graduating from secondary schools.[11] Favouritism and nepotism are so rampant that the agricultural schools which formerly trained chairmen of collective farms had students who were not even members of collective farms, young people with no practical experience in farming and even youth out of seven-year schools.[12]

Students admitted to higher educational institutions are carefully screened. With the application form they must present character references from party, YCL, trade union and other public organizations.[13]

In this case a Ukrainian is at a double disadvantage: firstly, in many leading positions sit Russians (they made up 26.6 percent of the party delegates at the Twenty-second Congress of the CPU in 1961[14] and 26.9 percent of the party membership in Ukraine in 1965[15]; secondly, parents of rural youth as a rule are not party members. In villages the only members are generally local officials and many of these very often are not Ukrainians.

Obviously the latter, especially if they are Russians, would be reluctant to recommend Ukrainian students. As party members they are guided by the party constitution, which states that a member must "carry on a struggle with survivals of nationalism".[16] Any emphasis on national customs, tradition or language can be and often is interpreted as such nationalism. One can imagine the attitude of a local party official to the son of a peasant who had strong attachment to custom and tradition.

In addition, the Russian central authorities have other plans for the students of secondary schools of Ukraine. In 1960, of 12,611 graduates of Vinnitsa region in Ukraine, 2,283 went to work in industry, 5,943 in agriculture and 1,393 in other branches of the national economy. A total of 9,619 or over 75 percent did not go on to higher studies. All the graduates of a school in the Poltava region remained to work on the collective farm. According to the same report from Ukraine, "more and more boys and girls go to work in industry after finishing school".[17]

Russian planners in Moscow also have programs of construction and industrialization in the eastern and northern regions of the USSR, which require "a significant number of Komsomol

members and youth, especially from among those who have completed secondary general education".[18] In the main they come
from Ukraine, Belorussia, Moldavia and Lithuania.[19] There are
no published statistics on the total number that were sent, but it
was estimated that in the period 1959-1965, the underdeveloped
regions required an additional two million for the labour force.[20]

While Ukrainians are moved out of Ukraine the Russians
move in. They numbered 3,164,800 and made up 8.2 percent of the
population in 1926 and 7,091,300 or 16.9 percent of the population
of Ukraine in 1959.[21] Another source has revealed that between
1959 and 1963 there were exchanges of population between Ukraine
and other republics, that more than 75 percent of this was with
the RSFSR and that, as a consequence, "Ukraine increased her
population".[22]

The result of this exchange is evident everywhere in Ukraine.
Russians from all parts of the RSFSR can be found occupying
every imaginable post. There is only one explanation for such
exchanges between Russia and Ukraine, Belorussia, Moldavia
and Lithuania which form the western regions of the USSR. The
Russians are following a policy of transplanting the indigenous
population to Russia where they will be assimilated, while the
western areas including Ukraine, are colonized with Russians to
speed up Russification and to tighten the Russian grip on these
border regions. In the exchange, Ukrainian youth who should
have proceeded to further education, end up in factories and on
construction sites in Siberia.

How strongly these and other factors affect the number of
Ukrainians in schools of higher learning in Ukraine is evident
from official statistics. In 1959 Ukrainians made up 76.8 and
Russians 16.9 percent of the total population of Ukraine (appendix
IV), but in 1960 only 62.5 percent of all the students in the higher
educational institutions were Ukrainians and 30 percent were
Russians (appendix III). Per 10,000 Ukrainian population in
Ukraine there were 81 Ukrainian students in higher educational
institutions of Ukraine; per 10,000 Russian population in Ukraine
there were 177 Russian students, or more than double the number

TABLE XIX

National Compositions of Students of Higher Educational Institutions
of the USSR, 1965

		%
USSR	**3,860,500**	**100**
Russians	**2,362,000**	**61.18**
Ukrainians	558,600	14.47
Belorussians	114,600	2.97
Uzbeks	95,600	2.48
Kazakhs	69,900	1.81
Georgians	70,100	1.82
Azerbaidzhans	54,000	1.40
Lithuanians	42,800	1.11
Moldavians	22,900	.59
Latvians	21,400	.55
Kirgiz	16,200	.42
Tadzhiks	17,500	.45
Armenians	61,800	1.60
Turkmans	15,600	.40
Estonians	18,800	.49
Others*	318,700	8.26

Source: *Narodnoe Khozaystvo 1965*, p. 701.

*Includes 26 other nationalities.

of Ukrainians. The relative position of Ukrainians in all higher educational institutions of the USSR is no better. In 1959 Ukrainians made up 17.84 percent of the total population of the USSR (appendix I) but in 1965 they made up only 14.47 percent of the student body of these higher educational institutions (table XIX). The Russians made up only 54.65 percent of the population and 61.18 of the student body. In other words there were 174 Russian students per 10,000 Russian population in the USSR and only 127 Ukrainian students per 10,000 Ukrainian population.

If a Ukrainian wishes to go on to postgraduate work he will find the discrimination even greater. It is apparently deemed by the Russian ruling hierarchy not safe to allow too many Ukrainians to achieve higher academic standing; they could become a threat to Russian hegemony in Ukraine. The Ministry of Higher and Secondary Special Education and the Academy of Sciences of the USSR impose restrictions on the number of students to be admitted to postgraduate work in all higher educational and research institutions. These bodies also have the right to establish and abolish postgraduate studies in all higher educational and research institutions of the USSR.[23]

On August 20, 1956, the CC of the CPSU and The Council of Ministers of the USSR empowered over two hundred institutions throughout the union to accept candidate and doctorate theses* for examination and to recommend students for these degrees. Of those institutions which had power to recommend the granting of candidate degrees only 56.7 percent were located in the RSFSR, which also had 75.7 percent of the institutions empowered to recommend granting both degrees. The UkrSSR had 17.1 percent in the first category and 8.7 in the second (table XX). Turkmenia, Tadzhikstan and Moldavia did not have any in the last category; all the other republics had a smaller proportion of such institutions than their proportion of the population.

---

*While these degrees may seem to be the equivalent of our master and doctorate degrees, no such direct relationship exists. The candidate degree in Ukraine, at some universities, could be equated to a doctorate here, while the Soviet doctorate is the highest degree available in the USSR.

TABLE XX

Number of Higher Educational Institutions in the Republics of the USSR
Having the Power to Recommend Students for (a) Candidate
(b) Both Candidate and Doctor Degrees

	(a)	%	(b)	%
USSR	217	100.	267	100.
Russian SFSR	123	56.7	202	75.7
Ukrainian SSR	37	17.1	23	8.7
Belorussian SSR	5	2.3	5	1.8
Uzbek SSR	8	3.7	8	3.0
Kazakh SSR	7	3.2	5	1.8
Georgian SSR	2	.9	7	2.7
Azerbaidzhan SSR	3	1.4	5	1.8
Lithuanian SSR	3	1.4	3	1.1
Moldavian SSR	3	1.4	0	.0
Latvian SSR	4	1.8	3	1.1
Kirgiz SSR	4	1.8	1	.4
Tadzhik SSR	3	1.4	0	.0
Armenian SSR	4	1.8	4	1.5
Turkmen SSR	6	2.8	0	.0
Estonian SSR	5	2.3	1	.4

Source: *Nauchnye kadry*, pp. 171-192.

Although their Russian equivalents are included, we find the following Ukrainian institutions in Kiev not among those that have the power to recommend students for doctorate degrees:

State Conservatory of Music
Karpenko-Kary State Institute of Theatrical Arts
State Institute of Fine Arts
Gorky Pedagogical Institute
Higher Party School of the CC of the CPU [24]

A Ukrainian cannot even be recommended for a doctorate degree in pedagogy in Ukraine. There are seven institutes in the USSR with this power; all are in the RSFSR.[25] For advanced studies in this field Ukrainians must go to Russia where Russians decide how many and who from among Ukrainians will be admitted.

The effect of these restrictions on the proportion of post-graduate students in Ukraine as compared with the RSFSR, is most unfavourable for Ukraine: in 1965 the latter had 12.95 percent of all postgraduate students in the USSR, while Russia had 67.86 (table XXI). This works out to four per ten thousand for Russia and only two for Ukraine.

If a student wishes to enroll for postgraduate work at an institute of the Academy of Sciences of the USSR or a higher educational institution of the USSR, he will be confronted with severe restrictions. Those accepted must be "worthy candidates", not only capable of achievement, but also politically reliable. In addition, students from the republican academies are accepted in the institutes of the Academy of Sciences of the USSR only in those disciplines in which locally there are no faculty advisors and no material and technical resources.[26]

The students who are accepted, receive their stipends not from the academy of the USSR, but from the republican academies. Since the RSFSR does not have one, the Academy of Sciences of the USSR which is financed by funds from all republics, is in reality the Academy of Sciences of the RSFSR and its facilities are basically reserved for Russians. A small percentage of the students are accepted from other republics. This is called "aid to the academies of science of the union republics . . ."[27]

TABLE XXI

Number of Postgraduate Students in
the Republics of the USSR, 1965

		%
SSR	90,294	100.
Russian SFSR	61,274	67.86
Ukrainian SSR	11,689	12.95
Belorussian SSR	2,409	2.67
Uzbek SSR	2,972	3.29
Kazakh SSR	1,743	1.93
Georgian SSR	1,494	1.65
Azerbaidzhan SSR	2,734	3.03
Lithuanian SSR	930	1.03
Moldavian SSR	771	.85
Latvian SSR	869	.96
Kirgiz SSR	734	.81
Tadzhik SSR	551	.61
Armenian SSR	1,109	1.23
Turkmen SSR	448	.50
Estonian SSR	569	.63

Source: *Narodnoe Khozaystvo 1965*, p. 716.

As one would expect, the policy of discrimination against postgraduate students in Ukraine is reflected in the number of scientists in that republic. In 1965 Ukraine had 14.35 percent of all candidates of science in the USSR, 12.77 percent of all doctors and 14.14 percent of all scientists. Russia had 66.16 percent of all candidates, 70.51 percent of all doctors and 68.85 percent of all scientists. Per 10,000 population in 1965 Russia had 33 scientists and Ukraine only 19. In every republic except Russia, Georgia, Azerbaidzhan and Armenia, the percentage of scientists was lower than the republic's percentage of the total population of the USSR (table XXII).

A comparative study of statistics for past years indicates that the percentage of scientists in Ukraine was considerably lower in 1965 than in 1940 as revealed by the following data:

Year	USSR	RSFSR	%	UkrSSR	%
1940	98,315	61,872	62.9	19,304	19.6
1950	162,508	111,699	68.7	22,363	13.7
1958	284,038	194,849	68.6	36,550	12.9
1960	354,158	242,872	68.3	46,657	13.2
1962	524,546	362,528	69.1	71,035	13.5
1963	565,958	389,326	68.8	78,866	13.9
1964	611,964	419,512	68.6	86,957	14.2
1965	664,584	457,538	68.9	93,984	14.1[28]

Although Ukraine's percentage of the total number of scientists in the USSR has very slowly climbed, it is still a long way from the pre-war level; Russia's percentage is considerably above the pre-war level.

If Russia has a higher percentage of all scientists in the union than the percentage of her total population in the USSR, it follows that in the non-Russian republics there will be a higher percentage of people employed in manual labour than in the RSFSR. In table XXIII we can see this relationship statistically. In 1959 in the USSR 79.3 percent of the population was engaged in physical and 20.7 in mental work. However, the percentage of those doing mental work in Russia is 22.6 and only 17.8 in Ukraine. In every republic except Georgia and Estonia the percentage of the population engaged in mental work is smaller than in Russia. In Moldavia it is 11.3, exactly half that of Russia. It should also be

TABLE XXII

Number of (a) Candidates of Science, (b) Doctors of Science and
(c) Total Number of Scientists in the Republics of the USSR, 1965

	(a)	%	(b)	%	(c)	%
Total in USSR	134,427	100.	14,757	100.	664,584	100.
Russian SFSR	88,940	66.16	10,405	70.51	457,538	68.85
Ukrainian SSR	19,291	14.35	1,885	12.77	93,984	14.14
Belorussian SSR	3,093	2.30	255	1.73	14,668	2.21
Uzbek SSR	3,879	2.89	314	2.13	16,329	2.46
Kazakh SSR	3,255	2.44	232	1.57	18,226	2.74
Georgian SSR	4,090	3.04	647	4.39	14,225	2.14
Azerbaidzhan SSR	2,999	2.23	329	2.23	12,350	1.86
Lithuanian SSR	1,349	1.00	58	.39	6,415	.96
Moldavian SSR	961	.72	64	.43	3,737	.56
Latvian SSR	1,325	.99	78	.53	6,019	.91
Kirgiz SSR	894	.67	71	.48	3,702	.56
Tadzhik SSR	737	.55	47	.32	3,538	.53
Armenian SSR	2,039	1.52	254	1.72	7,773	1.17
Turkmen SSR	602	.42	39	.26	2,607	.39
Estonian SSR	973	.72	79	.54	3,473	.52

Source: *Narodnoe khozaystvo 1965,* pp. 712-13.

TABLE XXIII

Percentage of Population Engaged in Physical and Mental Work
in the Republics of the USSR, 1959

	Percentage Engaged in PhysicalWork	Percentage Engaged in MentalWork
USSR	79.3	20.7
Russian SFSR	77.4	22.6
Ukrainian SSR	82.2	17.8
Belorussian SSR	85.1	14.9
Uzbek SSR	82.7	17.3
Kazakh SSR	77.8	22.2
Georgian SSR	77.1	22.9
Azerbaidzhan SSR	79.4	20.6
Lithuanian SSR	83.5	16.5
Moldavian SSR	88.7	11.3
Latvian SSR	77.9	22.1
Kirgiz SSR	81.0	19.0
Tadzhik SSR	84.1	15.9
Armenian SSR	78.2	21.8
Turkmen SSR	79.9	20.1
Estonian SSR	76.3	23.7

Source: *Itogi vsesoyuznoy perepisi,* p. 131.

borne in mind that in all republics a high proportion of those doing mental work are Russians. We can readily see who are the "hewers of wood and the drawers of water".

That Ukrainians as such are discriminated against, is also illustrated in the number of their graduate students in the USSR. The percentage of Ukrainians in the union in 1959 was 17.84 and of Russians 54.65 (appendix I), but the percentage of Ukrainian postgraduate students in the USSR in 1960 was 11.1 as against 58.53 Russians (table XXIV). The percentage of Ukrainian scientists in the USSR in 1965 was only 10.65; the percentage of Russians was 66.35 (table XXV). This same discrimination against Ukrainian specialists prevailed in the UkrSSR. In 1960 they made up only 58.3 percent of all specialists with higher education, Russians 26.5 and 33 other nationalities made up the remaining 15.2 percent (see appendix VI).

If Ukrainian specialists make up such a small percentage of the total number in Ukraine, there are two reasons for this: firstly, there are not enough Ukrainian specialists to fill all posts because Ukrainians are discriminated against in higher educational institutions of the USSR and the UkrSSR and secondly, of those that are trained, many are directed to work outside the UkrSSR. Thus in 1960, of 517,729 Ukrainian specialists with higher education in the USSR, only 399,931 or 77.2 percent worked in Ukraine. The rest were scattered throughout the republics of the USSR (see appendix VIII). It may be argued that not all Ukrainian specialists in the USSR are natives of Ukraine. However, only 13.7 percent of the Ukrainian population of the USSR lives outside the borders of the UkrSSR, whereas the percentage of Ukrainian specialists outside Ukraine is 22.8.

The policy of dispersing trained personnel beyond the borders of their native land is even more marked in the case of scientists. In 1960 only 22,523 or 48.3 percent of those in Ukraine were Ukrainians (table XXVI). However in 1960 there were in the USSR altogether 35,426 Ukrainian scientists.[29] This means that only 63.6 percent of all Ukrainian scientists were in Ukraine and 36.4 percent in other republics of the USSR.

TABLE XXIV

National Composition of Postgraduate Students in USSR, 1960

		%
USSR	36,754	100.
Russians	21,512	58.53
Ukrainians	4,081	11.10
Belorussians	902	2.45
Uzbeks	1,119	3.04
Kazakhs	591	1.61
Georgians	847	2.30
Azerbaidzhans	1,020	2.78
Lithuanians	415	1.13
Moldavians	145	.39
Latvians	276	.75
Kirgiz	185	.50
Tadzhiks	320	.87
Armenians	730	1.99
Turkmans	234	.64
Estonians	401	1.09
Others	3,976	10.83

Source: *Vysshee obrazovanie*, p. 223.

TABLE XXV

National Composition of Scientists in the USSR, 1965

		%
USSR	664,584	100.
Russians	440,976	66.35
Ukrainians	70,797	10.65
Belorussians	12,814	1.93
Uzbeks	6,734	1.01
Kazakhs	4,523	.68
Georgians	12,892	1.94
Azerbaidzhans	8,642	1.30
Lithuanians	5,700	.86
Moldavians	1,392	.21
Latvians	4,322	.65
Kirgiz	1,026	.16
Tadzhiks	1,390	.21
Armenians	13,491	2.03
Turkmans	1,232	.19
Estonians	3,448	.52
Others*	75,205	11.31

Source: *Narodnoe Khozaystvo 1965*, p. 711.

*Includes 26 other nationalities.

TABLE XXVI

(a) Total Number of All Scientists 1960, (b) Number of Scientists of
Indigenous Nationality 1960, (c) Percentage of Scientists of
Indigenous Nationality 1960, and (d) Percentage of Indigenous
Population in the Republics of the USSR 1959

	(a)	(b)	(c)	(d)
Russian SFSR	242,872	193,193	79.5	83.3
Ukrainian SSR	46,657	22,523	48.3	76.8
Belorussain SSR	6,840	3,209	46.9	81.1
Uzbek SSR	10,329	3,552	34.4	62.2
Kazakh SSR	9,623	2,064	21.4	42.7
Georgian SSR	9,137	7,658	83.8	64.3
Azerbaidzhan SSR	7,226	4,669	64.6	67.5
Lithuanian SSR	3,320	2,776	83.6	79.3
Moldavian SSR	1,999	516	25.8	65.4
Latvian SSR	3,348	2,189	65.4	62.0
Kirgiz SSR	2,315	573	24.7	40.5
Tadzhik SSR	2,154	727	33.8	53.1
Armenian SSR	4,275	4,000	93.6	88.0
Turkmen SSR	1,836	677	36.9	60.9
Estonian SSR	2,227	1,758	78.9	74.6

Source: *Vysshee obrazonvanie,* 215, *Itogi vsesoyuznoy perepisi,* pp. 206-208.

Consequently, not only is there discrimination against Ukrainians in higher education, but a large proportion of those that are fortunate enough to acquire advanced academic training end up beyond the borders of their native land—not by choice. They go where they are directed because, according to decree No. 1709 of the Council of Ministers of the USSR, May 22, 1948, "hiring of individuals who have completed postgraduate work while not employed, is forbidden without an assignment from a ministry".[30]

Another decree of the Council of Ministers of the USSR and the CC of the CPSU dated August 30, 1954 made it obligatory for all ministries and agencies:

> . . . to establish strict control over the timely arrival of young specialists at their designated places, to assess annually the summaries of the distribution of young specialists and to report the results to the Council of Ministers of the USSR and the CC of the CPSU.[31]

The minister of Higher and Secondary Special Education announced recently that a decree had been issued with instructions that:

> Graduates of day courses of higher educational institutions and technicums are obliged after graduating to work no less than three years according to assignment or contract made with an enterprise. It is strictly forbidden to hire young specialists who have not worked three years after graduating from an institution and without a travel order.[32]

After three years, if any such exiles wish to come back to their native land they generally find the avenue of return blocked. In order to live in a locality, a person must obtain a police permit. For a Ukrainian this is most difficult because the policy is to direct Russians to positions in Ukraine and let Ukrainians remain beyond their native land.

The discrimination also extends to the Ukrainian language. On occasion this practice has been officially condemned. In 1953 after Stalin's death, (according to reliable reports circulating in Ukraine) Beria wrote a memorandum to the CC condemning Russification and asking that the party return to Lenin's national policy of allowing non-Russians freedom to develop their languages and cultures. On June 13 of that year, the secretary of the CC of the CPU was dismissed from his post because among other things, he supported Russification of higher educational institutions in Western Ukraine (see p. 23). Subsequent plenums of the regional committees of the party of Lviv, Drohobych, Stanislav, Transcarpathia, Izmail and Chernivtsi, in identical language condemned "the changing of instruction to the Russian language" in various higher and other educational institutions in Western Ukraine.[33] On the heels of this a long editorial appeared in an official Kiev party organ which declared that:

> It is necessary to end decisively the underprivileged position of the Ukrainian language in the higher educational institutions and to organize instruction in the native language all over the country.[34]

Beria was liquidated before any changes could be made in the language of instruction in the educational institutions. As far as I could ascertain from speaking with many educators, graduates and students from various cities, in the universities of Dnipropetrovsk, Odessa and Kharkiv the instruction, except in the departments of Ukrainian language and literature, is entirely in Russian. In the other four universities—Kiev, Lviv, Uzhorod and Chernivtsi —Ukrainian is still used by some lecturers in some of the other faculties as well, especially in the social sciences. In Kiev, according to estimates of persons who are well acquainted with the situation, between 20 and 25 percent of the lectures are in Ukrainian. In Lviv, Uzhorod and Chernivtsi it may be slightly higher.

The other higher educational institutions: polytechnical, industrial, medical, trade and commerce, agricultural and economic, have all been completely Russianized except for those in Western Ukraine where the native tongue is used by some lecturers.

It is not openly admitted, but occasionally statements are unwittingly made in unguarded moments that confirm the fact that the language of instruction in higher educational institutions of non-Russian republics is Russian. In a pamphlet meant for internal distribution Bilodid wrote:

> Many students of various nationalities study in large scientific and educational centres of the country—Moscow, Leningrad,

Kiev, Kharkiv, Lviv, Novosibirsk, Minsk, Tbilisi and others. Possibility of such study for students of all nationalities is realized by a knowledge of the Russian language.[35]

A teacher in a national republic, pointing out that graduates of technicums do not have a full mastery of the Russian language, blames the condition on the insufficient number of hours assigned to Russian and, to strengthen her case, asks:

Will the graduates of the secondary special educational institutions of the national republics be able to complete the entrance examinations for the higher educational institutions of Moscow, Leningrad, Kiev and other cities where instruction is carried on in the Russian language?[36]

For the school year 1960-61, besides Ukrainians, there were listed as attending the higher educational institutions of Ukraine, students of thirty-three nationalities and some whose nationality was not listed (see appendix III). Altogether they made up 37.5 percent of all students of such institutions in Ukraine. However, non-Ukrainians made up only 23.2 percent of the total population of Ukraine (appendix IV). These students would not know the Ukrainian language and consequently instruction in classes they attended would have to be in Russian. Obviously this practice of accepting students from one republic in the schools of another is greatly encouraged and is a widely-used means of Russification of the educational institutions of the national republics. While in the USSR, I was informed by highly placed officials that there were even quotas for each institution for the number of students of each nationality that it was obliged to enroll.

The Ministry of Higher and Secondary Special Education of the USSR, which approves the entrance examinations and rules of admission to all higher educational institutions in the USSR[37] facilitates the enrollment of Russians and other non-Ukrainians in the institutions in Ukraine by including only the Russian language and literature among the compulsory subjects of entrance examinations and requiring Ukrainian language and literature only for those who enter Ukrainian institutions " in which instruction is conducted in the language of the republic".[38] This is a change from 1954 when higher educational institutions in Ukraine, among them Kiev and Lviv Universities and the Kiev Bohomolets Medical Institute, required entrance examinations in both Russian and Ukrainian language and literature.[39]

Russification is also advanced through the control over all higher education by the Ministry of Higher and Secondary Special Education. It issues in Russian a monthly *Byuleten ministerstva vysshego i srednego spetsialnogo obrazovaniya* (Bulletin of the Ministry of Higher and Secondary Special Education) in which are published its orders and instructions based on corresponding decrees and edicts of the Councils of Ministers of the USSR and the CC of the CPSU. These are binding on all republican higher educational institutions.

On August 20, 1956, the Council of Ministers and CC issued a decree giving the Higher Certification Commission, a committee of the ministry (referred to in Russian as VAK, Vysshaya attestat-sionnaya Komissiya) the power to appoint members of the academic councils of the higher and scientific research institutes; to supervise their granting of degrees below the candidate PhD. level; to grant candidate and doctorate degrees; and bestow titles of senior scientific researcher, assistant professor and professor.[40]

The Ministry of Higher and Secondary Special Education also approves and removes the heads of all higher educational institutions in the USSR.[41] Informed officials in the USSR whom I knew, claimed that republican ministers of higher and secondary special education are appointed by the CC of the CPSU and the Council of Ministers of the USSR. In view of the centralization of all control in Moscow, this is not improbable.

Everywhere Russians are given a wide preference. In every institute they hold many of the key posts: rectors, prorectors, faculty heads and professors. I took careful note of the names of officials in education in Ukraine. Typical Ukrainian names end in -enko, -yn, -uk, -yuk, -chuk, -ak or -yak, or -sky; typical Russian names end in -ov, -ev, or -in. It is true that one can find exceptions to this rule. There are cases of Ukrainians who had the ending -ov added to their names in the army or in some other Russian environment; there are also individuals who, feeling insecure, or hoping for easier advancement, have themselves made the addition or change. But exceptions do not disprove the rule. Generally, names ending in -ov, -ev, or -in are Russian. The Minister of Higher and Secondary Special Education of the UkrSSR is Dadenkov. The heads of some higher educational institutions in Kiev are:

Polytechnical Institute	Plegunov
Technological Institute of Light Industry	Orlov
Engineering Construction Institute	Vetrov
Ukrainian Academy of Agricultural Sciences	Peresipkin
State Institute of Physical Culture	Laputin
Kiev Institute for Improving Qualifications of Teachers	Kobyakov
Ukrainian Scientific Research Institute of Pedagogy	Chepilev
Karpenko-Kary Institute of Theatrical Arts	Kudin

Last autumn a new university opened at Donetsk in Ukraine. It too will have its share of "elder brothers" from Russia. We were informed that doctors of science from Moscow, Sverdlovsk, Kharkiv, Saratov, Lviv and Voronezh would arrive to fill posts on the staff.[42] All but Kharkiv and Lviv are in Russia.

The staffs of all higher educational institutions also have many Russians, especially in the key posts. There is only fragmentary data on the national composition of such faculties, but this is enough to reveal the discrimination against Ukrainians. In the 1949-50 academic year the national composition of the staff of Lviv University was as follows:

		Percentage
Total staff	297	100
Ukrainians	147	49.49
Russians	88	29.63
Belorussians	11	3.70
Poles	10	3.37
Jews	31	10.14
Unspecified	10	3.37 [43]

Ukrainians made up less than half the staff and Russians almost one third. Russification would also be advanced by many of the others who, not knowing Ukrainian, would also lecture in Russian.

In 1958-59, thirteen years after the end of the war, the picture was only slightly brighter in the University of Uzhorod in Transcarpathian Ukraine, as is evident from the data for that year:

		Percentage
Total staff	211	100
Ukrainians	130	61.61
Russians	50	23.70
Jews	17	8.06
Belorussians	5	2.37
Unspecified	9	4.26 [44]

It should be remembered that both these are universities. In technical institutes the percentage of Russians is even higher.

It is often argued that Russians are brought in because there are not enough Ukrainians available. It is true there have been insufficient trained local personnel in the western regions. The authorities made certain of that by limiting the number admitted to higher educational institutions. Of all those entering higher educational institutions in Lviv in 1953, only 51.8 percent were natives of the region and to Uzhorod University only 54 percent. Only 39.9 percent of the Chernivtsi Medical Institute's enrollment between 1944 and 1957 consisted of local students.[45]

When they graduated many were not allowed to remain in their native region, but were directed to all parts of the USSR and could be found "in the environs of Moscow, in Leningrad, the Urals, Siberia, Kazakhstan, Turkmenia, Kirgizia, Moldavaia, Estonia and so on".[46]

There are no statistics on the national composition of the staffs of all higher educational institutions of the UkrSSR, but approximate deductions can be made from available data. In 1960 there was a total of 46,657 scientists in the UkrSSR. Less than half of these were Ukrainian (table XXVI). In the same year nearly half of all scientists in the UkrSSR were employed in higher educational institutions.[47] There is little probability that in the science faculties even half of the members were Ukrainian.

In some of the social sciences and in the departments of Ukrainian language and literature Ukrainians predominate, but in many universities these departments are weak and inconsequential. In the 1960-61 academic year the Poetry Club of Kharkiv University discussed the works of nine Soviet poets; all were Russian.[48]

Not only is the Russian language dominant, but Russian chauvinism is so strong that many Ukrainians, through fear or in order to avoid unpleasantness, refrain from using their native tongue in the higher educational institutions. This was brought home to me on many occasions. The first of these was a small gathering of staff members in an institute in Kiev to which I was invited as a Ukrainian from Canada. There were two or three Russians present. All speeches were in Russian. Even the presence of a Ukrainian guest from abroad did not alter the standard procedure of using Russian when Russians were present. In another institution some staff members were very reluctant to reply to my greeting in Ukrainian if they passed me in the corridor when a Russian was within hearing distance.

There is also pressure on the students. Even I, a foreign student, was asked by a prorector why I did not use Russian instead of Ukrainian. In my second year in Kiev I was assigned to a class in the history of the party which was given in Russian. As a matter of principle I refused to attend and was transferred to a class given in Ukrainian; a native would have no choice.

Another means of Russification is through the language of the textbooks. The numbers of titles and copies of books and pamphlets published in Ukraine for higher educational institutions in 1964 as a percentage of the total for the USSR was as follows:

	USSR	RSFSR	%	UkrSSR	%	Others	%
Titles	5,668	3,845	67.84	813	14.34	1,010	17.82
Copies*	36,594	32,582	89.04	2,239	6.11	1,773	4.83[49]

*in thousands

Ukraine, with 19.68 percent of the population of the USSR published 14.34 percent of the titles and 6.11 percent of the copies of all books and pamphlets for higher educational institutions; Russia, with 54.87 percent of the population, published 67.84 percent of the titles and 89.04 percent of the number of copies; all the other republics published 17.82 percent of the titles and 4.83 percent of the copies.

Because books were published in Ukraine does not necessarily mean they were in Ukrainian. We have no data as to the language of these books, but there is a breakdown for 1965 giving the total number of titles and copies of textbooks and pamphlets for higher education published in (a) Russian and (b) non-Russian languages of the USSR and (c) foreign languages as follows:

	USSR	(a)	%	(b)	%	(c)	%
Titles	5,668	4,392	77.49	874	15.42	402	7.09
Copies*	36,594	29,797	81.43	2,125	5.81	4,672	12.76[50]

*in thousands

The number of titles published in non-Russian languages was 15.42 percent of the total in the USSR, but the percentage of copies was only 5.81. However the percentage of copies in foreign languages was 12.76. In other words, in *1965 there were over twice as many copies of books published for higher educational institutions in foreign languages as in all the non-Russian languages of the peoples of the USSR!*

There is further evidence that most of those published in Ukraine are in Russian. Following is a letter, dated June 22, 1964, and received at the Kiev publishing house Tekchnika, by the director G. P. Solnikov (a Russian of course):

> The Ministry of Higher and Secondary Special Education of the Ukrainian SSR is forwarding to you a list, authorized by the committee of the Ministry of Higher and Secondary Special Education of the USSR, of educational literature for 1965-66 (in Russian only) for higher educational institutions for which you publish.
>
> Deputy Minister, I. DZUBKO

To a person in the Western world it may sound unbelievable that an agency of the central government must approve textbooks for the republics, but such is the case. The CC of the CPSU and the Council of Ministers of the USSR on May 9, 1963, decreed:

> To entrust the Minister of Higher and Secondary Special Education of the USSR with the task of approving, in agreement with the organs administering higher and secondary special educational institutions, the summary annual plans of publication of textbooks and educational aids for higher and secondary special institutions regardless of the jurisdiction over those publishers and educational institutions. To establish that those plans are obligatory for all ministries, departments, publishers and educational institutions.[51]

A check of the 1965 catalogue of technical and scientific books published in Ukraine[52] reveals that Tekchnika was not slated to publish even one textbook in Ukrainian for either the higher educational institutions or the technicums (see figure 11). When we check the catalogue of publications of Kharkiv University for 1965[53] we find that there are 15 textbooks authorized for higher educational institutions—all are in Russian (see figure 12).

Reference books in libraries are also predominantly in Russian. The libraries of many educational institutions publish monthly bulletins of incoming books. For January 1965 the Kiev Gorky Pedagogical Institute lists a total of 236 new books, of which 205 are in Russian and only 31 or 13 percent in Ukrainian.[54] All books on philosophy, "scientific" communism, economics, history, cybernetics, astronomy, technology, linguistics, music, physiology, medicine and methods of teaching physics, languages and literature were in Russian (see figures 13 and 14). This is an institution that is still predominantly Ukrainian. In the technical and scientific institutions the library books are *all* in Russian.

In one higher educational institution with which the author was acquainted and where both English and Ukrainian were studied as subjects, there were no English-Ukrainian or Ukrainian-English dictionaries, although such had been published in Ukraine. When a student wished to find the English for a Ukrainian word, he first found the Russian equivalent and then looked it up in the

IV. УЧБОВА ЛІТЕРАТУРА

1. Для вузів

114. ОРНАТСКИЙ П. П., канд. техн. наук.— **Автоматические электроизмерительные приборы** (аналоговые и цифровые).

Издательство «Техніка», язык русский, 25 печ. лист. Цена 1 руб. 10 коп. Тираж 8000.

Выход в свет во II кв. 1965 г.

В книге рассматриваются критерии дискретности, методы регистрации и вопросы надежности автоматических измерительных приборов, анализируются основные свойства и погрешности автоматических аналоговых и цифровых приборов прямого преобразования и уравновешивания; описаны устройство звеньев и узлов автоматических приборов, схемы и конструкции приборов.

Книга предназначена для студентов вузов, а также может быть использована инженерами и техниками, работающими в области измерительной техники.

Темплан 1964 г., № 116.

Заказано . . . . экз.

115. ПЕРКОВ В. Г., канд. техн. наук — **Тепловой расчет и конструирование котельных агрегатов средней производительности** (пособие по курсовому проектированию).

Издательство «Техніка», язык русский, 7 печ. лист. Цена 30 коп. Тираж 5000.

Выход в свет в I кв. 1965 г.

В брошюре приведены расчетные, методические и справочные данные, необходимые при выполнении курсового проекта котельного агрегата.

Брошюра является пособием для студентов теплотехнических и энергомашиностроительных специальностей вузов.

Темплан 1964 г., № 114.

Заказано . . . . экз.

116. ОРНАТСКИЙ П. П., канд. техн. наук, **НЕСТЕРЕНКО А. Д.— Детали и узлы приборов** (изд. III).

Издательство «Техніка», язык русский, 25 печ. лист. Цена 1 руб. 30 коп. Тираж 15 000.

Выход в свет в I кв. 1965 г.

В книге рассматриваются вопросы расчета и конструирования деталей и узлов приборов: опор подвижных систем, упругих элементов, передач, регуляторов, успокоителей, отсчетных устройств, органов управления, контактов, соединений и корпусов приборов.

Рассчитана на студентов вузов и техникумов, специализирующихся в области приборостроения.

Заказано . . . . экз.

Figure 11. **Page from the catalogue of technical books published in Ukraine for 1965, listing text and reference books for higher educational institutions published by Tekhnika. All are in Russian.**

I. ПІДРУЧНИКИ І УЧБОВІ ПОСІБНИКИ

1. **Комарь Н. П.** МАТЕМАТИЧЕСКАЯ СТАТИСТИ-
КА В ХИМИИ. Изд-во Харьковского университета. Язык
русский; объем 20 уч.-изд. л.; тираж 5 тыс. экз.; цена
70 коп. Выйдет в свет во II квартале.

*Допущена Министерством высшего и среднего специ-
ального образования УССР в качестве учебника для студентов химических факультетов университетов и химических вузов.*

Книга может быть полезна также для химиков исследователь-
ских и заводских лабораторий.

В ней излагаются общие положения теории случайных погреш-
ностей и методов обработки результатов измерений. В качестве
иллюстраций используются многочисленные примеры, в которых по-
казана статистическая обработка опытных данных, взятых из различных литературных источников.

Тем. пл. 1965 г.   *Заказ . . . экз.*

2. **Зегжда Д. П.** ФИЗИЧЕСКАЯ ХИМИЯ СИЛИКА-
ТОВ. Изд-во Харьковского университета. Язык русский;
объем 12 уч.-изд. л.; тираж 7 тыс. экз.; цена 46 коп.
Выйдет в свет во II квартале.

*Допущена Министерством высшего и среднего специ-
ального образования УССР в качестве учебного пособия
по курсу физической химии силикатов.*

Основным содержанием книги являются вопросы приложения
общетеоретических закономерностей к изучению силикатных систем,
материалов и изделий. В ней собраны и обобщены имеющиеся ма-
териалы, данные и результаты исследований, касающиеся строения
и свойств силикатов в твердом, жидком и тепловидном состоянии,
и их поведения в различных условиях.

Много внимания уделяется реакциям, протекающим в твердой
фазе, механизму осуществления этих процессов, их кинетике и спо-
собам управления ими. Подробно рассматриваются также вопросы
растворения силикатных расплавов твердых и газообразных веществ.

Значительная часть книги посвящена учению о фазовых равно-
весиях в гетерогенных системах и его приложению к силикатам.
В ней приведены основные сведения по термо- и электрохимии силикатов и химии кремнесодержащих соединений.

Тем. пл. 1965 г.   *Заказ . . . экз.*

5

Figure 12. **Page from the catalogue of Kharkiv University for 1965, listing
text and reference books for students of higher educational institutions.
All are in Russian.**

Russian-English dictionary. Another Canadian student related to me this interesting experience. In the institute in which he was studying, textbooks were lent to students for the duration of the course. My friend asked for a copy of the text in political economy, a course which was compulsory for all first year students. It was available only in Russian. He expressed amazement that there were none in Ukrainian. The librarian replied that they had eight copies, but all had been borrowed. Here was an institution with about a thousand students, of which several hundred were taking the compulsory course in political economy and the library had only eight copies in Ukrainian. Of course, there was no shortage of the text in Russian.

Many higher educational institutes in Ukraine are directly under the jurisdiction of ministries or committees of the USSR. In 1964, of 125 institutes in Ukraine, 24, that is 20 percent, were in this category.[55] Among these the two Institutes for Mechanization of Agriculture, the two Veterinary Institutes, the Ukrainian Academy of Agricultural Sciences and the twelve Agricultural Institutes have been under control of the Ministry of Agriculture of the USSR since 1964 (see figure 15). Prior to that time they were under the Ministry of Agriculture of the UkrSSR (see figure 16). There is no question about the language of instruction in these institutions.

The feelings on this problem of jurisdiction of educational institutions was expressed at the fifth convocation of the second session of the Supreme Soviet of the USSR by representatives from the republics of Turkmen, Azerbaidzhan and Ukraine. Hrechukha, a Ukrainian, echoed the requests of the other two when he said:

> It seems to us that it would be more expedient to place the higher educational institutions . . . under the Ministry of Higher Education of the Ukrainian SSR.[56]

This was the wish of representatives of the national republics; the almighty gods in the Kremlin have decreed otherwise.

There are many foreign students enrolled in Ukrainian higher educational institutions. In 1965 there were over 200 from 20

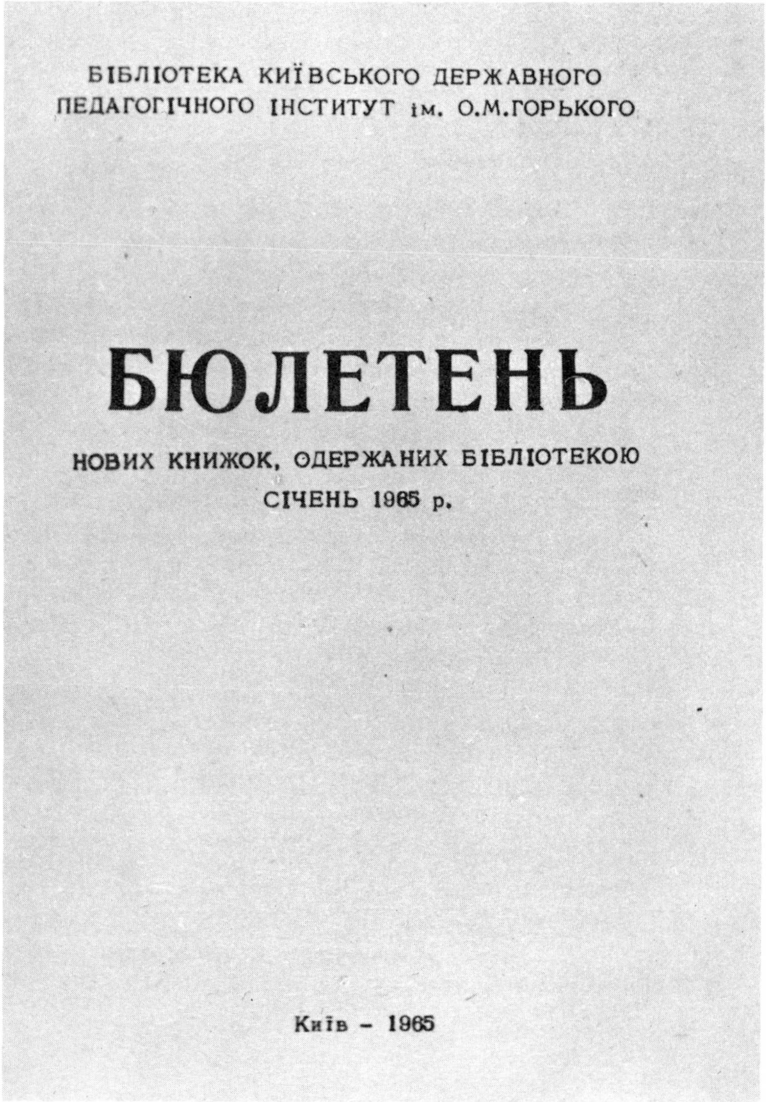

БІБЛІОТЕКА КИЇВСЬКОГО ДЕРЖАВНОГО
ПЕДАГОГІЧНОГО ІНСТИТУТ ім. О.М.ГОРЬКОГО

БЮЛЕТЕНЬ

НОВИХ КНИЖОК, ОДЕРЖАНИХ БІБЛІОТЕКОЮ

СІЧЕНЬ 1965 р.

Київ – 1965

Figure 13. Title page from the bulletin of the library of the Kiev Pedagogical Institute for January, 1965, listing all new books received for that month.

Сурдопедагогіка

371.9   М е щ е р я к о в А.И. и М а р е -
е в а Р.А. Первоначальное обучение
слепоглухонемого ребенка. /Для учите-
лей и воспитателей слепоглухонемых де-
тей/. М., "Просвещение", 1964, 55 с.

372.21   С п е р а н с к и й Г.Н. , З а б л у -
д о в с к а я Е.Д. Закаливание ребенка
раннего и дошкольного возраста. М.,
"Медицина", 1964, 204 с.

371.9   Р я б ч е н к о А.Т. Функциональные
нарушения голоса. М., "Медицина",1964,
102 с.

ІСТОРІЯ

9/6/   Б е к н а з а р - Ю з б а ш е в Б.Г.
Конго... третий акт трагедии. М.,"Зна -
ние", 1964, 32 с.

9/4 /7   Г о р е в Я. Я знал Зорге. М., "Прав-
да", 1964, 47 с.

91/98/   Г р о м о в Б.В. 104- на дрейфующей
М., Политиздат, 1964, 70 с.

9/с/   История СССР. Эпоха социализма.
/1917-1961. гг/. Учебник. М., Политиздат,
1964, 647 с.

9/6/   К е й т а М. Речи и выступления.Пер.
с франц. М., "Прогресс", 1964, 256 с.

9/49/   К о н д р а т ь е в В.К. Республика
Кипр. М., "Знание", 1964, 32 с.

9/с/27   К ю н г Н.Ф. Мужество непокоренных.
/Борьба советских людей в фашистских
застенках/. М., "Знание", 1964, 39 с.

Figure 14. Page from the bulletin of the library of the Kiev Pedagogical
Institute, for January, 1965, listing new books in surdopedagogics (the
education of handicapped children) and history. All are in Russian.

ІНСТИТУТИ
МЕХАНІЗАЦІЇ СІЛЬСЬКОГО ГОСПОДАРСТВА

1. МЕЛІТОПОЛЬСЬКИЙ ІНСТИТУТ МЕХАНІЗАЦІЇ СІЛЬСЬКОГО ГОСПОДАРСТВА

(Міністерство сільського господарства СРСР)
м. Мелітополь, просп. Б. Хмельницького, 18

Факультет механізації сільського господарства.
Спеціальність — механізація сільського господарства.
Строк навчання в інституті 5 років.
При інституті є загальнотехнічний факультет з усіх груп інженерних спеціальностей.
Строк навчання на загальнотехнічному факультеті 3 роки.
При інституті є заочний факультет для навчання студентів старших курсів за спеціальністю механізація сільського господарства.

2. ХАРКІВСЬКИЙ ІНСТИТУТ МЕХАНІЗАЦІЇ І ЕЛЕКТРИФІКАЦІЇ СІЛЬСЬКОГО ГОСПОДАРСТВА

(Міністерство сільського господарства СРСР)
м. Харків, Московський проспект, 45

1. Факультет механізації сільського господарства. Спеціальність — механізація сільського господарства.
2. Факультет електрифікації сільського господарства. Спеціальність — електрифікація сільського господарства.
Строк навчання в інституті 5 років.
При інституті є загальнотехнічний факультет. Спеціальності: механізація сільського господарства; електрифікація сільського господарства.
Строк навчання на загальнотехнічному факультеті 3 роки.
При інституті є заочний факультет для навчання студентів старших курсів за спеціальностями денного навчання.

УКРАЇНСЬКА АКАДЕМІЯ СІЛЬСЬКОГОСПОДАРСЬКИХ НАУК

(Міністерство сільського господарства СРСР)
м. Київ, Голосієво

1. Агрономічний факультет. Спеціальність — агрономія.
2. Факультет агрохімії та ґрунтознавства. Спеціальність — агрохімія та ґрунтознавство.
3. Факультет захисту рослин. Спеціальність — захист рослин.
4. Факультет механізації сільського господарства. Спеціальність — механізація сільського господарства.

5. Факультет електрифікації сільського господарства. Спеціальність — електрифікація сільського господарства.
6. Лісогосподарський факультет. Спеціальність — лісове господарство.
7. Зоотехнічний факультет. Спеціальність — зоотехнія.
8. Ветеринарний факультет. Спеціальність — ветеринарія.
9. Економічний факультет. Спеціальності: планування сільського господарства; бухгалтерський облік у сільському господарстві.

Строк навчання на факультетах механізації сільського господарства, електрифікації сільського господарства та ветеринарному 5 років; на факультетах агрономічному, агрохімії та ґрунтознавства, захисту рослин, лісогосподарському та зоотехнічному — 4 роки та 4 місяці; на економічному факультеті — 4 роки.
При академії є загальнонауковий факультет. Спеціальності: агробіологічні; економічні.
Строк навчання на загальнонауковому факультеті 2 роки.
При академії є заочний факультет. На I курс заочного факультету прийом проводиться за спеціальностями зоотехнія, ветеринарія, лісове господарство, механізація сільського господарства; електрифікація сільського господарства.
Строк навчання 6 років.
Навчання на старших курсах заочного факультету проводиться з усіх спеціальностей денного навчання.

СІЛЬСЬКОГОСПОДАРСЬКІ ІНСТИТУТИ

1. БІЛОЦЕРКІВСЬКИЙ СІЛЬСЬКОГОСПОДАРСЬКИЙ ІНСТИТУТ

(Міністерство сільського господарства СРСР)
м. Біла Церква, Київської області, площа Слободи, 8/1

1. Агрономічний факультет. Спеціальність — агрономія.
2. Ветеринарний факультет. Спеціальність — ветеринарія.
3. Зоотехнічний факультет. Спеціальність — зоотехнія.
Строк навчання 4 роки та 4 місяці, на ветеринарному факультеті — 5 років.
При інституті є загальнонауковий факультет. Спеціальності: гуманітарні; математичні; агробіологічні; економічні.
Строк навчання на загальнонауковому факультеті 2 роки, з математичних спеціальностей — 3 роки.
При інституті є заочний факультет. На I курс заочного факультету прийом проводиться з спеціальностей: зоотехнія; ветеринарія. Строк навчання 6 років.
Навчання на старших курсах заочного факультету проводиться з усіх спеціальностей денного навчання.

Figure 15. **Pages from a student's handbook of higher educational institutions for 1965, listing agricultural institutes in Ukraine, which are under the jurisdiction of the Ministry of Agriculture of the USSR.**

...ностей.

Строк навчання на заочному відділі 6 років.

ІНСТИТУТ ІНЖЕНЕРІВ ВОДНОГО ГОСПОДАРСТВА
УКРАЇНСЬКИЙ ІНСТИТУТ ІНЖЕНЕРІВ ВОДНОГО ГОСПОДАРСТВА

(Міністерство вищої і середньої спеціальної освіти УРСР)
м. Рівне, вул. Ленінська, 36

1. Гідромеліоративний факультет. Спеціальність — гідромеліорація.

2. Механічний факультет. Спеціальність: розробка торфових родовищ; будівельні та дорожні машини й устаткування; первинна технологія волокнистих матеріалів; механічна технологія волокнистих матеріалів; хімічна технологія волокнистих матеріалів.

3. Гідротехнічний факультет. Спеціальності: гідротехнічне будівництво річкових споруд та гідроелектростанцій; промислове та цивільне будівництво; водопостачання і каналізація.

Строк навчання 5—5,5 років.

При інституті є вечірній відділ з таких спеціальностей: промислове та цивільне будівництво; водопостачання і каналізація.

При інституті є загальнотехнічний факультет з усіх інженерних спеціальностей.

Строк навчання на загальнотехнічному факультеті 3 роки.

При інституті є заочний факультет для навчання студентів старших курсів. На 1-й курс заочного факультету проводиться прийом на спеціальності — Гідромеліорація, яка не входить в перелік спеціальностей загальнотехнічних факультетів.

ІНСТИТУТИ МЕХАНІЗАЦІЇ СІЛЬСЬКОГО ГОСПОДАРСТВА

1. МЕЛІТОПОЛЬСЬКИЙ ІНСТИТУТ МЕХАНІЗАЦІЇ СІЛЬСЬКОГО ГОСПОДАРСТВА

(Міністерство сільського господарства УРСР)
м. Мелітополь, просп. Б. Хмельницького, 18

Факультет механізації сільського господарства. Спеціальність — механізація процесів сільського виробництва.

Строк навчання в інституті 5—5,5 років.

груп інженерних спеціальностей.

Строк навчання на загальнотехнічному факультеті 3 роки.

При інституті є заочний факультет для навчання студентів старших курсів.

2. ХАРКІВСЬКИЙ ІНСТИТУТ МЕХАНІЗАЦІЇ І ЕЛЕКТРИФІКАЦІЇ СІЛЬСЬКОГО ГОСПОДАРСТВА

(Міністерство сільського господарства УРСР)
м. Харків, Московський просп., 45

1. Факультет механізації сільського господарства. Спеціальність — механізація процесів сільськогосподарського виробництва.

2. Факультет електрифікації сільського господарства. Спеціальність — електрифікація процесів сільськогосподарського виробництва.

Строк навчання в інституті 5—5,5 років.

При інституті є загальнотехнічний факультет. Спеціальності: механізація процесів сільськогосподарського виробництва; електрифікація процесів сільськогосподарського виробництва.

Строк навчання на загальнотехнічному факультеті 3 роки.

При інституті є заочний факультет для навчання студентів старших курсів с усіх спеціальностей денного навчання.

УКРАЇНСЬКА АКАДЕМІЯ СІЛЬСЬКОГОСПОДАРСЬКИХ НАУК

(Міністерство сільського господарства УРСР)
м. Київ, Голосієво

1. Агрономічний факультет. Спеціальність — агрономія.

2. Факультет ґрунтознавства та агрохімії. Спеціальність — ґрунтознавство та агрохімія.

3. Факультет механізації сільського господарства. Спеціальність — механізація процесів сільськогосподарського виробництва.

4. Факультет захисту рослин. Спеціальність — захист рослин.

5. Факультет електрифікації сільського господарства. Спеціальність — електрифікація процесів сільськогосподарського виробництва.

6. Лісогосподарський факультет. Спеціальність — лісове господарство.

7. Факультет економіки та організації сільського господарства. Спеціальність: економіка та організація сільського господарства; бухгалтерський облік (в сільському господарстві).

8. Ветеринарний факультет. Спеціальність — ветеринарія.

9. Зоотехнічний факультет. Спеціальність — зоотехнія.

Строк навчання в академії 5—5,5 років.

Figure 16. **Pages from a student's handbook of higher educational institutions in Ukraine for 1963, listing agricultural institutes in Ukraine which were under the jurisdiction of the Ministry of Agriculture of the UkrSSR.**

countries of the world studying in the Ukrainian Academy of Agricultural Sciences alone.[57] They begin attending regular lectures after a six-month basic course in Russian. In 1964 there were 401 from 32 countries taking such courses at the Preparatory Faculty for Foreign Citizens at Kiev University.[58] In June 1964, the faculty held a special conference on teaching Russian to foreign students.[59] There have even been six special textbooks published in Kiev recently to teach them the Russian language.[60] These students from abroad have become a pretext for Russification. Several educators who had personal knowledge of the incident, related that in the Lviv Polytechnical Institute a few such students were assigned to each class and the lecturers were ordered to switch over to Russian. When the head of one of the departments protested, Shpanova, a Russian and secretary of the party organization in the institute, accused him of bourgeois nationalism and demanded he be dismissed. However, other staff members came out strongly in his support. The foreign students were then organized into separate classes in which instruction was in Russian. In the Kiev Medical Institute several obdurate professors received orders direct from the Ministry of Higher and Secondary Special Education of the USSR in Moscow to lecture in Russian after the influx of foreign students.

To get a clearer picture of the process of Russification let us follow a student from a Ukrainian secondary school as he prepares to enter Kiev University. First he must write entrance examinations which will be in Russian and for which he studied from Russian texts (see figure 17). With him, trying the examinations, will be many Russians. They will have the advantage because he studied in a Ukrainian school and does not know Russian as well as they do. If he fails he will be reproached; "You should have attended a Russian school".

If successful he may be assigned to a student dormitory where notices on bulletin boards, slogans, wall and regular newspapers and magazines, will be for the most part in Russian. The attendants at the hostel will as a rule, also be Russian.

When he goes to the book kiosk and asks for Ukrainian text-

1) побудова обрисів технічних форм, що мають основні види сполучення, з нанесенням розмірів;
2) побудова за двома даними третього виду деталі із зображенням необхідних розрізів, а також її наочного зображення в аксонометричній проекції.

Список літератури на допомогу вступникам до вищих учбових закладів

Н. С. Моденов, С. И. Новоселов. Пособие по математике для поступающих в вузы. Изд-во Московского государственного университета, 1963.

К. У. Шахно. Как готовиться к приемным экзаменам в вуз. (Математика). Изд-во Ленинградского государственного университета, 1962.

К. У. Шахно. Пособие по математике для поступающих в высшие учебные заведения. (Сборник конкурсных задач по математике с решениями). Изд-во Министерства высшего, среднего специального и профессионального образования БССР, Минск, 1962.

В. Р. Саулит, В. Ю. Падалко. Как готовиться к приемным экзаменам в вуз. (Физика). Изд-во Ленинградского государственного университета, 1963.

Г. П. Хомченко. Пособие по химии для поступающих в вузы. Изд-во Московского государственного университета, 1963.

Д. Э. Розенталь. Пособие по русскому языку для поступающих в вузы. Изд-во Московского государственного университета, 1962.

В. А. Ежов, Ю. Д. Марголис, С. Л. Пештич. Как готовиться к приемным экзаменам в вуз. (История СССР). Изд-во Казанского государственного университета, 1961.

В. М. Макеева и др. Английский язык. (Учебное пособие для курсов по подготовке в вузы.). Изд-во «Высшая школа», 1961.

М. Г. Чернышева и др. Немецкий язык. (Учебное пособие для курсов по подготовке в вузы). Изд-во «Высшая школа», 1961.

Figure 17. **Page from a student's handbook of higher educational institutions for 1965, listing books for study in preparation for entrance examinations. All are in Russian.**

books, a Russian speaking clerk will measure him contemptuously from head to foot and snarl, "Nyet, tolko na russkom yazyke". ("No, we only have them in the Russian language".)[61]

The professors will in most cases lecture in Russian; there may be a lack of textbooks in Ukrainian; any Russian and foreign students present may demand that lectures be in Russian because they do not understand Ukrainian; the professor may be afraid to go against official policy; he may be a Russian born in Ukraine or directed there.

Our student will come in contact with the rector, prorectors, faculty heads and other officials. He will find that many of them are Russians. Since they speak their native tongue, others must answer in the same language because "it is not cultured not to reply in the tongue in which one is addressed". When he goes to the library to study, he will find that most reference books are also in Russian.

After graduating he will come before a government board to "choose" his place of employment. The choice may be wide: Siberia, Kazakhstan, the Urals or the Island of Sakhalin. His diploma, written in Russian, will be sent to the personnel department where he is assigned and will be made available to him after one full year of work.

If accepted, a graduate goes on to advanced studies. The degree of candidate is conferred by VAK in Moscow. There is no stipulation as to which language should be used in writing a thesis. A student may write it in Ukrainian, but in Moscow they read only Russian. Many of those who wrote in Ukrainian waited a long time before finding out that their theses were unacceptable.[62] The word gets around; most theses are now written in Russian. There is no pressure, you understand; it is all "voluntary". Of course, a few are still accepted in Ukrainian.

There are no complete official statistics on the language of theses, but enough data can be compiled to indicate a trend. In 1962 Lviv University published a bibliography of the works of all academic personnel at the university from 1944-1960, listing the titles of their theses and the language in which each was written.[63]

From that source has been compiled the following on the language of theses of the university staff:

Number of theses	Russian	%	Ukrainian	%
365	312	85.5	53	14.5

Of the 53 written in Ukrainian, 39 were by members of the faculties of philology and journalism and 14 by members of all the other faculties. By 1960, the pressure of Russification had increased. A report for that year indicated that in the faculties of philology of all the higher educational institutions of Ukraine there was a grand total of eleven theses in Ukrainian.[64]

A report for 1966 indicated that a total of 25 theses were presented in the Institute of Economics of the Academy of Sciences of the UkrSSR and by its staff members in other institutions. All theses were in Russian. Of the 25, three were for doctorate degrees. Two of the aspirants had typically Russian names, indicating that they were most likely "elder brothers".[65]

An official organ of the Party has recently listed the titles of theses on the history of the CPSU accepted by VAK between the years 1957-1966 for the doctorate degree from higher educational institutions of the republics of the USSR. *All the theses are in Russian.* Of the total of 70, nine or 13 percent are from Ukraine. Eight of the aspirants have typical Ukrainian names.[66]

Three other lists of thesis titles approved by the local Councils for the Coordination of Academic Research in the History of the CPSU in 1966 are all in Russian. Of the total of 90, only 12 are from Ukraine. This again makes up 13 percent of the total, but of the 12 students working for their doctorate degree, only six have Ukrainian names and five have typically Russian ones.[67]

Not only is Ukraine's percentage of doctors in this field of study smaller than her percentage of the population, but it appears from the 1966 data that Ukrainians are being discriminated against. The faculties of the history of the CPSU in Ukrainian institutions are heavily-weighted with Russians and also generally headed by Russians. The two most important in the capital are at Kiev

University and the Higher Party School of the CC of the CPU. Their heads are A. A. Borodin and V. M. Samofalov, both Russians.

Anyone wishing to work for his doctorate in an institute of the Academy of Sciences of the UkrSSR must be recommended by the ministry which has jurisdiction over the institution employing the applicant. The latter becomes attached to the institute in which he works for his doctorate, but is on full salary at his place of employment.[68] It is obvious that there is careful selection and close control over the training for doctorates.

In spite of all this planned and organized discrimination against Ukraine, the Ukrainians and their language, Brezhnev can shamelessly proclaim that:

> The Soviet Union has become for the peoples of the world an inspiring example of fruitful fraternal harmony of people of various races and nationalities.[69]

FOOTNOTES

1. "Polozhenie o vysshykh uchebnykh zavedeniyakh SSSR (Regulations Regarding Higher Educational Institutions of the USSR)", *O kommunisticheskom vospitanii,* p. 291.
2. L. M. Vidavsky and others, *Spravochnik po pravovym voprosam vysshey shkoly* (Handbook of Questions on Regulations in Higher Educational Institutions), Kiev, 1965, pp. 203-214.
3. Polozhenie o vysshykh uchebnykh zavedeniyakh, *O kommunisticheskom vospitanii,* p. 291.
4. *Narodnoe khozaystvo 1963,* p. 569. *Narodnoe khozaystvo 1965,* p. 691.
5. E. P. Pichugina, op. cit., p. 86.
6. *Vysshee obrazovanie v SSSR,* pp. 106-107.
7. *Narodnoe khozaystvo 1964,* p. 554.
8. E. P. Pichugina, op. cit., p. 86.
9. *Vysshee obrazovanie v SSSR,* p. 159.
10. Of the 7,090,813 Russians living in the UkrSSR in 1959, 5,726,476 or 80.8 percent lived in the cities. *Itogi vsesoyuznoy perepisi,* pp. 168, 170, 172.
11. *Izvestia,* April 19, 1958.

12. E. P. Pichugina, op. cit., p. 82.
13. *Dovidnyk dlya vstupnykiv do vyshchykh uchbovykh zakladiv Ukrayinskoyi RSR na 1965 rik* (Handbook for Entrants of Higher Educational Institutions of the Ukrainian SSR for 1965), Kiev University, 1965, p. 224.
14. *XXII Zyizd Komunistychnoyi Partiyi Ukrayiny* (Twenty-second Congress of the Communist Party of Ukraine), Kiev, 1962, p. 74.
15. U.R.E., *Ukrayinska Radyanska Sotsialistychna Respublika* (The Ukrainian Soviet Socialist Republic), Kiev, 1967, p. 201.
16. *Statut Komunistychnoyi Partiyi Radyanskoho Soyuza* (Statutes of the Communist Party of the Soviet Union), Kiev, 1963, p. 16.
17. O. H. Syvets, *Vyrobnyche navchannya v shkolakh Ukrayinskoyi RSR* (Industrial Training in the Schools of the Ukrainian SSR), Kiev, 1960, pp. 31-32.
18. N. N. Zabelin and others, *Planirovanie podgotovki i raspredeleniya rabochykh kadrov v SSSR* (Planning of Training and Distribution of Personnel in the USSR), Moscow, 1960, p. 91.
19. Ibid., p. 145.
20. Ibid., p. 134.
21. V. I. Naulko, *Etnichny sklad naselennya Ukrayinskoyi RSR* (The Ethnic Composition of the Population of the Ukrainian SSR), Kiev, 1965, p. 79.
22. V. I. Tovkun, "Osoblyvosti mihratsii naselennya Ukrayinskoyi RSR u 1959-1963 rr. (The Peculiarities of the Migration of the Population of the Ukrainian SSR in 1959-1963)", *Ukrayinsky Istorychny Zhurnal* (Ukrainian Historical Journal), No. 4, April, 1966, p. 56.
23. "Polozhenie ob aspiranture pri vysshykh uchebnykh zavedeniyakh i nauchno-issledovatelskikh uchrezhdeniyakh (Regulations Regarding Post Graduate Studies at Higher Educational and Scientific Research Institutes)".*Nauchnye Kadry v SSSR* (Science Cadres in the USSR), A. V. Topichev, ed. Collection of Documents and Reference Materials, Moscow, 1959, p. 16.
24. Ibid., p. 181.
25. Ibid., pp. 178-79.
26. "Rasporyazhenie Presidiuma AN SSSR ot 13 iyulya 1957 g. No. 2-1602 O Poryadke Zachisleniya Aspirantov iz Akademiy Nauk Soyuznykh Respublik v Nauchnye Uchrezhdeniya Akademii Nauk SSSR (Instruction of the Presidium of the AN USSR, July 13, 1957, No. 2-1602 Regarding the Order of Enrollment of Aspirants from the Academy of Science of Union Republics into the Scientific Institutes of the Academy of Sciences of the USSR), *Nauchnye Kadry, SSSR*, p. 30.
27. Ibid.
28. *Narodnoe khozaystvo 1963*, pp. 592-93; *Narodnoe khozaystvo 1964*, pp. 702-03; *Narodnoe khozaystvo 1965*, pp. 712-13.
29. *Vysshee obrazovanie v SSSR*, pp. 210-211.
30. *Polozhenie ob apiranture*, Nauchnye Kadry v SSSR, p. 21.

31. *KPSS o kulture, prosveshchenii i nauke* (The CPSU on Culture, Education and Science), Collection of Documents, Moscow, 1963, p. 407.
32. V. Elyutin, in Pravda, June 20, 1964.
33. *Pravda Ukrayiny,* June 18, 21 and 26, 1953.
34. *Radyanska Ukrayina,* June 28, 1953.
35. I. K. Bilodid, *Rosiyska mova—mova mizhnatsionalnoho spilkuvannya narodiv SRSR* (Russian, The Language of International Communion of the Peoples of the USSR), Kiev, 1962, p. 20.
36. A. Avayan, "Ob izuchenii russkogo yazyka v srednykh spetsialnykh uchebnykh zavedeniyakh Azerbaidzhanskoy SSR (Regarding the Study of the Russian Language in the Secondary Special Educational Institutions of the Azerbaidzhan SSR)", *Russky Yazyk,* No. 4, 1963, p. 76.
37. *Dovidnyk dlya vstupnykiv do vyshchykh uchbovykh zakladiv,* pp. 175, 223.
38. Ibid., p. 227.
39. *Radyanska Ukrayina,* July 4 and 10, 1954. See last page for announcements of opening of enrollment for these institutions.
40. "Polozhenie o vysshey attestatsionnoy komissii po prisuzhdeniyu uchenykh stepeney i zvaniy pri ministerstve vysshego obrazovaniya SSSR (Decree Regarding the Higher Certification Commission on Awarding Degrees and Titles of the Ministry of Higher Education of the USSR)", *Nauchnye Kadry,* v SSSR, pp. 167-170.
41. *KPSS o kulture,* p. 389. The power was originally (1936) bestowed upon the All-Union Committee on Higher Schools of the Council of Peoples' Commissars. In 1955 the board was reorganized into the Ministry of Higher Education of the USSR and in 1959 into the Ministry of Higher and Secondary Special Education.
42. *Radyanska Ukrayina,* September 1, 1965.
43. F. I. Stebliy, "Rozvytok vyshchoyi osvity v zakhidnykh oblastyakh URSR v 1944-1960 rr. (The Development of Higher Education in the Western Regions of the UkrSSR in 1944-1960)", *Z istorii Ukrayinskoyi RSR* (From the History of the Ukrainian RSR) No. 8, 1963, p. 90.
44. Ibid.
45. Ibid., p. 92.
46. Ibid., p. 101.
47. V. Titov, *Vysshaya shkola Ukrainskoy SSR v period perestroyki* (Higher Schools of the Ukrainian SSR in the Period of Reconstruction), Kiev 1962, p. 11.
48. Ibid., p. 188.
49. *Pechat SSR v 1965 godu,* pp. 42-43, 120-21.
50. Ibid., p. 50.
51. *KPSS o kulture,* p. 440.
52. *Zvedeny temalychny plan,* op. cit., pp. 40-50.

53. Derzhavny komitet rady ministriv Ukrayinskoyi RSR po presı (State Committee for Publishing of the Ukrainian SSR), *Tematychny plan vydavnystva Kharkivskoho universytetu na 1965 rik* (Catalogue of Publications of Kharkiv University Publishers for 1965), Kharkiv, 1964, pp. 5-12.

54. Biblioteka Kyyivskoho derzhavnoho pedahohichnoho instytuta im. O. M. Gorkoho (Library of the Gorky Kiev State Pedagogical Institute). *Byuleten novykh knyzhok oderzhanykh bibliotekoyu, Sichen 1965 r.* (Bulletin of New Books Received by the Library, January, 1965), Kiev, 1965.

55. *Dovidnyk dlya vstupnykiv do vyshchykh uchbovykh zakladiv Ukrayinskoyi RSR na 1964 rik,* pp. 3-72.

56. *Zasedanie Verkhovnogo Soveta SSSR,* p. 298.

57. *Vechirny Kiev,* January 6, 1965.

58. Ibid., November 23, 1964.

59. *Voprosy programirovannogo obucheniya russkomu yazyku inostrantsev* (Problems of Programmed Teaching of Russian to Foreigners), Kharkov, 1966.

60. G. Makarova, V *kosmos* (Into Space), Series 1, Kiev, 1966.
   — *Khimiya vchera, segognya i zavtra* (Chemistry Yesterday, Today and Tomorrow), Series 2, 1966.
   — *Ya izuchayu prirodu i cheloveka* (I Am Studying Nature and Man), Series 3, 1966.
   — *Mirniy atom* (The Peaceful Atom), Series 4, 1966.
   — *Khochu znat rodinu moyikh druzey—Sovetskiy Soyuz* (I Wish to Know the Motherland of My Friends—the Soviet Union), Series 5, 1967.
   — *Uchus govorit po russki* (I am Learning to Speak Russian), Series 6, 1967.

61. I was witness to this particular incident (as well as other similar ones) at a book kiosk in a higher educational institution in Kiev.

62. There is no complete data on the number of recommendations for degrees from higher educational institutions of Ukraine not confirmed by VAK, but for 1951-53 the numbers were, ten doctorate and fifty-four candidate. *Radyanska Ukrayina,* July 6, 1954.

63. N. P. Berezhna and others, *Drukovani pratsi profesoriv, vykladachiv i spivrobitnykiv Lvivskoho Universytetu za 1944-1960 roky* (Published Works of Professors, Lecturers and Co-workers of Lviv University for 1944-1960), Lviv, 1962.

64. "Zakhyst dysertatsiy z Ukrayinskoho i Rosiyskoho movoznavstva na Ukrayini v 1960 r. (Defense of Dissertations in Ukrainian and Russian Philology in Ukraine in 1960)", *Ukrayinska Mova v Shkoli,* No. 2, March-April, 1961, pp. 94-96.

65. *Ekonomika Radyanskoyi Ukrayiny* (The Economy of Soviet Ukraine), No. 5, May, 1967, p. 97.

66. *Voprosy Istorii KPSS,* No. 6, June, 1967, pp. 152-154.

67. *Voprosy Istorii KPSS,* No. 1, January, 1967, p. 156; No. 3, March, 1967, pp. 154-155; No. 8, August, 1967, p. 156.

68. *Radyanska Ukrayina,* October 29, 1952.

69. *Izvestiya,* December 30, 1962.

7

Bureaucratic merging
versus democratic development

The accumulated evidence clearly indicates that the Russians are discriminating against education in Ukraine in all its aspects (see appendix VIII) and against Ukrainians as a nationality both in Ukraine (see appendix X) and in the USSR as a whole (see appendix XI). Russian domination is asserted by means of the imposition of directives from Moscow; control over republican ministries by all-union ministries of education; the concentration in Russia of educational institutions, especially those empowered to recommend the granting of candidate and doctorate degrees; the appointment of Russians to fill academic posts in education; the imposition of Russian as the language of textbooks and instruction on all levels of education.

The aim of Russian policy is to maintain a tight control over education in Ukraine and the other national republics, to restrict Ukrainians and other nationals from progressing beyond the elementary and general secondary level, to denationalize them, to direct many of those who obtain a higher education beyond the borders of their native land and to increase Russian hegemony in the republics by the continuous influx of Russians to occupy posts in government, education, science and other fields.

This differs very little from the policies pursued by the Tsarist government, except that the latter openly and clearly proclaimed its aims and policies. In an official pronouncement in 1870, the Minister of Education of Russia, D. Tolstoy, wrote:

> To be sure, the aim of the education of all those of other nationality, living within the boundaries of our Fatherland, uncontestably ought to be their Russification and merging with the Russian people.[1]

The Seventh Congress of the Nobility, held in Moscow in 1911, resolved that:

> The state school cannot have an alien character. In it the state language ought to dominate without any concessions. Instruction should be in the Russian language . . . We, the noblemen proclaim that the school should be Russian and Russia for the Russians![2]

The present Russian rulers, although more skillful, more efficient and more ruthless than their Tsarist predecessors, are not as honest, nor do they call their policies Russification. A completely new terminology has been invented. Khrushchov, speaking at the Twenty-second Congress in 1961 described it thus:

> In our country there is going on a drawing together of nations . . .
> In the process of the unfolding construction of communism there will be achieved the complete unity of nations.[3]

This has since been widely commented upon, explained and expanded by official high priests, as in the following:

> In the period of the development of communism there is objective intensification of the aspiration of peoples to an all-sided drawing together on the basis of unfolding communist relationships. The development of this tendency takes place under conditions of further consolidation of a new international community of people—the Soviet Union . . . This community of people of various nationalities is a transitional stage on the road to the complete future merging of nations.[4]

What this merging means for the languages of the non-Russian peoples of the USSR is revealed in many official articles and pronouncements. The editorial of an official publication in reference to the languages of the peoples of the USSR, stated that:

> There are, among them, languages with a rich literary tradition. These are first the great Russian language and also those of the peoples of the union republics, such as Armenian, Georgian, Latvian, Lithuanian, Estonian and others. They fulfill all the complex of functions of literary languages, that is, they serve in all spheres of life and activity of the given peoples. However, there are languages whose functions have not gone beyond the circle of the local production and family sphere.[5]

Ukrainian which is the language of 40,000,000 people is not even mentioned as being among those with a rich literary tradition. But then, in the 1930's the Russians had by means of terror, mass murder, starvation and exile, destroyed the Ukrainian government, party and academic personnel and imposed the Russian language "in all spheres of life and activity".

The extent of the penetration of Russian in some republics, among them Ukraine, is described as follows:

> A significant part of state, social and political activity in the republic (regional) and not infrequently on the district level is carried on in the Russian language. This means that various congresses, conferences and meetings are carried on mainly in the Russian language. In it most frequently is conducted official documentation and business correspondence.[6]

What is to happen to the languages of the non-Russian peoples? One authority argues against the compulsory study of the national languages in the schools of the respective republics and their legalizing as official,[7] thus opening wide the door for Russian. Another confines the national languages to the role of mediums of expression of the national cultures, but does not see much "prospect in the expansion of the sphere of their use".[8]

The slogan regarding national cultures had been "Socialist in content and national in form". Now pressure is applied to force national writers to exchange their native language for Russian. The resulting Russification is hailed with pride as in the following quotation:

Thus the basic tendency of cultural development of Soviet nations is turned in the direction of the transformation of a culture which is socialist in content and national in form into a culture which is communist in content and international in form.[9]

The Kremlin leaders do not limit their ambitions to imposing their language on the subject peoples of the USSR. One of the latest works on the question of the development of communism states that:

The development and rapprochement of nations will continue to their complete merging after the victory of communism all over the world.[10]

That merging is synonymous with Russification was made clear in an article which appeared while I was living in Kiev and which caused considerable excitement and anger in the Ukrainian community. The author criticized Stalin's thesis (and Lenin's, without mentioning the latter's name) of the merging of "all national languages into a common one", and added that:

History indicates that the emergence of linguistic unity proceeds through the wide adoption of one of the more diffused national languages, which, under conditions of Soviet reality, is the Russian language.[11]

There were many reports circulating in Ukraine about attempts to accelerate merging and the popular opposition to them. According to these, Khrushchov had planned before the Twenty-second Congress to proclaim Russian as the official language in the USSR. Opposition in the republics was so strong that he was forced to abandon his plan. Another attempt to make a major breakthrough in Russification was made at an all-union conference of linguists which was held on November 20-24, 1962 in Alma Ata in Kazakhstan. Its theme was *The Laws of Development of National Languages in Connection With the Development of Socialist Nations.* The power behind the conference was V. V. Vinogradov, director of the Institute of Linguistics of the Academy of Sciences of the USSR. The keynote speaker was M. D. Kammari, a philosopher and corresponding member of the Academy of Sciences of the USSR. He was selected to fly a trial balloon; his thesis was that, in view of the rapprochement of all peoples of the USSR, their full mastery of Russian as a native language and the rapid advancing of Soviet society to communism, the need for local national languages no longer existed. He proposed that newspapers and schools change over to Russian. Reaction from representatives of the republics was immediate and decisive. The first to speak was a Georgian, who denounced Kammari's proposal and asserted that for Georgia the native tongue would be adequate as a language of expression even under communism. He was supported by speakers from other republics. The conference ended in a complete defeat for the advocates of Russification.[12]

Almost a year later on October 9 to 12, 1963, another conference was held in Frunze, the capital of the Kirgiz SSR, on the problem of relations between the Soviet nationalities during the period of transition from Socialism to Communism. Again the main speaker was Kammari; his subject was the merging of Soviet nations and the full adoption of Russian.[13]

This was followed by an all-union conference in Moscow University on December 24 to 28, 1963, of instructors of the Russian language in the higher educational institutions of the republics. Its avowed purpose was to "further improve the teaching of the Russian language". Its real aim was the extension of Russian as the language of instruction in those institutions where the national languages are still used. Russian criticism was especially directed against Latvia, Estonia and Moldavia[14] where hostility to the study of Russian is most marked. The pressure to adopt Russian as the language of instruction in higher educational institutions became intensified after the conference, according to reports that circulated in academic circles.

On September 22 to 25, the following year, another all-union conference was held in Kazan, the capital of the Tatar ASSR, on the problems of mutual interaction on each other of the languages of the peoples of the USSR. In the scheduled addresses the speakers praised the beneficent influence of Russian on the Tatar language. However the Tatars were not so enthusiastic about this blessing; in the discussion they protested that Russian was displacing their native tongue. Even the Minister of Education of the Tatar ASSR displayed veiled opposition to Russification when he questioned the effect of the change of the language of instruction from Tatar to Russian, on the development of logical thinking in the pupils.[15]

Not only are the non-Russians not accepting Russification, but they are opposing it with every means at their disposal. The destruction of a person's language and culture—the most sacred treasures of his national birthright bequeathed to him by his forefathers—condemns him to the basest degradation, strips him of his national dignity and denies him the nourishing intellectual sustenance of his cultural heritage. Perhaps few have better described the feelings engendered by such denial than the Ukrainian writer I. K. Mykytenko. An avowed Communist who participated in the Ukrainian renaissance in the 1920's and 1930's, he believed that the revolution spelled national freedom. Even in 1935 when the Stalinist drive against the Ukrainian nation was in full swing, still believing, or pretending to believe, that Soviet power brought freedom from national oppression, he described his reaction to Russification under the Tsarist regime in these emotion-packed words:

> They taught me in school that I should repudiate the age-old culture of my people; that I should forget my language; that I should learn to be like a person of the ruling nation; that I should serve its culture. They denied me the right to create and obliged me to imitate.
> This was more than coercion. This was poison, which they raised and proposed as a choice: death or existence with one's soul placed under lock . . .[16]

Two years later in 1937, Mykytenko, the faithful and fiery Communist fell victim to the Russian campaign of terror against Ukraine. His words however have survived, to stand in silent condemnation of the intruder's ceaseless campaign to annihilate by the right of Russian might, Ukrainian speech and culture.

To justify their present policy the Kremlin rulers quote from Lenin who wrote in one of his earlier works that:

> The proletarian party . . . aspires to the drawing together and further merging of nations, but this aim it wishes to achieve not

by force, but by an exclusively free, fraternal union of the labour-
ing masses of all nations.[17]

Like all great men he looked into the dim and distant future and
in his vision saw a great community of free people, drawn together
by common bonds based on the brotherhood of man, and speaking
a common language. But this was to be a new language freely
forged in the process of developing civilization. To Lenin merging
was not synonymous with Russification. Faced with the practical
problem of ruling a multi-national state, he vehemently opposed
the imposition of the Russian language on the non-Russians and
emphasized that each nation was to have the full right to free
national development.

Not only is the present policy of the Russian rulers at variance
with what was advocated and practiced in the early years after the
achievement of Soviet power, but it is a complete violation of
every principle on the national question propounded by Lenin,
every resolution and decree of the party and the government of
this period and even the constitution of the USSR of which article
121 guarantees "instruction in the schools in the native language".

The present Russian rulers and their satraps, while prophe-
sying full merging of all languages under what they term a universal
communist system, do not even wait for this system to be achieved
in the USSR, but are frantically merging the non-Russian languages
now by the forceful imposition of Russian. Can this convince
anyone that they believe their own forecasts? If merging is to
come naturally, why do they force it? Is it not clear that the
theory is a mere smokescreen for Russification? Is not this policy
naked Russian chauvinism? Is this not national oppression,
subjugation and domination? Do not these hideous policies spell
IMPERIALISM in large ugly script?

In the light of recent developments the Russian prediction of
one language to be achieved under a universal communist system
appears ludicrous. Both Russia and China claim to be rapidly
advancing to what they choose to call communism. Can there be
detected any merging of the Russian and Chinese languages?[18]
Have not the opposition of the non-Russian peoples in the USSR

to merging, the developments in China and the demands of the Romanians for the return of Moldavia proved the complete bankruptcy of the policy of merging? Is not this Russian theory of one universal Communist system under the leadership of the most revolutionary proletariat (Russian) and one universal language (the Russian), a mad dream of world empire?

Let us assume that milleniums from now there will emerge one world wide linguistic medium. Does that justify denying to living languages today the right to full and free development? We are told by scientists that millions of years from now life on our planet will become extinct. Is anyone vindicated in starting an atomic holocaust to hasten that extinction? By the very laws of nature my neighbour is doomed to die. Would I be justified in killing him now? We know that all things born will pass away, including civilizations, cultures and languages. But should they not be allowed to live out their full span? Why must the Ukrainian language be denied the right to bud, to flower, to run its full course and make its contribution to civilization? Why must it be annihilated in the bud? We have examples of civilization, destroyed. Are we not the poorer for this? Did not part of our heritage perish when Carthage was destroyed?

Other nations than Russia respect and value the cultures and languages of smaller peoples. The theory of merging is opposed in practice by nearly every country, socialist or otherwise, which is made up of two or more nations or which has significant national minorities (see chapter VIII).

In countries like Canada and the United States where immigrants from various nations live together with native-born citizens, but do not form separate language communities due to their wide dispersion, sociologists have recently noted a surprising phenomenon. For decades there has prevailed in the United States the "melting pot" theory according to which all national groups were to merge to form a distinctly new nationality. Now it turns out that the national groups are not merging but are maintaining their separate national characteristics in a dominantly Anglo-Saxon environment even to the fourth generation. The melting pot theory is being discarded as at variance with reality and the best interests of the nation. Ethnic languages are now recognized as an asset and the U.S. government has recommended that they be cultivated along with English.[19]

Moreover, a bill has been sponsored by Senator Ralph Yarborough and cosponsored by Senator Jacob K. Javits, Senator Robert F. Kennedy and other senators to set up a bilingual education program in the United States for Puerto Rican and Mexican children, in which Spanish would be taught as the native and English as a second language. This program would endeavour in working with the children "to impart a knowledge of and pride in ancestral culture and language".[20]

The General Conference of UNESCO decided in 1950 to undertake a study of the use in education of the vernacular or mother tongues of peoples who are dominated socially and politically by nations speaking different languages. A committee made up of philologists from various countries ranged over five continents in its investigations. Recognizing and analyzing the many objections and difficulties to the use of the native languages of small dependent nations as mediums of instruction in education it reported that:

> Every child is born into a cultural environment; the language is both a part of, and an expression of that environment. Thus the acquiring of this language (his "mother tongue") is a part of the process by which a child absorbs the cultural environment; it can then be said that this language plays an important part in moulding the child's early concepts. He will therefore find it difficult to grasp any new concept which is so alien to his cultural environment that it cannot readily find expression in his mother tongue . . .
>
> Ideas which have been formulated in one language are so difficult to express through the modes of another, that a person habitually faced with this task can readily lose his facility to express himself. A child, faced with this task at an age when his powers of self-expression even in his mother tongue are but incompletely developed, may possibly never achieve adequate self-expression.
>
> For these reasons it is important that every effort should be made to provide education in the mother tongue . . .

On educational grounds we recommend that the use of the mother tongue be extended to as late a stage in education as possible. In particular, pupils should begin their schooling through the medium of the mother tongue, because they understand it best and because to begin their school life in the mother tongue will make the break between home and school as small as possible.

We consider that the shock which the young child undergoes in passing from his home to his school life is so great that everything possible should be done to soften it ... He passes from being one of a few children under his mother's eye to being one of a large group under a teacher. Instead of running about and playing and shouting he is usually expected to sit still and be quiet; to concentrate, to do what he is told instead of what he wants to do, to listen and learn and answer questions. New information and ideas are presented to him as fast as he can possibly absorb them, and he is expected to show evidence that he has absorbed them. Almost everything is different from home and it is not surprising that many children find difficulty in adjusting themselves to their new surroundings. If the language in which all these bewildering new communications are made is also different from the mother tongue, the burden on the child is correspondingly increased.

Even when the child has been at school long enough to be familiar with school life, he still has to cope with the incessant stream of lessons in many different subjects. He will find a lesson in geography or almost any other subject easier if he is taught it in his mother tongue. To expect him to deal with new information or ideas presented to him in an unfamiliar language is to impose on him a double burden, and he will make slower progress.[21]

Among the committee's conclusions were the following:

Every pupil should begin his formal education in his mother tongue.
. . . .

There is nothing in the structure of any language which precludes it from becoming a vehicle of modern civilization.
. . . .

If the mother tongue is adequate in all respects to serve as the vehicle of university and higher technical education, it should be so used.[22]

The committee consisted of fourteen members; there was no representative from Russia of the USSR. But there was a time when the Russians also condemned the replacing of the native tongue as the language of instruction. On March 13, 1938, a decree of the Communist Party and the Soviet government stated that:

> . . . the native tongue is the means of instruction in the schools of the national republics and regions; that exceptions to this rule, which are prevalent in some autonomous republics of the RSFSR, can only be temporary; that the tendency to transform the Russian language from a subject of study to the language of instruction and at the same time infringe on the native tongue is harmful and incorrect.[23]

If the replacing of the native tongue by Russian was harmful and incorrect in 1938, how can it be right now? If it was wrong to Russify Ukrainian schools in 1953, why is it correct now? If the principles worked out by Lenin of allowing free development of national languages and cultures was Leninist, how can the present policies of Russification also be termed Leninist?

While most Socialist countries in Europe oppose in practice the present Russian policy of linguistic annihilation, one of them, Yugoslavia, has explicitly condemned it in theory and in practice.

Edward Kardelj, the one-time foreign minister and today's president of the Federal Assembly of Yugoslavia, in an exhaustive discussion of the national question criticized Stalin's concept that the nation is a "bourgeois creation" and defended the right of the nations of Yugoslavia to the maintenance of their separate identities. He attacked the advocates of centralization on the grounds that this would threaten the achievements of socialism and the development of socialist democracy and added that:

> . . . on the basis of such bureaucratic centralist tendencies endeavours are made here and there at renewing the old chauvinistic concept of an "integral Yugoslavia" as an attempt to deny the existence of Yugoslav nations in the interests of some sort of a new "Yugoslav nation".[24]

Calling the idea of the creation of a single Yugoslav nation absurd, Kardelj described the consequences of such a policy thus:

> The consolidation of endeavours of bureaucratic centralization with their aspects of chauvinistic great statism would undermine not only the correct socialist and democratic principles on which

is founded the unity of the peoples of Yugoslavia, but also the political stability of the socialist system in general. It would surely lead to the restoration of bureaucratic despotism and to the alienation of the masses from the leading political forces of the state.[25]

Turning his attention to the question of languages Kardelj vehemently criticized the proponents of merging, asserting that:

> Various languages existed before there were nations and only a narrow nationalist logic does not admit that in the future there can be a diversity of languages and a wealth of cultural forms without the existence of nations in today's meaning of that term.[26]

The right to full and free development of national languages and cultures is also clearly outlined in the Yugoslav constitution as follows:

ARTICLE 42

The languages of the peoples of Yugoslavia and their scripts shall be equal.

Members of the peoples of Yugoslavia on the territories of republics other than their own shall have the right to school instruction in their own languages, in conformity with republican law.

As an exception, in the Yugoslav People's Army, commands, military drill and administration shall be in the Serbo-Croatian language.

ARTICLE 43

With the view of attaining the freedom of the citizen to express his nationality and culture, every nationality — national minority, shall have the right to use its language freely, to develop its culture, and to found organizations to this end, and it shall enjoy the other rights determined by the Constitution.

In schools for the members of the nationalities, instruction shall be in the languages of those nationalities . . .[27]

More recently the question of nationalities was discussed by Marshal Tito in his report to the Eighth Congress of the League of Communists of Yugoslavia, held in Belgrade on December 7 to 13, 1964. In the speech which was a strong reaffirmation of national rights and a scathing denunciation of the advocates of centralization, he said:

> For many years after the First World War, an acute struggle went on in the ranks of the Communist Party of Yugoslavia, or

rather in the top echelons of the Central Committee, over the manner in which the nationalities question in Yugoslavia should be solved. The view that finally won out was the Marxist-Leninist concept according to which the question should be settled on the basis of the principle of equality among all nationalities, by voluntary association, including the right of secession . . . The Party's position on the nationalities question won it the confidence of all our peoples. This is a major achievement of which we Communists may be justifiably proud. But we must take care to nurture this confidence in the future phases of the development of socialist social relationships, which have got to be in line with the proper development of relations between the nationalities in our community. The substance of these relations must ensure further consolidation of unity and brotherhood among our peoples. There are, however, certain people, and there are even Communists among them, who have already grown tired of this powerful slogan from our Liberation War and who feel that the nationalities have become obsolete in our socialist social development and should wither away. These people have the confused idea that the unity of our peoples means the elimination of nationalities and the creation of something new and artificial, that is a single Yugoslav nation, rather on the lines of assimilation and bureaucratic centralization, unitarianism and hegemony.

. . . To be true to internationalism means to be a consistent internationalist first and foremost in one's country, particularly in a multi-national social community like ours. The internationalist idea within one's own country does not imply an amalgamation of all the nationalities and ethnic groups and a denial of their identity as members of the socialist social community.

Marshal Tito's statement on the national question is clear and unequivocal; policy is in strict conformity with these pronouncements. In Yugoslavia as in nearly every other country from the most backward to the most developed, the languages of smaller nations and minorities are freely flourishing and developing. The Russians are almost alone in their drive to impose linguistic uniformity on subordinate nations.

FOOTNOTES

1. *F. F. Sovetkin,* op. cit., p. 14.
2. Ibid., p. 14.
3. *XXII ziyzd komunistychnoyi partiyi Radyanskoho Soyuzu, 17-31 zhovtnya 1961 roku* (Twenty-second Congress of the Communist Party of the Soviet Union, October 17-31, 1961), Stenographic report, I, Kiev, 1962, pp. 205-206.
4. A. M. Gindin and S. G. Markin, "O nekotorykh osobenostyakh novogo etapa v razvitii druzhby narodov SSSR (Regarding Some of the Peculiarities of the New Stage in the Development of Friendship of the Peoples of the USSR)", *Voprosy istorii KPSS* (Problems of History of the CPSU), No. 2, February, 1965, p. 15.
5. "XXII Sezd KPSS i zadachi izucheniya zakonomernostey razvitiya sovremennykh natsionalnykh yazykov Sovetskogo Soyuza (The Twenty-second Congress of the CPSU and the Problems of the Study of the Orderly Development of Contemporary National Languages of the Soviet Union)", *Voprosy Yazykoznaniya,* No. 1, January, 1962, p. 5.
6. Ibid.
7. I. P. Tsameryan, "Razvitie natsionalnykh otnosheny v period razvernutogo stroitelstva kommunizma (The Development of National Relations in the Period of the Unfolding Construction of Communism)", *Voprosy Filosofii,* No. 7, July, 1959, p. 42.
8. "XXII Sezd KPSS . . .", p. 5.
9. A. M. Gindin and S. G. Markin, op. cit., p. 21.
10. *Stroitelstvo kommunizma i razvitie obshchestvennykh otnosheniy* (The Building of Communism and the Development of Social Relations), Moscow, 1966, p. 250.
11. N. V. Mansvetov, op. cit., p. 51.
12. There is mention of the conference in I. K. Bilodid, *Rozvytok mov sotsialistychnykh natsy SRSR* (The Development of Languages of Socialist Nations of the USSR), Kiev, 1963, p. 7.
13. No published confirmation of the conference is available to the author.
14. A report of the conference was printed in *Radyanska Ukrayina,* December 25, 1963.
15. See report of Conference in *Russky Yazyk,* No. 1, 1965, pp. 87-88.
16. The excerpt is from a speech delivered at a congress of writers in Paris. It was reprinted in *Ukrayina,* No. 17, 1957, pp. 19-20.
17. T. Yu. Burmistrova, "Iz istorii borby Lenina za printsipy natsionalnoy politiki partii (1910-1914 gg.) (From the History of Lenin's Struggle for the Principles of the National Policy of the Party (1910-1914)" *Voprosy istorii KPSS,* No. 2, February, 1965, p. 46.
18. There is a story told in Ukraine that when Khrushchov visited China he asked Mao Tse-tung when the Chinese were going to start learning Russian. The latter is supposed to have retorted, "There are more of us. When are *you* going to learn Chinese?"

19. See: M. M. Gordon, *Assimilation in American Life,* New York, 1964; J. B. Gittler (ed.), *Understanding Minority Groups,* New York, 1964; U. S. Department of Health, Education and Welfare, *Improving English Skills of Culturally Different Youths in Large Cities,* Washington, D.C., 1964.

20. *New York Times,* July 22, 1967, p. 54.

21. UNESCO, *The Use of Vernacular Languages in Education,* Paris, 1953, pp. 47-48.

22. Ibid., pp. 68-69.

23. *Natsionalnye shkoly,* p. 12.

24. Edward Kardelj, *Razvoj slovenackog nacionalnog pitanja* (The Development of the Slovenian National Question), Belgrade, 1960, p. 41.

25. Ibid.

26. Ibid., p. 49.

27. *The Constitution of the Socialist Federal Republic of Yugoslavia, adopted on April 7th, 1963,* Belgrade, 1963, pp. 39-40.

28. *Practice and Theory of Socialist Development in Yugoslavia,* Belgrade, 1965, pp. 36, 38.

8

Where minority
languages flourish

When Ukrainians and other non-Russians in the USSR are being
denied the right to education in their native languages, smaller
nations and minorities in other states are enjoying various degrees
of national autonomy. On the USSR's north-western border lies
the little country of Finland. Of its population of 4,500,000 about
8.5 percent are Swedes. For this minority there are elementary
and high schools, a school of economics and a university in their
native language. In addition, nearly all courses at the Institute of
Technology and the University of Helsinki are given in both
languages. Finnish is compulsory as a language in all Swedish
schools and vice versa. Both languages are used on street and
other signs, in broadcasting, government and parliament. There
are Swedish newspapers and periodicals and Swedish units in the
Finnish army.[1]

The central European country of Switzerland also has a
population of about 4,500,000, of which 69 percent are German,
19 percent French, 10 percent Italians and 1 percent Romansh.
Although the Germans form over two-thirds of the population,
there is no attempt to impose that language on the three minorities.
Each national group has elementary and secondary schools in its

native tongue. A second national language, German or French is compulsory in all schools from grade two. Instruction in the universities is in one of the three national languages; in a few, instruction is in two languages. In social and economic life the language of the local inhabitants is used. German, French and Italian, have the constitutional status of official languages with the first two being used in diplomacy. Government communications are written in the native tongue of the addressee. The Romansh language is also regarded as a national language and even though it is spoken by only 50,000 people, every measure is taken for its preservation.[2]

A most interesting example of how the national problem can be resolved is provided by Belgium. Of the total population of about 9,500,000 over 5,000,000 are Flemish speaking. However, French, the language of the 3,000,000 inhabitants of the south, at one time predominated to the extent of becoming the official language. In 1963 the Belgian parliament passed laws regulating the use of languages. Belgium was divided into four linguistic areas: the provinces of the north with Flemish as the official language; the provinces of the south with French as the official language; Brussels and its environs, inhabited by both French and Dutch, where both languages were accorded equal status; a small area in the eastern part of Belgium, inhabited by 80,000 Germans where the official language is German, but French is also to be used in public enactments. Instruction in schools is in the official language but Dutch or French is compulsory as a subject from the first grade, the former in French schools and the latter in Dutch and German schools.[3]

In The Federal Republic of Germany, in Southern Schleswig, there is a small Danish minority of 60,000. The rights of this group were recognized by *The Bonn-Copenhagen Declaration of 1955*. Consequently Danes in Germany have been enjoying full national rights. They have 48 kindergartens and 72 schools of which three are secondary. All instruction is in their native tongue. Textbooks are printed locally or purchased from Denmark. There are Danish churches; Danish clubs for young people, farmers, artisans and housewives; Danish music clubs, libraries, a theatre and a Danish newspaper. The Danes have representation in municipal, county and state government and the Danish language is used in the courts and government offices.[4]

Perhaps most to be envied for their national rights are Italy's German-speaking citizens. They inhabit the Alto-Adige area in the province of Bolzano on the Alpine frontier which borders Austria and Switzerland. The province, 65 percent of whose population is German-speaking, enjoys full local autonomy. The Provincial Council is made up of 22 members, of whom 15 are German. Their language is used in local public life, in notices, courts, documents, correspondence and administration. Two-thirds of the local public employees must be German-speaking citizens who have passed an examination in that language. Sums are allocated for scholarships to public employees who wish to study in German-speaking countries to improve their knowledge of German.

The Italian National Broadcasting in the Alto-Adige region devotes 26 out of 33 hours a week to German programs which are produced with the collaboration of representatives of that minority. There are 28 German newspapers and periodical publications of which one is a daily and five are weeklies. Movie houses show original Austrian and German as well as American films dubbed in German.

For the education of this minority there are 453 elementary and secondary German schools with German-speaking teachers under the authority of a Deputy Supervisor of Education, inspectors and principals whose mother tongue is German. Place is given in the curriculum to local history, tradition and customs. Textbooks for most courses are imported from Austria, Germany or Switzerland.

There is full freedom to form national organizations, associations and cultural circles. Political representation is through the Südtiroler Volkspartei which has deputies in local, provincial and national elected bodies. In parliament this party is represented by three deputies and two senators.[5]

For centuries the dispersed Jewish people had been mercilessly persecuted as minorities in every corner of the globe. Having established their own state of Israel, they granted national, political and religious rights to the 250,000 Arabs living within its borders. Consequently the Arabs have seven deputies in the fourth Knesset (parliament). With state aid mosques were reconstructed and at present 78 are in regular use. There are Moslem religious courts which deal with personal matters such as marriage, divorce, alimony, guardianship, adoption, wills, legacies and others which are settled on the basis of Koranic law. Much has been done to foster their language and culture. Arabic is given the status of an official language: it appears with Hebrew on coins, banknotes and postage stamps, is used in the Knesset and as the language of administration in areas inhabited by Arab-speaking citizens. There are also a variety of newspapers, magazines and books in Arabic. The State Broadcasting Service devotes eight hours per day to Arabic programs, which include readings from the Koran. Education in schools is also in the native tongue with Hebrew as a compulsory subject. In 1959 there were about 50 Arab mission and church schools and 268 state kindergarten, elementary and secondary schools with 1300 teachers. The number of secondary schools has increased from six in 1959 to 12 in 1963. There has also been an increase in the number of Arabs attending higher educational institutions.[6]

In Turkey the minorities are estimated to number approximately 500,000. Most of them are organized in separate communities which occupy sections of Istanbul and exist as semi-autonomous islands in the Turkish state. They worship in their own churches, carry on their own cultural activities, publish newspapers, magazines and books in their languages and maintain private schools for their children from the elementary to the secondary levels. Among these groups are the Armenians, Greeks, Jews, French, Germans and Italians. Instruction in the schools is partly in Turkish and partly in the mother tongue of the pupils.

In 1966 there were 30 Armenian schools, of which ten were elementary from grade 1-5, 16 were middle schools from grades 1-8 and four were full secondary from 1-12. Geography, history, sociology and the Turkish language and literature were taught by Turkish teachers in Turkish, while arithmetic, geometry, Bible history, foreign and native languages and other subjects were taught in the mother tongue of the pupils. Financial assistance for these institutions has been rendered by Armenians in the United States and elsewhere. The greatest benefactor is the renowned Armenian oil magnate, Kalust Gulbenkian, who lives in England.[7]

There are numerous other examples of national minorities with schools in their native tongues. Among these are the Slovenians in Austria, the Greeks in Egypt and the Armenians in Iran. Aleut, the language of the indigenous population of the Danish territory of Greenland is used in elementary schools.[8] In Burma where many languages are spoken, the mother tongue of the pupils is also the medium of instruction in elementary schools.[9] In African territories under British administration 91 native languages were used in schools.[10]

There are also many other countries in which more than one official language prevails. Afghanistan has two: Pushtu and Persian.[11] Pakistan has four: Urdu, the national language, and three official regional languages, Bengali, Sindki and Pushtu.[12] In India, Hindi was proclaimed the federal language with 14 official regional and 86 local ones. The language of instruction in schools is in the native tongue.[13]

In Canada, of a population of 18,238,247 (1961 census), 5,540,346 were French Canadians whose ancestors first settled here over three centuries ago. Approximately 75 percent of them live in the province of Quebec. Education is under the complete control of the province. No one holds a gun to the head of a parent and asks him whether he wishes his child to go to a French or English school. The French language is used exclusively in all educational institutions from elementary to university, except in schools for the English-speaking minority in Montreal. French is also the official language; it prevails in government, business and military units of the Canadian Army in Quebec. When the Queen visited the Quebec Legislature in October 1964, the Honourable Jean Lesage, Premier of Quebec, addressed her in French; she replied in the same language. French-Canadians in Ontario, Saskatchewan, Alberta, Manitoba and New Brunswick also have elementary and secondary schools in their native tongue in areas where they live in sufficient numbers. In the Dominion of Canada French is an official language and is used with English on all official publications, documents, paper currency and postage stamps.

Most of the Socialist countries are no less zealous in promoting the cultures and languages of their national minorities. Czechoslovakia has a population of 9,000,000 Czechs and nearly 4,000,000 Slovaks. Both are official state languages. Slovakia has full and complete national autonomy; its language prevails in all walks of life. There is not one Czech school in all of Slovakia. If a traveller enters Czechoslovakia through Slovakia, he is greeted by Slovaks in their native language.[14] In addition there are three other large minorities—about 425,000 Hungarians, 165,000 Germans and 85,000 Poles—for whom there are elementary schools in their native languages. For Hungarians, the largest minority, there are also special secondary schools and a section of the Pedagogical Department of the Slovak University in Bratislava with instruction in their native tongue.[15]

Romania began setting up schools for national minorities in 1947. By 1956-57 instruction was being conducted in 2,354 schools in the languages of 15 minorities, among whom were Hungarians, Germans, Ukrainians, Russians, Serbs, Slovaks, Jews, Tatars and Turks. The two largest minorities, Hungarians and Germans, enjoy education in their native tongues from elementary through secondary, vocational, technical to university levels. Five other groups, Ukrainians, Russians, Serbs, Slovaks and Tatars have elementary, secondary and teacher training schools in their languages. The author has heard complaints of injustices to national minorities. These may be well-founded, but the fact remains that schools for national minorities do exist and pupils are being taught in their native tongues.[16]

In the German Democratic Republic, along the Spree River in

the area of Dresden live the Lusatian Sorbs, a national Slav minority numbering 130,000. They are descendents of Slavs who had originally lived in the area between the Oder and the Elbe. From the sixth century they were subjected to attacks by the stronger and more numerous Germanic tribes who conquered them by the tenth century. In the second half of the nineteenth century there began the forceful process of their Germanization. Hitler planned to wipe them out as a distinct national group. However the Sorbs managed to preserve their culture and their language. These Slavs now enjoy full national autonomy. They publish newspapers, journals and books by Lusatian authors and poets in their native tongue and have an ethnographic institute, a national theatre, musical ensembles and radio programs. Their language prevails in local administration and in elementary schools. At Leipzig University there is a faculty of Lusatian philology and a department of Lusatian history.[17]

In Hungary, also, the national minorities have the right to education in their native tongues. There are schools on the elementary and in some cases on the secondary level, with instruction in German, Slovak, Slovene, Croat, Serbian and Romanian. Courses are given in German, Croat, Serbian and Romanian at Budapest University.[18]

Another multi-national state is Yugoslavia, whose population is about 18,500,000. In three of the six federal republics—Serbia, Bosnia-Herzogovina and Montenegro—the population, totalling nearly 8,000,000, is Serbian. In Croatia, whose population is nearly 4,500,000, the language has much in common with the Serbian, but there are differences in accentuation, the alphabet is Latin instead of Cyrillic and Croatian literature has its own national characteristics.

Slovenes with a population of 1,600,000 and Macedonians[19] with about 1,000,000 are related to the Serbs, but have separate languages and literatures. All four: Serbian, Croatian, Slovenian and Macedonian, have complete equality in government, economic life and education. Schools exist in all four languages from the elementary to the university level. The official organ of the party is *Kommunist*; it is published in four languages: Serbian, Croatian, Slovenian and Macedonian.

In addition to the four nations which have separate republics, there are many minorities in Yugoslavia. The largest of these, the Albanian, numbers about 900,000. In 1964-65 for Albanians, Czechs, Slovaks, Italians, Hungarians, Romanians, Turks, Bulgarians and Ukrainians there were 1,419 elementary schools in their native tongues; for the first eight there were thirty-one secondary and for the first seven there were eighty-nine vocational schools. There are also teacher training institutions for national minorities, and language departments at Belgrade and other universities in German, Hungarian, Czech, Slovak, Polish, Russian and Ukrainian.[20]

We are particularly interested in the fate of Ukrainian minorities, which are found in a number of countries. In Poland they number 200,000, but unfortunately, are rather widely dispersed. However, there are three elementary and two secondary schools where the language of instruction is Ukrainian and 138 elementary and secondary Polish schools where Ukrainian is taught as a subject if seven or more pupils register for it. Normal schools and the University of Warsaw provide advanced classes in the Ukrainian language and literature. Ukrainians have organized a cultural society with nine choirs, two musical and one dance ensemble and twenty-three drama groups. They publish a weekly newspaper, a monthly literary supplement, an annual almanac, school texts and the works of Ukrainian writers in Poland. For the last several years they have also organized four weekly Ukrainian radio programs.[21]

Czechoslovakia has 70,000 Ukrainians, who live in a compact mass in the eastern regions of Slovakia. They have over 200 elementary and secondary schools with nearly 20,000 pupils. Ukrainian is also taught in the pedagogical institute and the university in Prashiv. There is a very active Ukrainian cultural organization, a national theatre, a professional song and dance ensemble, cultural centres with their choirs and dance and drama groups, libraries, a weekly newspaper, a children's magazine, a literary journal and an almanac. Ukrainians in Czechoslovakia have produced a number of prominent writers whose works are published in Ukrainian, and several talented artists and sculptors. The centre of the Ukrainian community is the town of Prashiv from where originate Ukrainian broadcasts, totalling twenty-two hours per week.[22]

Romania's Ukrainian minority numbers 60,000, but they do not live as compactly as those in Czechoslovakia. In 1956-57 they had 98 four-year schools, 20 seven-year, three full secondary classes in Ukrainian in other schools and facilities for training teachers in Ukrainian at three teacher-training schools.[23] There are Ukrainian cultural societies with libraries, choirs, dance and drama groups. Ukrainians publish a weekly paper, school text-books and literary works of their own writers.

In Yugoslavia there are only 45,000 Ukrainians who are quite widely dispersed. Yet in 1964 they had four elementary schools with 1,257 pupils,[24] a Shevchenko cultural society, a publishing firm that produces books for their schools, a weekly newspaper and a monthly literary journal. Lately they have expanded their activities with a weekly radio program.

The Ukrainian population of the United States numbers about 1,500,000, but is widely scattered throughout the country. However they have hundreds of cultural and religious institutions, museums, dozens of newspapers and journals, book publishing firms and academic societies where Ukrainian culture flourishes without interference. There are private Ukrainian schools with classes for children in the evenings and on Saturdays and regular schools with elementary and secondary programs. Ukrainians have achieved prominence in many walks of life as scientists, professors, artists, writers and professionals. In 1964 they erected in Washington a monument to T. H. Shevchenko, the national poet of Ukraine.

Canada has about 500,000 Ukrainians scattered from the Atlantic to the Pacific. They also have their cultural and religious centres, libraries, museums, newspapers and journals. There are two monuments to Shevchenko, one at Palermo near Toronto and one on the legislative grounds in Winnipeg. Ukrainian is taught in private cultural centres at night and on Saturdays, in the regular program of the secondary schools of Alberta, Manitoba and Saskatchewan and in many universities. The Ukrainian community has produced prominent scientists, educators and professional men. There are Ukrainians in provincial legislatures and provincial cabinets, in the House of Commons and in the Senate. In the previous federal cabinet an outstanding Ukrainian, the Honourable Michael Starr, was minister of labour.

The largest Ukrainian group outside the UkrSSR lives in the RSFSR. According to the census of 1959 they numbered 3,359,083.[25] In reality there are many more. It is unpopular in the RSFSR to proclaim oneself a Ukrainian; many, therefore, give their nationality as Russian. The millions of Ukrainians in the RSFSR have not one social or cultural society, not one choir, dance or drama group, not one newspaper. Moreover, it is often even difficult for a Ukrainian in the RSFSR to obtain a Ukrainian newspaper, because subscriptions are not readily accepted by Soyuzpechat, the agency through which they must be channelled. There is an equal problem with Ukrainian books which must be ordered from Kiev. The Ukrainian schools that did exist were arbitrarily closed in the early 1930's. Stalin has died; his misrule was denounced, but the schools remain closed despite requests to the government, the CC and the Twenty-second and Twenty-third Congresses of the party from the Ukrainians in the RSFSR and the UkrSSR that they be reopened.[26]

Requests on behalf of these Ukrainians were made by a very prominent Ukrainian lawyer from Canada (now deceased) who visited the USSR three times and on each occasion raised the question with Krushchov. The first time the premier replied that he would investigate it, the second time he said that Ukrainians in the RSFSR were not interested in having their own schools and the third time he simply told his visitors not to stir up the national question.

This same policy, dictated by the CC in Moscow, is applied to other national minorities. In Ukraine the Czech, Slovak, Greek,

Bulgar and Romanian population totals over 450,000 (see appendix IV). Not only do they not have any schools, but there was not even one student listed as attending any higher educational institution in the UkrSSR in 1960 from any of these groups (see appendix III). This is not, of course, the fault of the Ukrainians. In the 1920's and 1930's when they could still make independent decisions on these matters, schools were organized for Russians, Jews, Poles, Bulgarians, Belorussians, Tatars, Germans and Moldavians. In 1940, after the western regions of Ukraine were annexed to the UkrSSR from Poland and Romania, 131 Jewish schools were opened in the whole area[27] and 12 Jewish and Polish schools in Bukovina.[28]

There were 840,311 Jews in Ukraine according to the 1959 census (see appendix IV), but not one Jewish school. During a discussion of this question, I asked a Jewish citizen of Kiev whom I had met several times why he did not organize a private school in the synagogue which is still open in Kiev, in order to provide night classes for Jewish children. He looked at me in horror and by way of reply asked, "Do you want me to be sentenced to Siberia?"

This is how the Russians solve the national problem. They are not alone in using these methods; others have practiced them. In territories conquered in the last war the Japanese established schools only in their language; Franco allows no schools in Spain in the Basque or Catalan languages; Mussolini tried to denationalize the German-speaking citizens of Italy and Hitler aimed at destroying the Lusatian Sorbs.

In the meantime, not only are the languages of the smaller nations not merging, but several, whose use had been narrowed to a very small number of people in isolated areas are now being revived. One of these is the Celtic language, which was spoken in the British Isles before the Saxon invasions.

In Scotland, whose population numbers over five million, Celtic (or Gaelic as it is known in Scotland) was the native tongue of a large part of the country to the seventeenth century, by which time it had its own literature. After the Protestant Reformation in the sixteenth century, English began to displace Gaelic and the latter's use as a language of daily intercourse was confined to the northern region. In the twentieth century began its revival. *The Education Act (Scotland) of 1918* made provisions for its teaching as a subject in the schools.

In 1946 the Advisory Council on Education in Scotland advocated the preservation of the 'Gaelic cultural heritage and recommended that:

> . . . all Scottish children should learn something of Gaelic life and legends and traditions. Some pupils as they grow older may wish to learn the Gaelic language and read its literature; and for these, opportunities at selected schools may one day be provided. As for the Gaelic-speaking areas themselves, we recommend that all possible steps be taken to get an adequate number of Gaelic-speaking teachers and an ample supply of suitable class books and texts in the Gaelic language.[29]

At first some were indifferent to the revival and some even opposed the teaching of Gaelic in school. However a positive attitude has been developing since the Second World War. A publication of the Scottish Education Department was able to note in 1955 that:

> . . . there is evidence that many Gaels awakened to a conscious-ness of the loss which they and their children would sustain if their language should perish, are making persistent efforts to ensure that the rich heritage of their language, literature and music is maintained and developed.[30]

This growth of Scottish national sentiment is reflected in the political field. In a by-election on March 9, 1967, in the constituency of Pollock, George Leslie, the Scottish national candidate, campaigned for separate armed forces, a separate parliament in Edinburgh and separate negotiations with the European Common Market. He received 10,884 votes; the victorious Tory candidate obtained 14,270.[31]

In the south-west of Britain, in a mountainous region, lies the small country of Wales. Most of its 2,693,000 people are also descendents of the original Celts who were pushed back into their present location by the invading Anglo-Saxons. The original schools were in English. Even the speaking of the native tongue during school hours was in some cases forbidden. The demand to introduce the language into the schools as a medium of instruction gathered momentum at the turn of the century. In 1907 a Welsh Department was set up in the Ministry of Education and the language was introduced in some schools.

The attitude and policy of the British government toward Welsh has undergone a fundamental change. It was summarized by R. A. Butler, President of the Board of Education, June 16, 1942, in the House of Commons as follows:

> I regard as obscurantist the attitude of the Commission of Inquiry exactly 100 years ago which went to Wales and took the view that to keep alive a knowledge of this beautiful tongue was tantamount to crippling Welsh initiative and penalizing Welsh endeavour. I wish now, a hundred years later, to make amends for that attitude.[32]

In 1963 the Council for Wales and Monmouthshire, in its *Report on the Welsh Language Today,* recommended that Welsh be given official status with the right to be used in courts of law, public enquiries, tribunals, on public signs and notices, in business and administration; that there be an increase in the use of Welsh on radio and television; that there be subsidies for Welsh language publications.[33]

The revival of Welsh national consciousness has also manifested itself in the political arena. A nationalist party has been formed numbering seventeen thousand members. In the last general election in 1966 it elected one of its candidates, Gwynfor Evans, to the House of Commons. The Welsh are demanding self-government and have organized a Free Welsh Army which has financial supporters abroad, among them the famous moviemaker, Howard Hughes. In a by-election on March 9, 1967, in Rhondda West, their candidate polled 39.9 percent of the votes as compared to 8.7 in the previous general election.[34]

Celtic was also the original language of the people of Ireland. By the end of the nineteenth century it had been replaced in all but the western counties by English, the language of her conquerors. A movement to restore Irish (as Celtic is known in Ireland) began in the middle of the last century and gained popularity through the Gaelic League which reflected the views of Thomas Davies a passionate advocate of Irish, who wrote that:

> ... the language which grows up with a people, is conformed to their organs, descriptive of their climate, constitutions and manners, mingled inseparably with their soil, is fitted beyond any other language to express their prevalent thoughts in the most natural and efficient way.[35]

With the establishment of the Irish Free State in 1921, the Provisional Government decreed that from March 17, 1922, Irish should be taught in schools. Although much progress was made, the revival was far from complete. In July, 1958, a commission was appointed by the government to study the problem and make recommendations. In 1962 Irish characters were replaced by Latin script. January, 1964, witnessed the completion of the commission's report, which "contained 288 recommendations designed to bring Irish into regular use in state and semi-state bodies, to revive the districts where it is still spoken, and to extend and improve its use in all spheres of education".

It is beyond the scope of this study to speculate on the future of the Celtic languages. We have, however, witnessed the complete revival of Hebrew, which ceased to be used in common speech after the destruction of Judea in 132 A.D. The pogroms against the Jews in Russia in the 1880's intensified national consciousness and gave birth to a new interest in the revival of the Hebrew language and the establishment of a national state. The subsequent campaign to revive it in literary writing, in everyday speech and in schools was so successful that by 1918 no less than 40 percent of the Jewish population in Palestine spoke Hebrew. Today, not quite 80 years after the idea was raised, the revival is complete and Hebrew rules in all spheres of the life of the new state of Israel.[37]

There are also examples of smaller national groups, denied national rights in the past, who are today raising their voices. These include the minorities of Spain among which are the nearly 5,000,000 Catalans, most of whom live in the four north-eastern provinces centered around the city of Barcelona and the 600,000

Basques, descendents of the oldest inhabitants of the Iberian peninsula, who live in the north of Spain. The policy of the Franco government toward these and other national minorities was suppression and assimilation. However, lately there have been indications that even Franco is altering his policy toward these minorities. Recent immigrants to Canada from Spain report that Basques and Catalans have been demanding national recognition with some positive results. Before me is the twenty-fifth issue of the weekly journal *Telestel* published in Barcelona January 6, 1967 in the Catalan language. It is reported that a scientific monthly journal, *Serra d' Or,* has also begun publication in Catalan recently. In addition, the question of schools for Basques and Catalans in their native tongues is now being raised.

The principle of the right to free development of national cultures of all nations and minorities, the cornerstone of which is education in the native tongue, has almost universal recognition and approval. In practice it has such wide application that attempts are even made to revive languages that were considered dead. There are a few examples of denial of this principle. Among them are the Russians, who stand today as the greatest national oppressors through their campaign to destroy the languages and cultures not only of the small minorities that inhabit the USSR, but the historically-established and culturally-developed nations, the largest of which is the 40,000,000 Ukrainian nation.

FOOTNOTES

1. Information obtained through the courtesy of the Finnish Consulate in Toronto and the Finnish language newspaper *Vapaa Sana.*
2. From sources provided by the Consulate of Switzerland in Toronto.
3. Based on information supplied by the Consulate General of Belgium in Toronto.
4. Information obtained through the cooperation of the Danish newspaper, *Flensborg Avis,* in Flensburg, Germany.

5. Data is from a publication of the Presidency of the Council of Ministers of Italy, *German-Speaking Inhabitants of the Alto-Adige,* Rome, 1960, provided by the Consulate of Italy in Toronto.

6. M. Avidor, *Education For a Growing Nation,* Israel Today Series, No. 1, Jerusalem, 1964, provided by the Consulate of Israel in Toronto.

7. The data on Turkey was obtained from three sources: The Turkish Embassy in Ottawa, a colleague in the teaching profession who taught English in Istanbul for two years and an Armenian immigrant to Canada who was closely associated with the national minorities in Istanbul.

8. UNESCO, op. cit., p. 23.

9. Ibid., p. 32.

10. Ibid., p. 17.

11. Ibid., p. 28.

12. Ibid., p. 29.

13. Ibid., p. 29.

14. This information was obtained from travellers to Czechoslovakia who know the language.

15. J. S. Roucek and K. V. Lattich, *Behind the Iron Cutain,* Caldwell, Idaho, 1964, pp. 221-23.

16. Randolph L. Braham, *Education in the Romanian People's Republic,* Washington, 1963, pp. 76-77.

17. *U.R.E.,* VIII, Kiev, 1962, p. 285.

18. J. S. Roucek and K. V. Lattich, op. cit., p. 312.

19. There are large Macedonian minorities in Bulgaria and Greece; neither country recognizes them as a separate national group.

20. *ABC Facts About Yugoslavia,* Zagreb, 1966, pp. 17, 108, provided by the Yugoslav Consulate in Toronto.

21. M. Yavorsky, "Desyat rokiv isnuvannya Ukrayinskoho suspilno-kulturnoho tovarystva v Polshchi (Tenth Anniversary of the Founding of the Ukrainian Social-Cultural Society in Poland"), *Ukrayinsky Istorichny Zhurnal, No.* 6, June, 1966, pp. 40-49.

22. V. U. Pavlenko, "Rozvytok kultury ukrayinskoho naselennya Chekhoslovatskoyi Sotsialistychnoyi Respubliky (1945-1966 rr.) (The Development of the Culture of the Ukrainian Population of the Czechoslovak Socialist Republic 1945-1966)", *Ukrayinsky Istorychny Zhurnal,* No. 12, December, 1965, pp. 55-64.

23. Randolph L. Braham, op. cit., p. 76.

24. *ABC Facts About Yugoslavia,* p. 108.

25. *Itogi vsesouznoy perepisi, RSFSR,* p. 300.

26. The question has even been raised in a Soviet publication. A writer, in discussing the need in the eastern regions of the USSR for new recruits for the labour force which can only come from the overpopulated areas of Ukraine, Belorussia, Moldavia and Lithuania, suggests that as an enticement, schools and cultural clubs should be set up for these national groups in their native languages where they live in compact masses. V. V. Pokshishev-

sky, "Perspektivy migratsiy naseleniya v SSSR (The Prospects of Migration of the Population of the USSR)", *Geografiya naseleniya Vostochnoy Sibiri* (Geography of the Population of Eastern Siberia, Moscow, 1962, p. 79.

27. S. K. Hutyansky, *Lenin i Ukrayinska Radyanska kultura* (Lenin and Ukrainian Soviet Culture), Kiev, 1963, p. 24.

28. P. I. Melnyk, "Rozkvit narodnoyi osvity na Bukovyni (The Flowering of Public Education in Bukovina)", *Radyanska Shkola,* No. 2, February, 1957, p. 21.

29. Stuart W. Semple, *The Problem of Bilingualism in the Schools of Wales and Scotland,* Educational Research Series No. 35, Department of Educational Research, Ontario College of Education, University of Toronto, 1964, p. 31.

30. Ibid.

31. Ron Poulton, *The Toronto Telegram,* March 25, 1967, p. 7.

32. *Education in Wales (Addysg yng Nghymru) 1847-1947.* Welsh Department, Ministry of Education, Pamphlet No. 2, Reprint, 1960, p. 25.

33. Stuart W. Semple, op. cit., p. 18.

34. Ron Poulton, op. cit.

35. John Macnamara, *Bilingualism and Primary Education,* Edinburgh, 1966, p. 3.

36. T. J. McElligott, *Education in Ireland,* Dublin, 1966, pp. 35-36.

37. Chaim Rabin, *The Revival of Hebrew,* Israel Today Series, No. 5, Jerusalem, 1958, provided by the Consulate of Israel in Toronto.

9

In defense of language

Soviet propaganda is constantly proclaiming the eternal and undying love of the Ukrainian people for the Russians and their willing and enthusiastic acceptance of the Russian language, even to the point of exclusion of their own native tongue. Yet during Lenin's time and for almost a decade after his death there was a period of rapid development of the Ukrainian language and culture. Beginning in the early 1930's the leaders of this movement were arrested and physically destroyed along with millions of common people, while the rest were subjected to terror and persecution. From whence then this sudden emergence of "fraternal friendship"?

The fact is that Ukrainians have always fought to preserve their heritage. During the war vague rumours circulated that with the return of peace there would also be a return to the policies of Lenin and Skrypnyk. The Russians nourished this hope to encourage more active participation of the Ukrainians in the war, even to the extent of establishing Ukrainian schools for children evacuated from Ukraine. When they were under military attack and needed support the Russians were very careful to respect the national rights of Ukrainians. According to one source:

> Everywhere the Soviet principle in education, schools in the native tongue, was safeguarded. For that reason, for example, schools with instruction using the Ukrainian language for evacuated Ukrainian children were opened in the RSFSR (in the Urals), in Kazakhstan and in Uzbekistan.[1]

Ukrainians hoped, fought and died. Their hope was given added substance on February 1 1944, when the Supreme Soviet of the USSR passed amendments to the constitution granting national republics the right to establish commissariats (ministries) of foreign affairs, with the right to enter into direct relations with foreign powers, and commissariats of defense with the right for each republic to organize its own troop formations.[2] The war ended and the provisions of the amendment have only partially been implemented. Ukraine acquired a figurehead minister "without foreign affairs" (as he is characterized by citizens in Ukraine) and without ambassadors or consuls. A minister of defense was never appointed and there are no Ukrainian troop formations.

When Khrushchov denounced the misrule of Stalin in 1956 and began to rehabilitate those who had perished, Ukrainians again dared to hope that the period of arbitrary rule was over and looked forward to the return of the days of Lenin and Skrypnyk. Frequently individual protests against Russification and demands to return to the national policy of Lenin began to manifest themselves in letters to the press, to various governmental bodies and to the CC of the party in Kiev and Moscow. Later these protests and demands took on sharper verbal forms, first in closed committees and then at mass public meetings.

One of the earlier and more significant of such demonstrations took place at the Republican Scientific Conference on the Problems of the Culture of the Ukrainian Language, held in Kiev, February 11-15, 1963. Among numerous unscheduled speakers who participated in the discussion and condemned Russification, were Lydia Orel from the movie studio of Kiev University, M. Shestopal, a brilliant, dynamic and popular young assistant professor from the faculty of journalism of Kiev University and V. F. Lobko, a war veteran, former army captain and an engineer from the Academy of Sciences. In a speech interrupted by intermittent outbursts of loud and enthusiastic applause he said:

> The people of the Soviet Union, among them the Ukrainians, supporting the decisions of the party congresses regarding the liquidation of the band of criminals, waged a decisive struggle

with all the evil, which came as an offspring of the personality cult, and how strange if not painful, that the consequences of this cult are with us today. Apparently the Stalin-Kaganovich disciples have power, because due to their opposition the Ukrainian people have not been able to reclaim that which was forbidden by these criminals, have not been able to achieve that which is ordinary and natural, but which is most basic, most important and most sacred, that which all people possess—the privilege of education in the Ukrainian language . . . and the wide use of this language in all spheres of the life of our people . . . The Ukrainian community has already more than once placed this question before responsible organizations of the republic, but there have not been any results to this day. Moreover, they do not even reply to our proposals regarding the introduction of instruction in the native Ukrainian language in secondary and higher educational institutions and the reestablishment of Ukrainian cultural institutions in those districts where millions of Ukrainians live—Siberia, Kazakhstan, the Far East and Kuban.

When he finished, the audience rose and gave him a tumultuous, standing ovation. No Soviet publication mentioned the speech or the demands of the participants, among whom were many engineers and other technical personnel. One of those present, a retired teacher, wrote a report entitled *The Fate of Our Native Language,* for the monthly supplement of the Ukrainian paper, *Nashe Slovo* (Our Word) in Poland[3] and listed the demands for Ukrainianization made by the participants in the discussion.

There is evidence from official sources that representatives of the national republics have also raised the question of inequitable distribution of financial resources to the republics. Khrushchov admitted at the Twentieth Congress of the party in 1956 that:

> Some comrades complain that in determining appropriations for education, public health, construction of housing and cultural accommodation, town planning etc., no proper procedure is followed and, as a result, there is sometimes a deficiency in the amount of these appropriations for some republics.[4]

After the ousting of Khrushchov, the criticism of Russification became stronger, louder and bolder. A participant informed me that in November 1964, at a meeting of the members of the Communist Party of the Writers' Union of Ukraine, V. Rechmedin voiced misgivings about the party's national policy in Ukraine.

He was followed by M. Shumylo who has tirelessly wielded his facile pen in defense of the Ukrainian language. The latter began his criticism of party policy in Ukraine by remarking that Russia will reach communism, but Ukraine will never make it because she will be destroyed long before then. He cited examples of discrimination against Ukraine's rights, attacks on her culture, such as the fire in the library of the Ukrainian Academy of Sciences,[5] Russification of Ukrainian schools and imposition of the newspapers *Pravda* and *Izvestia* in the Russian language.

A. D. Skaba, the hated Stalinist third secretary of the CC of the CPU who is in charge of Agitation and Propaganda, rose and in reply stated that one must view the national question not through nationalist, but through party spectacles. After the meeting he approached Rechmedin and asked him to write a memorandum outlining his disagreement with the policy being pursued on the national question. The writer gave Skaba a laconic and caustic reply: "Why should I spend my time writing what has already been so well stated by Lenin; read him."

Early in January 1965, one of Ukraine's great lyric poets, V. Sosyura, passed away. He had often been attacked as a nationalist for his expressions of deep attachment to his native land. At the funeral on January 11, one of his close friends, poet A. S. Malyshko, in a deeply emotional tribute to Sosyura took the occasion to level a sharp attack on Russification by reaffirming his faith in Ukraine and its language.[6] He said that:

> The stone will disintegrate and the thousand year-old tree will blossom and die, but your poetry will remain. And let not the snobs wait for our language and our native Ukraine to pass away, because Ukraine is eternal, as you are eternal in it.

The excitement over this sensation had not died down, when on January 16, I. M. Dzyuba, an outstanding literary critic and an opponent of Russification, in speaking at a memorial meeting for V. Simonenko, a young national poet who died in 1963, made a most devastating indictment of Russification when he said:

> It is true that Leonid Mikolaiovich Novichenko, who sits here in the presidium, assures us that the ideas "national concept",

"national consciousness" are now obsolete, unwarranted, out-
dated and non-Marxist. I would advise him to tell this to the
Chinese Communists, or the Italian Communists, or the English
Communists, or the Polish Communists, or, finally, the Russian
Communists . . . Obviously, the national concept exists and will
continue to exist.

. . . .

Dostoyevsky once asked: "Would you agree to build a system of
universal harmony on one single tear of one innocent child?"
And similarly we ask: "Can there be universal harmony, can
there be a universal society, can there be universal human
justice for the attainment of which is necessary even the smallest
injustice to any one nation, in this case the Ukrainian nation?
No, there cannot be such a society and such "harmony" established on such foundations."[7]

The oration had a stirring effect on the Ukrainians; the authorities were dumbfounded. In the meantime the speech which had
been recorded on tape, began circulating illegally in hand and
typewritten copies. Dzyuba's courageous attack was followed in
February by another bold protest against Russification by S. Yo.
Karavansky, a Ukrainian philologist, newspaperman and trans-
lator from Odessa. It was in the form of a petitition to the attorney-
general of Ukraine to arraign the Minister of Higher and Secondary Special Education, Yu. M. Dadenkov, under the criminal
code on charges of violating the national rights of the Ukrainians.
Copies of this document also began to circulate secretly throughout Ukraine (see appendix XI for full text).

In the meantime there was a growing agitation in Ukrainian
circles; students were especially active in voicing opposition to
Russification. At the beginning of the year students of Ukrainian
philology sent a petition, a copy of which I saw, to the rector of the
university requesting that all courses in their department be given
in the Ukrainian language. On April 13, 1965, an informal group
gathered at the Kiev University to discuss an article in a Moscow
newspaper by a controversial Russian writer, V. Soloukhin, who
raised some problems of culture associated with the age of mechanization. He decried the fact that people had forgotten their
national handicrafts, customs, folklore and songs. Instead of

creators of beautiful wood carvings and hand-embroidered cos-
tumes, inspiring folk songs and national pageants in which all
participated, they had become bored and passive spectators.[8]

Before adjourning the participants decided to continue their
discussion the following week. In the meantime the word was
spread around and on April 20 several hundred students and
graduates from various higher educational institutions gathered
at the university. The discussion very quickly passed from problems of culture to the national problem. Among the questions
raised was the directing of graduates to work outside Ukraine, the
sending of army recruits for training and service to all parts of
the USSR and the failure to use Ukrainian as the language of
instruction in the higher educational institutions of Ukraine. As
the discussion progressed each speaker became bolder. One
student drew a parallel between colonial countries which had
achieved national liberation and were fighting for economic freedom (socialism) and countries which had achieved economic freedom but were fighting for their national liberation. These remarks
were greeted by a storm of applause.

The meeting formed an organization, The Society to Aid the
Dissemination of Ukrainian Culture, and elected an executive.
A delegation was selected to see Shelest, the first secretary of the
CC of the CPU to ask for a permanent meeting place for the new
organization and present their views on the national question.
It was to report back to a meeting scheduled for April 27, a week
later.

At the CC the emissaries were informed that Shelest did not
meet such delegations. Instead they were directed to see N. Popov
who looked after matters pertaining to higher educational institutions in the Department of Science and Culture of the CC of the
CPU. The latter, a Russian and hostile to any national aspirations
of the Ukrainians, was in no mood to entertain protests against
Russification or reports of the formation of an organization to
promote Ukrainian culture. His reaction was a gruff remark that
such an organization "was not necessary". Then he proceeded to
take down the names of the members of the group. The following

day the delegates were taken out of their classes by members of the KGB, questioned and terrorized.

On April 27, the evening they were to report, students and others began to arrive at the social science building of the university shortly after 6 p.m. Police admitted only those who could prove that they had scheduled classes. Those not admitted began assembling in front of the entrance on Shevchenko Boulevard. Soon the crowd was spilling onto the roadway and blocking traffic. Someone suggested they meet in the Shevchenko Park across the road and the crowd began to move thither.

In the meantime a group of high officials had arrived and, occupying a vantage point, carefully followed developments. Then suddenly police and plainclothes agents of the KGB began to disperse the crowd. The operation was directed by an official shouting commands in Russian, who had mounted the pedestal of the Shevchenko Monument which is centrally located in the park. Some of those present claimed he was the chief of the KGB in the Kiev Region. Several of the demonstrators who did not disperse quickly enough were arrested and taken away.

Questioning of people involved in this affair went on for some time. One participant in the formation of the organization had drawn up a draft constitution and a program that was almost word for word a copy of resolutions of the party and decrees of the government on the national question dating from the days of Lenin and shortly after. The KGB questioned him for several days and then tried to gather up all copies of the draft. I had obtained a copy but, like the rest, it ended up in the files of the secret police.

The protests against Russification continued in spite of these police measures. An outspoken young psychologist and literary critic of independent and original views, speaking at a convention of teachers in the city of Lutsk in May, launched into a bold criticism of Russification which contained pointed remarks about Ukrainians being "prisoners of alien ideas".[9]

Several Kiev citizens, among them the son of one of Ukraine's most outstanding poets, drew up a petition which was forwarded to the CC of the CPSU to be presented to the Twenty-third Congress, requesting that the national schools for the Ukrainian minority in areas of the USSR outside Ukraine which had functioned before their closing in the early thirties, be reopened. At the beginning of July, I was informed, although I did not see one, that copies of a sharply-worded protest to the authorities in Ukraine against Russification of education, written by Evhenia Kuznetsova, of Kiev University, were also being secretly circulated.

Obviously such protests are not to the liking of the authorities who are constantly on the alert for any manifestations of national consciousness. They proclaim full merging but admit that this:

> ... rapprochement of nations, the attainment of their full unity ... will not occur spontaneously ... Here the subjective factor plays a great role and first of all the correct Leninist national policy of the Communist Party.[10]

To aid this merging there is a ceaseless campaign of mass agitation denouncing nationalism and glorifying Russification as a natural development in the march to communism. The intensity of this campaign was revealed by the secretary of the CPU in charge of Agitation and Propaganda, who wrote that:

> After the Twenty-first Congress of the party, the army of agitators in the republic grew to one million.[11]

Khrushchov himself laid special emphasis on this question at the Twenty-second Congress when he said:

> It is necessary to intensify the education of the masses in the spirit of proletarian internationalism and Soviet patriotism. With all Bolshevik implacability, we must root out even the smallest manifestation of nationalist survivals.[12]

The terms "proletarian internationalism" and "Soviet patriotism" are sugar-coated terms for Russification. What happens if one million propagandists in Ukraine do not convince each other? How do you then deal with "manifestations of nationalist survivals?" Obviously it becomes necessary to use more "concrete" measures. The "subjective factor" takes over in the form of mass terror, arrests, jail sentences and exiles. When he visited Kiev on

January 30, 1964, Khrushchov was asked by Ukrainian party leaders, according to a report by one who was present, whether they should not ease up on Russification. Khrushchov was adamant:

> Nyet! Tighten the screw. We will continue to implore and persuade that it is imperative to adopt the Russian language. However, if necessary, we will repeat 1937!

In the spring of 1965 after Khrushchov had become a mere memory, P. N. Demichev, acting secretary of the CC of the CPSU in charge of ideological work, gave instructions to the secretaries in charge of Agitation and Propaganda of the national parties to take the offensive against manifestations of nationalism. There had always been a close scrutiny of those who championed the Ukrainian language. Every higher educational institution has a "special department", a branch of the security organs, which keeps a file on every student and professor, thus exerting a tight control on the life of the institution. All professors who insist on lecturing in Ukrainian are on a special list and carefully watched as dangerous enemies of the Soviet state. All classrooms are connected by an inter-communications system to a central recording room. Periodically lectures are taped and carefully scrutinized for any nationalist sentiment and deviation from the prevailing ideological line.

After Demichev's instructions the offensive began; Khrushchov's threats were being translated into reality by his successors. Lydia Orel was relieved of her post; Shestopal was expelled from the party and dismissed from his position (V. Lobko had already been ousted from the Academy of Sciences). The Kiev writer Shumylo, who spoke up at the party conference of writers, was summoned to the CC by A. D. Skaba and given a thorough dressing down and a stern warning; some of the students involved in the campaign to propagate the Ukrainian language, after being detained and terrorized, were expelled from Kiev University.

All summer, tension was building up; the security police became more active; detentions and interrogations increased, assuming mass proportions in Kiev after my return to Canada in August 1965. Later news arrived that among the arrested were Dzyuba and another uncompromising opponent of Russification, the literary critic Svitlychny. Although others were sentenced, the latter two were released after wide public protests in Europe and North America. Names of some of those jailed were revealed later; among them was Karavansky who was exiled to Siberia and Kuznetsova who received four years.

The case of Karavansky is especially interesting because of his background, his courage and his fate. When his Red Army detachment was cut off by the Germans in Belorussia he escaped capture and found his way through enemy occupied territory back to his native Odessa where he lived through the occupation, suffering persecution and detention. When the Nazi armies were driven back and Odessa was reoccupied by Soviet forces, he was arrested, convicted in typical Stalinist fashion of being a Nazi collaborator and sentenced to 25 years by a Russian military tribunal. In 1960, after spending 16 years in concentration camps, Karavansky was released. In the autumn of 1965 he was arrested again and sent off to complete the balance of his 25-year sentence.

After rumours of his incarceration had reached the West I asked a Soviet official, who was visiting Canada, about Karavansky. He confirmed the arrest. When I enquired the reason, he snapped back, "Karavansky was a German spy".

In 1937 Marshal Tukhachevsky and other outstanding military leaders were court-martialed and shot on the same false charge. Almost 30 years later, after the denunciation of Stalin, the revelation of his crimes and the rehabilitation of the victims, Russian authorities are still using the same worn-out charge to condemn the innocent.

A reliable account recently received from Ukraine revealed that Karavansky was subjected to rigorous interrogation and torture. When his wife was allowed to visit her husband she did not recognize him. But the prisoner was not questioned about spying. His crime was writing the petition to the attorney-general and then clandestinely circulating it.

The arrests and convictions which the authorities tried to keep secret, caused loud protests in Europe and America. In the meantime, opposition to Russification did not subside but manifested itself more boldly and strongly than ever at the Congress of Writers of Ukraine held in Kiev, November 19 to 23, 1966. The tone of criticism was set by the president Oles Honchar, one of Ukraine's most talented writers who deplored the fact that in secondary schools and higher educational institutions "the native tongue often finds itself in a worse position than the foreign language". He praised the republics of Czechoslovakia, Poland, Romania and Yugoslavia which,

> . . . guided by principles of internationalism create favourable conditions for the cultural development of the Ukrainian population, open Ukrainian schools, introduce Ukrainian literature into university programs, create conditions for literary creativity for their citizens who write in the Ukrainian language.[13]

Others followed, among them Vitaliy Korotych, a talented young poet who has visited Canada and the USA under the auspices of UNESCO, criticizing various aspects which thwarted the free and full development of Ukrainian culture.[14]

To head off the strong criticism, S. Barudzin one of the delegates from the RSFSR, employed an old tactic; having a handy scapegoat in the person of Khrushchov, he laid the blame for the campaign of Russification at his door. It was time, he stated, to raise questions "which agitate our literatures" and over which "there was much confusion" before the October plenum of 1964 (i.e. before the ousting of Khrushchov). He admitted there had been much ill-feeling engendered among non-Russians and reminded the delegates of Stalin's formula: "National in form and socialist in content".

Baruzdin was referring to the campaign of merging of the national cultures, but he did not denounce the aim; his objection was against the method. He stated that:

> To me a Russian, the haste with which we spoke of the merging of cultures was not always understandable.[15]

Two Ukrainian delegates, L. M. Novichenko and V. P. Kozachenko, both of them notoriously slavish in following the wavering party line, echoed and supplemented Baruzdin's "criticism".[16] A. D. Skaba, who would normally have spoken on behalf of the CC of the CPU as the secretary in charge of Agitation and Propaganda, but who was completely compromised by his persecutions of those who opposed merging, was silent. Instead the report was delivered by P. Yu. Shelest the first secretary, who mouthed platitudes about the development of the Ukrainian language depending on the Ukrainian writers whom the party would always support.[17]

Impressive as the reports of criticisms printed in the Soviet press appear to us, latest information brought back by visitors to Ukraine from Canada is that these are incomplete. Accordingly, the report of Honchar's speech was heavily censored, while Korotych's was not even recognizable and Malyshko's eloquent and fervent criticism was not even reported.

The heavy hand of Soviet bureaucracy also excluded from the Congress such young literary talents as Mykola Vinhranovsky, Lena Kostenko, Ivan Dzyuba, Evhen Sverstyuk and Ivan Svitlychny. On this question the delegates also showed their feelings. When S. Kryzhanivsky mentioned the name of Dzyuba[18] the delegates, according to reports coming out of Ukraine, almost raised the roof with their thunderous applause.

It is quite obvious that many of the events at the congress were not anticipated and proved embarrassing to say the least. As a result, Russification may have slowed down, but it did not stop. The events, however, encouraged further opposition. Editorials criticizing past policy and defending the right of Ukrainian culture to free development appeared in an organ of the Union of Writers of Ukraine[19] and a teachers' magazine[20]. Reports of recent visitors to Ukraine indicate that criticism is widespread and quite open among the populace.

The outside world is only vaguely aware of the Russian campaign to destroy the Ukrainian culture or the courageous opposition put up by the Ukrainian people. There are some, who although not in possession of incontrovertable evidence, have strongly suspected the existence of a policy which denied non-Russians their national and personal rights. One such was Palmiro Togliatti, outstanding Italian communist leader. He could not have known all the facts, but he sensed these injustices when he wrote in his *Testament,* published after his death:

> The problem meriting the greatest attention . . . is however, that of restrictions and suppressions of the democratic and personal freedoms which were introduced by Stalin . . . The general impression is that there exists a slowness and a resistance against the return to the Leninist norms that ensured within the party, as well as outside it, a broad freedom of expression and debate on questions of culture, art and politics. We cannot understand this slowness and this resistance, especially when taking into account the existing conditions, when capitalist encirclement no longer exists.[21]

Togliatti's words were greeted with enthusiasm by the peoples of the USSR. They were greatly encouraged that a man of international renown had raised his voice on their behalf. In the meantime we continue to be flooded with Soviet propaganda such as the following:

> Only malicious provocateurs can maintain that Moscow chains Ukrainian culture and condemns it to vegetation.[22]

The world is taken in by this Russian hypocrisy. We hear about the oppressed of Asia, Africa and South America, but people are unaware of the oppressed nations of the USSR. In the meantime, fighting with their backs to the wall to preserve their cultures and languages, these people wonder why the world has forgotten them. The feelings of Ukrainians are best given substance by a grade 6 student of a Kiev school in a couplet which reads:

> The world shouts: "Freedom for Asia, freedom for Africa!" When will it shout: "Freedom for Ukraine!"?

FOOTNOTES

1. F. F. Sovetkin, op. cit., p. 12.
2. J. Stalin, *On the Draft Constitution of the USSR. Constitution (Fundamental Law) of the Union of Soviet Socialist Republics,* Foreign Languages Publishing House, Moscow, 1945, Appendix I, II, pp. 83-86.
3. *Nasha Kultura* (Our Culture), March, 1963, pp. 5-6.
4. *XX syezd,* I, p. 89.
5. He was referring to a fire in the State Public Library of the Academy of Sciences of the UkrSSR which broke out May 24, 1964, under very suspicious circumstances and raged for two days. It was first reported in the local paper, *Vechirny Kiev,* on May 27.
6. Part of Malyshko's speech, without the sections where he is critical of official policy, was printed in *Literaturna Ukrayina* (Literary Ukraine), January 12, 1965.
7. The author was present when the speech was delivered. Novichenko, mentioned by Dzyuba, is a literary critic who is usually in the forefront of those paying lip service to the official line in literature in Ukraine.
8. "Dialogue", *Literaturnaya Gazeta,* December 3, 1964.
9. A tourist from Ukraine who visited Canada recently, informed me that Sverstyuk is now employed in a publishing house.
10. *Stroitelstvo kommunizma,* p. 251.
11. S. Chervonenko, "Tesnaya svyaz s zhiznyu-zalog uspekha ideologicheskoy roboty (Close Contact with Life—The Guarantee of Success of Ideological Work)", *Kommunist,* No. 10, October, 1959, p. 31.
12. *XXII zyizd,* I, p. 206.
13. *Literaturna Ukraina,* November 17, 1966.
14. Ibid., November 20, 1966.
15. Ibid., November 22, 1966.
16. Ibid., November 25, and November 20, 1966.
17. Ibid., November 17, 1966.
18. Ibid., November 20, 1966.
19. Ibid., November 29, 1966.
20. *Ukrayinska Mova i Literatura v Shkoli,* No. 1, January, 1966.
21. *Pravda,* September 10, 1964.
22. *Radyanska Ukrayina,* July 25, 1965.

Epilogue

Since the book went to press I have received new data which indicates that Russification is not subsiding. Commencing in the 1967/68 school year Russian will be taught as a subject from Grade 1 in all Latvian schools.[1]

The Kirgiz SSR is now blessed with 266 mixed schools compared to 1027 schools in the Kirgiz language in which Russian is also taught from the first grade. To further advance Russification, preparatory pre-school classes in Russian were organized in 1966. In 1967 there were 135 such classes embracing about 4,000 children.[2]

In all native schools in Dagestan, the language of instruction is Russian beginning in Grade 3. In the schools of many regions "in accordance with the wishes of the parents", Russian is now being introduced in place of the native tongue in Grade 1. Of 127,000 pupils in beginning classes in village schools in the 1967/68 school year, 60,000 were taught in Russian.[3]

The contempt in which the national languages are held by the Russians was revealed by a Russian educator who arrogantly asserted that a good knowledge and command of the Russian language should become for the national youth a mark of education and high culture.[4]

In Ukraine, in the meantime, the proportion of Russian personnel has been increasing as is evident from the following data:

Percentage of Specialists with Secondary Special Education

Year	Ukrainians	Russians	Others
1957	66.9	23.0	10.1
1960	67.4	24.5	8.1
1962	67.4	24.7	7.9
1964	66.7	25.3	8.0

Percentage of Specialists with Higher Education

Year	Ukrainians	Russians	Others
1957	56.8	25.0	18.2
1960	58.0	26.7	15.3
1962	58.5	27.0	14.5
1964	58.1	28.1	13.8[5]

The low percentage of Ukrainian specialists in Ukraine has already been noted. But here, in addition, a comparison of statistics for several years indicates the continuing increase in the proportion of Russian specialists.

Ukraine is also consistently losing control over its higher educational institutions. In 1966 ministries of the UkrSSR still had jurisdiction over the following institutions;[6] Kharkiv Institute of Medicine, Crimean Institute of Medicine, Kharkiv Institute of Aviation, Dnipropetrovsk State University. In 1967 all four were placed under ministries of the USSR.[7]

My fears and suspicions, set out in previous pages, that the appointment of P. P. Udovychenko at the beginning of 1967 as Minister of Education of the UkrSSR would be followed by intensified Russification of general education, have now been confirmed. According to a recent official report:

The Ministry of Education of the UkrSSR deems it necessary to carry on work in the further ... raising of the quality of students' achievement in the Russian language.[8]

However there are no measures to improve achievement in Ukrainian, but, of course, a knowledge of Ukrainian is not "a mark of education and high culture."

Meanwhile new information has come out of the USSR concerning the persecution of opponents of Russification in Ukraine. Recently a collection of materials was published in the West[9] including biographic sketches of those arrested shortly after my departure from Kiev, reports of the proceedings of the closed trials at which they were sentenced, letters by the prisoners from the camps in the Mordvinian ASSR where they are incarcerated, and other materials. Those arrested were accused of disseminating anti-Soviet propaganda which turned out to be protests against the very Russification I have described in this book.

Furthermore from these letters we learn that in one of the camps there is a group of Ukrainian intellectuals from the city of Karaganda in Kazakhstan. This group was imprisoned for demanding schools in the Ukrainian language for the large Ukrainian minority there.[10]

The compiler of the above-mentioned collection was Vyacheslav Chornovil, a Candidate in Marxist-Leninist philosophy, a former secretary of a Komsomol organization and a critic and reporter for Kiev radio and television. In the last capacity he attended the closed trials and took down reports. The latest news from Ukraine is that V. Chornovil has been arrested.

Fifty years of Soviet power! Persecution of opponents of Russification in Ukraine has reached an intensity unheard of in Tsarist times. Evidence of this is so overwhelming that even the staunchest supporters of the Soviet system cannot refrain from condemning Russian national policy, and the brutal persecution of those who are striving to maintain their national cultures.

FOOTNOTES

1. Russky yazyk v natsionalnoy shkole, No. 5, 1967, page 22.
2. Ibid., pp. 22-23.
3. Ibid., p. 31.

4. Ibid., p. 76.
5. Tsentralne statystychne upravlinnya pry Radi Ministriv Ukrayin-skovi RSR (Central Statistical Administration of the Council of Ministers of the UkrSSR), *Narodne hospodarstvo Ukrayinskoyi RSR v 1964 rotsi.* (The National Economy of the UkrSSR in 1964), Statistical Yearbook, Kiev, n.d., p. 476.
6. *Dovidnyk dlya ustupnykiv do vyshchykh uchbovykh zakladiv Ukrayinskoyi RSR na 1966 rik,* Kiev 1966, pp. 60, 86, 110-111.
7. Ministerstvo Vysshego i Srednego Spetsialnogo Obrazovaniya SSR (Ministry of Higher and Secondary Special Education of the USSR). *Spravochnik dlya postupayushchikh v vysshie uchebnye zavedeniya SSSR v 1967 g.* (Handbook for Entrants of Higher Educational Institutions of the USSR for 1967), Moscow, 1967, pp. 65, 166, 277, 280.
8. Russky yazyk, No. 5, 1967, p. 9.
9. *Lykho z rozumu* (Woe from Wit), A Collection of Materials compiled by Vyacheslav Chornovil, Paris, 1967.
10. Ibid., p. 330.

GLOSSARY

ASSR. Autonomous Soviet Socialist Republic. Areas comprised of small nationalities not large enough to form a national republic. There are 19 in the USSR. Of these, 15 are in the RSFSR.

Bolshevik. The term is applied to members of the majority in the Russian Social Democratic Labour Party. They later formed the Communist Party.

Bourgeois nationalist. Term applied by Soviet authorities and official propagandists to members of the non-Russian nationalities of the USSR who are conscious of their national heritage and oppose encroachment on their languages and cultures. Such people are regarded as the most dangerous enemies of the USSR and treated accordingly.

CC. Central Committee.

Central Rada. The latter word means council. This was a convention in Ukraine of representatives of political parties and other organizations. Called in 1917, after the overthrow of the Tsar, it formed a government in Ukraine.

Council of People's Commissars. Now called the Council of Ministers. The equivalent of the cabinet. Its chairman is the prime minister.

CPSU. Communist Party of the Soviet Union.

CPU. Communist Party of Ukraine. When first formed the letter (b) was inserted (CP(b)U) denoting Bolsheviks. In the text the (b) is omitted.

District. A division of a region. In Russian the word is *rayon*.

KGB. Committee of State Security, the Russian secret police.

Kurkul. Term applied to peasants of average wealth. The policy of the Soviet government was to confiscate their property and to exile or destroy them.

Petlura, Simon. Political and military leader in Ukraine from 1917 to 1920.

Region. A large area similar to our county. The Russian word is *oblast*.

RSDLP. Russian Social Democratic Labour Party.

RSFSR. The Russian Soviet Federated Socialist Republic, the largest of the 15 republics of the USSR. The population is for the most part Russian, but includes many smaller nations which inhabited the areas before they were added to the Russian Empire. Also referred to as Russia.

Supreme Soviet. The house of representatives organized along the lines of the House of Commons, but without any real powers.

UkrSSR. Ukrainian Soviet Socialist Republic, the second largest of the republics. Also referred to in the text as Ukraine.

USSR. Union of Soviet Socialist Republics.

YCL. Young Communist League, the youth organization of the Communist Party.

APPENDIX I
National Composition of the Population of the USSR, 1959

	Population	%
USSR	208,826,650	100
Russians	114,113,579	54.65
Ukrainians	37,252,930	17.84
Belorussians	7,913,488	3.79
Uzbeks	6,015,416	2.88
Kazakhs	3,621,610	1.73
Georgians	2,691,950	1.29
Azerbaidzhans	2,939,728	1.41
Lithuanians	2,326,094	1.11
Moldavians	2,214,139	1.06
Latvians	1,399,539	.67
Kirgiz	968,659	.46
Tadzhiks	1,396,939	.67
Armenians	2,786,912	1.34
Turkmans	1,001,585	.48
Estonians	988,616	.47
Others	21,195,466	10.15

Source: *Itogi vsesouznoy perepisi,* Summary volume, p. 185.

APPENDIX II
Population of the Republics of the USSR

	1959	%	January, 1965	%
Total in USSR	208,246,874	100	229,198,000	100
Russian SFSR	117,239,586	56.30	125,768,000	54.87
Ukrainian SSR	41,720,596	20.03	45,100,000	19.68
Belorussian SSR	8,030,634	3.87	8,533,000	3.72
Uzbek SSR	8,079,599	3.88	10,130,000	4.42
Kazakh SSR	9,297,838	4.42	11,853,000	5.17
Georgian SSR	4,030,981	1.93	4,483,000	1.96
Azerbaidzhan SSR	3,684,240	1.77	4,518,000	1.97
Lithuanian SSR	2,696,718	1.30	2,949,000	1.29
Moldavian SSR	2,879,409	1.39	3,303,000	1.44
Latvian SSR	2,079,948	1.00	2,241,000	.98
Kirgiz SSR	2,064,712	.99	2,569,000	1.12
Tadzhik SSR	1,987,148	.96	2,482,000	1.08
Armenian SSR	1,765,297	.85	2,134,000	.93
Turkmen SSR	1,507,740	.73	1,862,000	.81
Estonian SSR	1,191,428	.58	1,273,000	.56

Source: *Itogi vsesouznoy perepisi,* Summary Volume, p. 17. (1959)
   Narodnoe Khozaystvo, 1964, p. 9. (January, 1965)

APPENDIX III

National Composition of Students in Higher Educational Institutions
of the UkrSSR, 1960

	Number	%
Total	417,748	100
Ukrainians	260,945	62.5
Russians	125,464	30.0
Jews	18,673	
Belorussians	4,377	
Moldavians	1,030	
Armenians	909	
Georgians	527	A
Tatars	517	L
Azerbaidzhans	192	L
Chuvash	139	
Ossetians	129	O
Lithuanians	106	T
Uzbeks	104	H
Kazakhs	101	E
Latvians	84	R
Mordvinians	78	S
Yakuts	68	
Komi	62	7.5
Dagestans	55	
Bashkirs	51	
Estonians	51	
Kirgiz	44	
Kalmyks	42	
Balkars	40	
Abkhaz	38	
Buryats	29	
Tadzhiks	28	
Turkmans	28	
Kabardians	22	
Maris	21	
Karelians	17	
Udmurts	17	
Ingush	8	
Chechen	6	
Others	3,746	

Source: *Vysshee obrazovanie,* op. cit., p. 130.

APPENDIX IV

National Composition of the Population of the UkrSSR, 1959

	Number	%
Total population	41,869,046	100
Ukrainians	32,158,493	76.8
Russians	7,090,813	16.9
Jews	840,311	
Poles	363,297	
Belorussians	290,890	
Moldavians	241,650	
Bulgarians	219,409	
Hungarians	149,229	
Greeks	104,359	
Romanians	100,863	
Tatars	61,527	A
Armenians	28,024	L
Hahauz	23,530	L
Gypsies	22,515	
Czechs	14,539	O
Slovaks	13,991	T
Georgians	11,574	H
Mordvinians	11,397	E
Chuvash	8,925	R
Lithuanians	8,906	S
Uzbeks	8,472	
Latvians	6,919	6.3
Azerbaidzhans	6,680	
Kazakhs	4,694	
Estonians	4,181	
Dagestans	3,823	
Albanians	3,809	
Bashkirs	3,345	
Ossetians	3,325	
Karais	3,301	
Udmurts	2,828	

Source: *Itogi vsesoyuznoy perepisi,* Ukrainskaya SSR, p. 168.

APPENDIX V

National Composition of Specialists with
Secondary Special Education in the UkrSSR, 1961

	Number	%
Total	1,051,680	100
Ukrainians	711,541	67.66
Russians	255,962	24.34
Jews	54,521	
Belorussians	8,986	
Moldavians	1,709	
Tatars	1,205	
Armenians	1,043	
Georgians	522	
Mordvinians	318	
Chuvash	292	
Latvians	205	
Estonians	153	
Lithuanians	131	A
Ossetians	119	L
Azerbaidzhans	117	L
Komi	101	
Karelians	85	O
Udmurts	84	T
Maris	60	H
Kazakhs	49	E
Bashkirs	47	R
Balkars	42	S
Dagestans	37	
Uzbeks	37	8.0
Yakuts	28	
Altays	27	
Buryats	21	
Tadzhiks	20	
Abkhasians	19	
Turkmans	17	
Cherkesses	14	
Kabardians	13	
Chechens	11	
Adygeys	10	
Others *	14,134	

Source: *Srednee spetsialnoe obrazovanie*, p. 44.

*This includes 34 whose nationality is given; for the remainder it is not specified.

APPENDIX VI

National Composition of Specialists with Higher Education
in the UkrSSR, 1960

	Number	Percentage
Total in UkrSSR	685,851	100
Ukrainians	399,931	58.3
Russians	181,489	26.5
Jews	83,689	
Belorussians	6,272	
Armenians	1,800	
Moldavians	823	
Tatars	806	
Georgians	578	
Chuvash	228	
Latvians	209	
Ossetians	183	
Mordvinians	175	
Lithuanians	143	A
Komi	123	L
Udmurts	118	L
Estonians	114	
Azerbaidzhans	101	O
Maris	61	T
Yakuts	45	H
Bashkirs	40	E
Karelians	32	R
Dagestans	31	S
Uzbeks	31	
Kazakhs	23	15.2
Tadzhiks	18	
Balkars	14	
Buryats	11	
Abkhasians	9	
Kabardians	7	
Turkmen	6	
Kirgiz	4	
Kalmyks	3	
Chechens	2	
Ingush	2	
Karakalpaks	2	

Source: *Vysshee obrazovanie*, p. 70.

APPENDIX VII

Distribution of Ukrainian Specialists with Higher Education
in the republics of the USSR, 1960

	Number	Total Percentage
Total in USSR	517,729	100
Ukrainian SSR	399,931	77.2
Russian SFSR	85,155	16.4
Kazakh SSR	10,984	
Moldavian SSR	5,702	A
Belorussian SSR	5,441	L
Uzbek SSR	2,984	L
Kirgiz SSR	2,201	
Latvian SSR	1,135	O
Tadzhik SSR	1,108	T
Turkmen SSR	787	H
Azerbaidzhan SSR	615	E
Georgian SSR	579	R
Lithuanian SSR	519	S
Estonian SSR	420	
Armenian SSR	168	6.4

Source: *Vysshee obrazovanie*, pp. 70-71.

APPENDIX VIII

Comparison of Various Areas of Education of the RSFSR
and the UkrSSR in Percentage of Totals for the USSR (Summary)

	Year	RSFSR	UkrSSR
Population	1965	54.87	19.68
Workers who improved their qualifications while employed	1965	65.67	17.94
Budget for all education	1965	55.98	17.39
Budget for kindergartens	1965	61.73	14.93
Budget for elementary and general secondary education	1965	54.22	17.42
Budget for technicums	1965	60.48	17.46
Budget for higher education	1965	62.14	16.79
Textbooks for technicums (titles)	1955	76.	6.
Textbooks for technicums (copies)	1955	94.51	2.93
Textbooks for higher education institutions (titles)	1964	67.84	14.34
Textbooks for higher educational institutions (copies)	1964	89.04	6.11
Kindergartens & crèche-kindergartens	1965	64.27	14.38
Children in them	1965	63.04	15.65
General education schools of all types	1965	55.88	16.15
Pupils in them	1965	54.66	17.97
Out-of-town Pioneer camps	1965	67.53	15.91
Children accommodated in them	1965	69.46	15.51
Secondary special educational institutions	1965	58.35	18.25
Higher educational institutions	1965	57.14	17.46
Students in secondary special educational institutions	1965	61.74	17.65
Students in higher educational institutions	1965	60.97	17.87
Students in higher educational institutions receiving stipends	1960	60.73	17.66
Students in higher educational institutions sponsored by enterprises	1960	61.1	16.1
Institutions with power to recommend students for candidate degrees	1959	56.7	17.1
Institutions with power to recommend students for candidate and doctorate degrees	1959	75.7	8.7
Graduates of vocational — technical schools	1965	63.70	16.36
Postgraduate students	1965	67.86	12.95
Specialists with secondary specialized education	1964	60.80	19.09
Scientists	1965	68.85	14.14
Scientists with candidate degrees	1964	66.66	14.32
Scientists with doctorate degrees	1964	70.69	12.77
Associate professors in higher educational institutions	1951–5	72.	13.0
Doctors in higher educational institutions	1951–5	76.	10.4
Professors in higher educational institutions	1951–5	79.	8.7

APPENDIX IX

Comparison of Russians and Ukrainians in Various Areas of Education
as Percentages of the Total for the USSR (Summary)

	Year	Russians	Ukrainians
Population	1959	54.65	17.84
Students in secondary specialized educational institutions	1965	64.44	15.00
Specialists with secondary special education	1964	65.08	15.92
Students in higher educational institutions	1965	61.18	14.47
Postgraduate students	1960	58.53	11.10
Scientists	1965	66.35	10.65

APPENDIX X

Comparison of Russians and Ukrainians in Various Areas of Education
as Percentages of the Total for the UkrSSR (Summary)

	Year	Russians	Ukrainians
Population	1959	16.9	76.8
Students in secondary special educational institutions	1961	24.8	69.1
Students in higher educational institutions	1960	30.	62.5
Specialists with higher education	1960	26.5	58.3
Scientists	1960	Not given	48.3

APPENDIX XI

Languages of Non-Russian Peoples of the RSFSR Used in Schools of the RSFSR Prior to 1958.

The schools of many peoples of the RSFSR conduct education using the native tongue in the first four grades. Beginning in the fifth grade all instruction is conducted wholly in the Russian language. This is the case in Abazin, Avar, Adygey, Balkar, Mountain-Altay, Dargin, Ingush, Kabardian, Karachay, Kalmyk, Kumyk, Lak, Lezgin, Nogay, Ossetian, Tabasaran, Turkmen, Khakass, Cherkess and Chechen schools.

A significant group is made up of people in whose schools, as a rule, instruction using the native tongue is carried on in seven grades of the middle schools. To this group belong the Buryat-Mongol, Zyryan-Komi, Permyak-Komi, Korean, Mari (of the plains), Mari (of the hills), Erzyan-Mordvinian, Mokshan-Mordvinian, Tuvinian, Udmurt, Chuvash and Yakut.

Instruction using the native tongue in all subjects in all grades of the middle schools (grade 10) is carried on in Tatar, Bashkir, Armenian, Azerbaidzhan, Georgian and Kazakh schools of the RSFSR.

In the schools of the peoples of the Far North, who have their written language, instruction using the native language is carried on in the preparatory and the first two grades of the elementary school. Of these people, the following have their written language and textbooks: Nentsi, Evenki, Khanty, Chukchi, Nanaytsi, Koryaks, Eskimos and Eveny.

Source: *Natsionalnye Shkoly RSFSR,* p. 23. The book was published in 1958, which would mean that the above applied prior to the new education law of 1958, when planned Russification of the schools of these peoples began.

APPENDIX XII

Petition of S. Ya. Karavansky to the attorney-general of the UkrSSR that Yu. M. Dadenkov, Minister of Higher and Secondary Special Education be Arraigned on Charges of Promoting Russification.

To the Attorney-general of the Ukrainian SSR.
From citizen Karavansky Svyatoslav Yosipovich, who resides in the city of Odessa, at 59 Choronomorsky Road, Apartment 47.

PETITION

I request you to arraign on criminal charges the Minister of Higher and Special Secondary Education of the Ukrainian SSR, Dadenkov Yuri Mikolaiovich, under sections of the criminal code of the Ukrainian SSR which provides penalties for:

1. Violation of national and racial equality. (Sec. 66. CC, UkrSSR)
2. Opposition to the restoration of Leninist principles in the practical organization of higher education of the Ukrainian SSR. (Sec. 167, CC, UkrSSR)
3. Failure to implement the resolutions of the Twentieth Congress of the CPSU regarding the liquidation of the consequences of the cult of the individual[1] and impeding the restoration of normal conditions of development of the Ukrainian socialist nation. (Sec. 66. CC, UkrSSR)
4. Training of unqualified personnel and disorganization of the pedagogical process in the system of higher and specialized secondary education. (Sec. 167. CC, UkrSSR)[2]

In accordance with the rules of admission to higher and specialized secondary educational institutions, Russian language and literature are among the subjects of the entrance examinations. Graduates of Russian schools are more successful in this examination than graduates of Ukrainian schools. In addition to this, entrance examinations in specialized subjects are conducted in Russian; this also makes it more difficult for graduates of Ukrainian schools to write these subject examinations. Therefore they achieve fewer points on these competitive examinations.

Of the total number of those who study in the higher educational institutions, Ukrainians make up a significantly lower percentage than they do in the sphere of production of material goods on the territory of the Ukrainian SSR. Thus, among those who entered the Odessa Polytechnical Institute in the school year 1964-65, Ukrainians made up 43 percent. Of 1126 Ukrainians who made entrance applications, 453 were accepted, i.e. 40 percent. But of 1002 Russians who applied, 477 were accepted, or 46 percent. The procedure of admittance to higher and specialized secondary educational institutions of the republic now in force is anti-Leninist and a direct restriction of the rights of citizens as regards their nationality. Acts of this nature are subject to penalty under Sec. 66, Criminal Code, Ukrainian SSR.

> Sec. 66. Violation of national and racial equality. Propaganda or agitation with the view of inciting to racial or national animosity as a direct or indirect limitation of rights, or the establishment of direct or indirect privileges of citizens as regards their racial or national affiliation.—Punishable by imprisonment for a term of from 6 months to 3 years, or by banishment for a period of from 3 to 5 years.

In the overwhelming majority of higher and specialized secondary educational institutions of Kiev, Kharkiv, Odessa, Dnipropetrovsk and others, instruction is not in the Ukrainian language.

The teaching personnel in higher educational institutions of the Ukrainian SSR "do not understand the Ukrainian language". Thus in the Odessa Pedagogical Institute which trains teachers for secondary schools, lectures are in Russian because the lecturers "do not know" the Ukrainian language. In the Odessa State University, even in the Ukrainian department of the philological faculty which trains Ukrainian philologists, the majority of subjects (history of the CPSU, foreign languages, logic, psychology, foreign literature, Marxist philosophy) are not taught in Ukrainian. This is the direct result of the negligent attitude of the minister of higher education to his responsibilities:

a) failure to have published a whole series of textbooks for higher educational institutions e.g. foreign language, logic, foreign literature;

b) failure to train national (i.e. Ukrainian) personnel as lecturers.

Such conditions in higher education in Ukraine destroys the normal conditions for the development of the Ukrainian Socialist nation.

As a result of relegating the Ukrainian language to second place, graduates of universities and pedagogical institutes are not proficient in its use. Teaching in Ukrainian schools, such teachers do not employ the Ukrainian language. Fifty percent of the graduates of Odessa University and the Odessa Pedagogical Institute refuse to teach in Ukrainian schools, giving as their reason ignorance of the language.

I beg you to study the above facts and to determine the degree of guilt of Yuri Mikolaiovich Dadenkov.

FOOTNOTES

1. The resolution reads as follows:

Having heard the report of comrade Khrushchov N. S. regarding the personality cult and its consequences, the Twentieth Congress of the Communist Party of the Soviet Union approves the theses of the report of the Central Committee and entrusts the CC of the CPSU to consistently carry through measures which will guarantee the full overcoming of the personality cult which is foreign to Marxism-Leninism, the liquidation of its consequences in all spheres of party state and ideological work, the strict introduction of norms of party life and principles of collective party leadership worked out by the great Lenin.

Source: *XX Sezd Kommunisticheskoy partii Sovetshogo Soyuza* (Twentieth Congress of the Communist Party of the Soviet Union). Stenographic Report, Vol. II, Moscow, 1956, p. 498.

2. Section 167 of the Criminal Code of the UkrSSR is not included in the text of the petition. It reads as follows:

Negligence. Failure to perform or improper performance by an official of his duties due to a negligent or disinterested attitude which would cause fundamental harm to state or community interests or to the rights and interests of individual citizens protected by the law.—Punishable by imprisonment for a term up to two years or corrective labour for a term up to one.

Source: *Kriminalny Kodeks Ukrayinskoyi RSR* (Criminal Code of the Ukrainian SSR), Kiev, 1961.

BIBLIOGRAPHY

1. Books and Pamphlets

ABC Facts About Yugoslavia. Zagreb, 1966.

Akademiya Nauk SSSR, Institut Filosofii (Academy of Sciences of the USSR, Institute of Philosophy), *Stroitelstvo kommunizma i razvitie obshchestvennykh otnosheniy* (The Building of Communism and the Development of Social Relations). Moscow, 1966

Akademiya Nauk SSSR, Sibirskoe Otdelenie, Institut Geografii Sibiri i Dalnego Vostoka (Academy of Sciences of the USSR, Siberian Division, Institute of Geography of Siberia and the Far East). *Geografiya naseleniya Vostochnoy Sibiri* (Geography of the Population of Eastern Siberia). Moscow, 1962

Akademiya Nauk Ukrayinskoyi RSR (Academy of Sciences of the Ukrainian SSR). *Ukrayinska Radyanska Entsyklopediya* (Ukrainian Soviet Encyclopedia). 17 vols. Kiev, 1959-1965

Akademiya Nauk Ukrayinskoyi RSR, Institut Suspilnykh Nauk (Academy of Sciences of the Ukrainian SSR, Institute of Social Studies). *Z istoriyi Ukrayinskoyi RSR* (From the History of the Ukrainian SSR). No. 8, 1963

Avidor, M. *Education for a Growing Nation.* Israel Today Series, No. 1. Jerusalem, 1964

Berezhna, N. P. and others, *Drukovani pratsi profesoriv, vykladachiv i spivrobitnykiv Lvivskoho Universytetu za 1944-1960 roky* (Published Works of Professors, Lecturers, and Co-Workers of Lviv University for 1944-1960). Lviv, 1962

Bilodid, I. K. *Rosiyska mova-mova mizhnatsionalnoho spilkuvannya narodiv SRSR* (Russian, the Language of International Communion of the Peoples of the USSR). Kiev, 1962

— *Rozvytok mov sotsialistychnykh natsiy SRSR* (The Development of Languages of the Socialist Nations in the USSR). Kiev, 1963

Braham, Randolph L. *Education in the Romanian Peoples' Republic.* Washington, 1963

Cherkashyn, L. V. *Zahalne navchannya v Ukrayinskiy RSR 1917-1957* (General Education in the Ukrainian SSR 1917-1957). Kiev, 1958

Chistyakov, V. M. (ed.) *Uchitelyu nachalnykh klassov natsionalnoy shkoly* (For the Teacher of Beginning Classes of the National Schools). Moscow, 1964

Deneyko, M. M. *40 let narodnogo obrazovaniya v SSSR* (Forty Years of Public Education in the USSR). Moscow, 1957

Education in Wales (Addysg yng Nghmru) 1847-1947. Welsh Department, Ministry of Education, Pamphlet No. 2. reprinted 1960

Galkin, K. I. *Vysshee obrazovanie i podgotovka nauchnykh kadrov v SSSR* (Higher Education and the Training of Science Cadres in the USSR). Moscow, 1958

Gittler, J. B. (ed.) *Understanding Minority Groups.* New York, 1964

Goncharov, N. K. and Korolev, F. F. *Novaya sistema narodnogo obrazovaniya v SSSR* (The New System of Education in the USSR). Moscow, 1960

GORDON, M. M. *Assimilation in American Life.* New York, 1964

HRYSHCHENKO, M. S. *Narysy z istoriyi shkoly v Ukrayinskiy RSR 1917-1965* (Outline of the History of Schools in the Ukrainian SSR 1917-1965). Kiev, 1966

HUTYANSKY, S. K. *Lenin i Ukrainska Radyanska kultura* (Lenin and the Ukrainian Soviet Culture). Kiev, 1963

ILYUSHIN, I. and UMREYKO, S. *Narodnoe obrazovanie v Belorusskoy SSR* (Public Education in the Belorussian SSR). Minsk, 1961

Institut Istorii Partiyi Ts K, KP Ukrayiny—Filial Institutu Marksyzmu—Leninizmu pry Ts K, KPRS (Institute of the History of the Party of the CC of CP of Ukraine—An Affiliate of the Institute of Marxism—Leninism of the CC of the CPSU). V. I. Lenin pro Urayinu (V. I. Lenin on Ukraine), Kiev, 1957

KARDELJ, EDWARD. *Razvoj slovenackog nacionalnog pitanja* (The Development of the Slovenian National Question). Beograd, 1960

KOMAROV, L. A. *Planirovanie podgotovki i raspredeleniya spetsialistov v SSSR* (The Planning of Training and Distribution of Specialists in the USSR). Moscow, 1961

KONDRASHENKO, L. *Respublika krasnykh galstukov* (The Republic of Red Ties). Simferopol, 1964

KRAVTSEV, I. E. *Razvitie natsionalnykh otnosheniy v SSSR* (The Development of National Relations in the USSR). Kiev, 1962

Lenin's Last Articles and Pamphlets. Progress Publishers, Moscow, (no date)

LENIN, V. I. *Pro natsionalne i natsionalno-kolonialne pytannya* (Concerning the National and National-Colonial Question). Kiev, 1957

MACNAMARA, JOHN. *Bilingualism and Primary Education.* Edinburgh, 1966

MCELLIGOTT, T. J. *Education in Ireland.* Dublin, 1966

MEDYNSKY, E. N. *Prosveshchenie v SSSR* (Education in the USSR). Moscow, 1955

MEKHTI-ZADE, M. M. *Ocherki istorii Sovetskoy shkoly v Azerbaidzhane* (Outline of the History of the Soviet School in Azerbaidzhan). Moscow, 1962

Ministerstvo Osvity URSR (Ministry of Education of the UkrSSR). *Zyizd uchyteliv Ukrayinskoyi RSR, 14-16 zhovtnya, 1959 roku* (Convention of Teachers of the Ukrainian SSR, October 14-16, 1959). Kiev, 1960

Ministerstvo vyshchoyi i serednoyi spetsialnoyi osvity Ukrayinskoyi RSR (Ministry of Higher and Secondary Special Education of the Ukrainian SSR). *Heohrafiya Kyyivskoyi oblasti: Atlas* (Geography of the Kiev Region: An Atlas). Kiev State University. Kiev, 1962

PICHUGINA, E. P. *Pravo na obrazovanie v SSSR* (The Right to Education in the USSR). Moscow, 1957

POSTYSHEV, P. P. *Borotba za Leninsko-Stalinsku natsionalnu polityku partiyi* (The Struggle for the Lenin-Stalin Nationality Policy of the Party). Kiev, 1935

PUTILIN, V. G. *Organizatsiya uchebnoy i vospitatelnoy raboty v tekhnikume* (Organization of the Work of Education and Training in a Technicum). second edition. Kharkiv, 1959

RABIN, CHAIM. *The Revival of Hebrew.* Israel Today Series, No. 5. Jerusalem, 1958

ROUCEK, J. S. and LATTICH, K. V. *Behind the Iron Curtain.* Caldwell. Idaho, 1964

RUDCHENKO, P. O. and LUZHNY, V. M. (compilers). *Khrestomatiya khoro-vykh tvoriv* (Anthology of Choir Compositions). Kiev, 1965

SEMBAEV, A. I. *Ocherki po istorii Kazakskoy Sovetskoy shkoly* (Outline of the History of the Kazakh Soviet School). Alma-Ata, 1958

SEMPLE, STUART W. *The Problems of Bilingualism in the Schools of Wales and Scotland.* Educational Research Series No. 35. Department of Educational Research, College of Education, University of Toronto, 1964

SOVETKIN, F. F. *Natsionalnye shkoly RSFSR za 40 let* (Forty Years of National Schools in the RSFSR). Moscow, 1958

STALIN, J. *Works.* 13 vols. Foreign Languages Publishing House. Moscow, 1952-1955

SYVETS, O. H. *Vyrobnyche navchannya v shkolakh Ukrayinskoyi RSR* (Industrial Training in the Schools of the Ukrainian SSR). Kiev, 1960

The Program of the Communist Party of the Soviet Union. Foreign Languages Publishing House. Moscow, 1961

The Use of Vernacular Languages in Education. UNESCO. Paris, 1953

TITOV, V. *Vysshaya shkola Ukrayinskoy SSR v period perestroyki* (Higher Schools of the Ukrainian SSR in the Period of Reconstruction). Kiev, 1962

TSAMERIAN, I. P. and RONIN, S. L. *Equality of Rights Between Races and Nationalities in the USSR.* UNESCO. Paris, 1962

U.S. Department of Health Education and Welfare. *Improving English Skills of Culturally Different Youths in Large Cities.* Washington, D.C., 1964

VESELOV, A. N. *Profesionalno-tekhnicheskoe obrazovanie v SSSR* (Voca-tional-Technical Training in the USSR). Moscow, 1961

YASNYTSKY, H. I. *Rozvytok narodnoyi osvity na Ukrayini 1921-1932 rr* (The Development of Public Education in Ukraine 1921-1932). Kiev, 1965

ZABELIN, N. N. and others. *Planirovanie podgotovki i raspredeleniya rabochykh kadrov v SSSR* (The Planning of Training and Distribution of Labour Cadres in the USSR). Moscow, 1960

2. Collections of Documents

Akademiya Nauk SSSR, Institut Prava (Academy of Sciences of the USSR, Institute of Law). *Sezdy sovetov soyuza SSR, soyuznykh i avtonomnykh sovetskikh sotsialisticheskikh respublik 1917-1936 gg.* (Congresses of the Soviets of the USSR, Union and Autonomous Soviet Socialist Republics 1917-1936). Vol. I, 1959, Vol. III, 1960

Desyaty sezd RKP(b), Mart, 1921 goda (The Tenth Congress of the RCP(b), March, 1921). Stenographic Report. Moscow, 1963

Dvenadtsaty sezd rosiyskoy kommunisticheskoy partii (bolshevikov) (The Twelfth Congress of the Russian Communist Party [Bolsheviks]). Stenographic Report. April 17-25, 1923, Moscow, 1923

Khrestomatiya z istoriyi Ukrayinskoyi RSR. 2 vols. Kiev, 1959-1961

Komunistychna partiya radyanskoho soyuzu v resolutsiyakh i rishennyakh zyizdiv konferentsiy i plenumiv Ts K (The Communist Party of the Soviet Union in Resolutions and Decisions of Congresses, Conferences and Plenums of the CC). 1898-1954, 3 vols. translation of 7th Russian ed. Kiev, 1954

Komunistychna partiya Ukrayiny v resolutsiyakh i rishennyakh zyizdiv i konferentsiy 1918-1956 (The Communist Party of Ukraine in Resolutions and Decisions of Congresses and Conferences 1918-1954). Kiev, 1958

KPSS o kulture, prosveshchenii i nauke (The CPSU on Culture, Education and Science). Moscow, 1963

Ministerstvo Kultury Ukrayinskoyi RSR (Ministry of Culture of the Ukrainian RSR). *Kulturne Budivnytstvo v Ukrayinskiy RSR* (Cultural Development in the Ukrainian SSR). *Vazhlyvishi rishennya komunistychnoyi partiyi i radyanskoho uryadu 1917-1959 rr* (The More Important Decisions of the Communist Party and the Soviet Government 1917-1959). 2 vols. Kiev, 1959-1961

Na blago i schaste naroda (For the Welfare and Happiness of the People), A Collection of Documents, Moscow, 1961

O kommunisticheskom vospitanii i ukreplenii svyazi shkoly s zhiznu (Regarding Communist Education and the Strengthening of Relationships of School and Life). A Collection of Documents. Moscow, 1964

Practice and Theory of Socialist Development in Yugoslavia. Beograd, 1965

Presidency of the Council of Ministers of Italy. *German-Speaking Inhabitants of the Alto-Adige.* Rome, 1960

Sbornik zakonov SSSR i ukazov presidiuma Verkhovnogo Soveta SSSR 1938-1958 (Collection of Laws of the USSR and Decrees of the Presidium of the Supreme Soviet of the USSR, 1938-1958). Moscow, 1959

STALIN, J. *On the Draft Constitution of the USSR. Constitution (Fundamental Law) of the Union of Soviet Socialist Republics.* Foreign Languages Publishing House. Moscow, 1945

Statut Komunistychnoyi Partiyi Radyanskoho Soyuzu (Statutes of the Communist Party of the Soviet Union). Kiev, 1962

The Constitution of the Socialist Federal Republic of Yugoslavia, adopted on April 7, 1963. Beograd, 1963

TOPICHEV. A. V. (ed.) *Nauchnye kadry v SSSR* (Science Cadres in the USSR). A Collection of Documents and Reference Materials. Moscow, 1959

XX Sezd Kommunisticheskoy Partii Sovetskogo Soyuza, 14-25 fevralya, 1956 (Twentieth Congress of the Communist Party of the Soviet Union, February 14-25, 1956). Stenographic Report. vol. I. Moscow, 1956

XXII Zyizd Komunistychnoyi Partiyi Radyanskoho Soyuzu, 17-31 zhovtnya, 1961 roku (The Twenty-second Congress of the Communist Party of the Soviet Union, October 17-31, 1961). Stenographic Report. 3 vols. Kiev, 1962

XXII Zyizd Komunistychnoyi Partiyi Ukrayiny (Twenty-second Congress of the Communist Party of Ukraine). Kiev, 1962

Zasedaniya Verkhovnogo Soveta SSSR, sozyv 5, sessia 2 (Sessions of the Supreme Soviet of the USSR, 5th Convocation, 2nd Session). December 22-25, 1958. Stenographic Report. Moscow, 1959

ZENOV, M. S. (compiler). *Dokumenty i materialy po perstroyke shkoly* (Documents and Materials on the Reconstruction of School). Moscow, 1960

3. Statistical and Other Handbooks

Dovidnyk dlya vstupnykiv do serednikh spetsialnykh uchbovykh zakladiv Ukrayinskoyi RSR na 1963 rik (Handbook for Entrants of Secondary Special Educational Institutions of the Ukrainian SSR for 1964). Kharkiv State University. Kharkiv, 1964

Dovidnyk dlya vstupnykiv do serednikh spetsialnykh uchbovykh zakladiv Ukrayinskoyi RSR na 1966 rik. Kharkiv, 1966

Dovidnyk dlya vstupnykiv do serednikh spetsialnykh uchbovykh zakladiv Ukrayinskoyi RSR na 1967 rik. Kharkiv, 1967

Dovidnyk dlya vstupnykiv do vyshchykh uchbovykh zakladiv Ukrayinskoyi RSR na 1963 rik (Handbook for Entrants of Higher Educational Institutions of the Ukrainian SSR for 1963). Kharkiv State University. Kharkiv, 1963

Dovidnyk dlya vstupnykiv do vyshchykh uchbovykh zakladiv Ukrayinskoyi RSR na 1964 rik. Kharkiv, 1964

Dovidnyk dlya vstupnykiv do vyshchykh uchbovykh zakladiv Ukrayinskoyi RSR na 1965 rik. Kiev University Publishers. Kiev, 1965

Dovidnyk dlya vstupnykiv do vyshchykh uchbovykh zakladiv Ukrayinskoyi RSR na 1966 rik, Kiev, 1966

Gosudarstvenny Komitet Soveta Ministrov SSR po Pechati (State Committee for Publishing of the Council of Ministers of the USSR). Vsesoyuznaya Knizhnaya Palata (All-Union House of Books). *Pechat SSR v 1964 godu* (Publishing in the USSR in 1964). Statistical Materials. Moscow, 1965

— *Pechat SSSR v 1965 godu.* Moscow, 1966

Kharkov: Spravochnaya Kniga (Kharkov: A Guidebook). Kharkov, 1957

Ministerstvo Kultury SSSR (Ministry of Culture of the USSR). Glavizdat, Vsesoyuznaya Knizhnaya Palata (Glavizdat, All-Union House of Books). *Pechat SSSR v 1955 godu* (Publishing in the USSR in 1955). Statistical Materials. Moscow, 1956

— *Pechat SSSR v 1956 i 1957 godakh.* Moscow, 1958

— *Pechat SSSR v 1958 godu.* Moscow, 1959

— *Pechat SSSR v 1959 godu.* Moscow, 1960

— *Pechat SSSR v 1960 godu.* Moscow, 1961

— *Pechat SSSR v 1961 godu.* Moscow, 1962

— *Pechat SSSR v 1962 godu.* Moscow, 1963

— *Pechat SSSR v 1963 godu.* Moscow, 1964

— *Pechat SSSR za sorok let 1917-1957* (Forty Years of Publishing in the USSR 1917-1957). Statistical Data. Moscow, 1957

Ministerstvo Finansov SSR, Budghetnoe Upravlenie (Ministry of Finances of the USSR, Budgetary Administration). *Gosudarstvenny byudghet SSSR i byudghety soyuznykh respublik* (State Budget of the USSR and the Budgets of the Union Republics). Statistical Handbook. Moscow, 1962

—*Gosudarstvenny byudghet SSSR i byudghety soyuznykh respublik.* Moscow, 1966

Ministerstvo Vysshego i Srednego Spetsialnogo Obrazovaniya SSSR (Ministry of Higher and Secondary Special Education of the USSR). *Spravochnik dlya postupayushchikh v vysshie uchebnye zavedeniya SSSR v 1967 g.* (Handbook for Entrants of Higher Educational Institutions for 1967). Moscow, 1967

Odessa: Spravochnik (Odessa: A Guide). Odessa, 1957

Tsentralne statystychne upravlinya pry Radi Ministriv Ukrayinskoyi RSR (Central Statistical Administration of the Council of Ministers of the Ukrainian SSR). *Narodne hospodarstvo Ukrayinskoyi RSR v 1964 rotsi* (The National Economy of the Ukrainian SSR in 1964). Statistical Yearbook. Kiev, 1965

Tsentralnoe statisticheskoe upravlenie pri Sovete Ministrov RSFSR (Central Statistical Administration of the Council of Ministers of the RSFSR). *Narodnoe khozaystvo RSFSR v 1963 godu* (The National Economy in the RSFSR in 1963). Statistical Year Book. Moscow, 1965

—*Narodnoe khozaystvo RSFSR v 1964 godu.* Moscow, 1965

—*Narodnoe khozaystvo RSFSR v 1965 godu.* Moscow, 1966

Tsentralnoe statisticheskoe upravlenie pri Sovete Ministrov SSSR (Central Statistical Administration of the Council of Ministers of the USSR). *Itogi vsesoyuznoy perepisi naseleniya 1959 goda* (Totals of the All-Union Population Census, 1959). Summary Volume: USSR, Moscow, 1962

—*Itogi vsesoyuznoy perepisi naseleniya 1959 goda, RSFSR.* Moscow, 1963

—*Itogi vsesoyuznoy perepisi naseleniya 1959 goda, Ukrayinskaya SSR.* Moscow, 1963

—*Kulturnoe stroitelstvo SSSR* (Cultural Development in the USSR). Statistical Handbook. Moscow, 1956

—*Narodnoe khozaystvo SSSR v 1958 godu* (National Economy in the USSR in 1958). Statistical Year Book. Moscow, 1959

—*Narodnoe khozaystvo SSSR v 1959 godu.* Moscow, 1960

—*Narodnoe khozaystvo SSSR v 1960 godu.* Moscow, 1961

—*Narodnoe khozaystvo SSSR v 1961 godu.* Moscow, 1962

—*Narodnoe khozaystvo SSSR v 1962 godu.* Moscow, 1963

—*Narodnoe khozaystvo SSSR v 1963 godu.* Moscow, 1965

—*Narodnoe khozaystvo SSSR v 1964 godu.* Moscow, 1965

—*Narodnoe khozaystvo SSSR v 1965 godu.* Moscow, 1966

—*Srednee spetsialnoe obrazovanie v SSSR* (Secondary Special Education in the USSR). Statistical Handbook. Moscow, 1962

—*Vysshee obrazovanie v SSSR* (Higher Education in the USSR). Statistical Handbook. Moscow, 1961

Tsentralnoe statisticheskoe upravlenie RSFSR (Central Statistical Administration of the RSFSR), *Kulturnoe stroitelstvo RSFSR* (Cultural Development in the RSFSR), Statistical Handbook, Moscow, 1958.

VIDAVSKY, L. M. and others. *Spravochnik po pravovym voprosam vysshey shkoly* (Handbook of Questions on Regulations in Higher Educational Institutions). Kiev, 1965

4. Publishers' and Other Book Catalogues

Biblioteka Kyyivskoho derzhavnoho pedahohichnoho instytuta im. O. M. Horkoho (Library of the O. M. Gorky Kiev State Pedagogical Institute). *Byuleten novykh knyzhok oderzhanykh bibliotekoyu sichen, 1965 r.* (Bulletin of New Books Received by the Library January, 1965). Kiev, 1965

Derzhavny komitet Rady Ministriv Ukrayinskoyi RSR po presi (State Committee for Publishing of the Council of Ministers of the Ukrainian SSR). *Zvedeny tematychny plan vypusku literatury vydavnytstv Ukrayiny na 1965 rik: Tekhnika, Khimiya, Budivnytstvo, Arkhitektura, Komunalne Hospodarstvo* (Summary of Publications of Literature of Publishers of Ukraine for 1965: Technology, Chemistry, Construction, Architecture, Communal Economy). Kiev, 1964

— *Tematychny plan vydavnytstva Kharkivskoho universytetu na 1965 rik* (Catalogue of Publications of Kharkiv University for 1965). Kharkiv, 1964

Mezhdunarodnaya Kniga (International Book). *Gazety i zhurnaly SSSR na 1967 god* (Newspapers and Magazines of the USSR for 1967). Moscow, 1966

Ministerstvo Kultury SSSR (Ministry of Culture of the USSR). Vsesoyuznaya knizhnaya palata (All-Union House of Books). *Periodicheskaya pechat SSSR, 1917-1949* (Periodical Publications, 1917-1949). Journals and Transactions. Moscow, 1963

Ministerstvo Osvity Ukrayinskoyi RSR (Ministry of Education of the Ukrainian SSR). *Tematychny Plan "Radyanska Shkola" na 1958 rik* (Catalogue of Publications of "Soviet School" for 1958). Kiev, 1959

— *Tematychny Plan "Radyanska Shkola" na 1963 rik.* Kiev, 1963

Ministerstvo Zvyazku URSR, "Soyuzpechat" (Ministry of Communications of the UkrSSR, "Soyuzpechat"). *Kataloh respublikanskykh hazet i zhurnaliv Ukrayinskoyi RSR na 1965 rik* (Catalogue of Republican Newspapers and Journals of the Ukrainian SSR for 1965). Kiev, 1964

Zhurnaly izdalelstva "Prosveshchenie" (Journals of "Prosveshchenie" [Education] Publishing House), Moscow, 1965

5. Journals and Other Periodical Publications

Bilshovyk Ukrayiny (Bolshevik of Ukraine)

Ekonomika Radyanskoyi Ukrayiny (Economy of Soviet Ukraine)

Kommunist (Communist)

Komunist Ukrayiny (Communist of Ukraine)

Litopis knyh (Annual of Books)

Nasha kultura (Our Culture)

Radyanska Shkola (Soviet School)

Russky yazyk v natsionalnoy shkole (The Russian Language in the National School)

Ukrayinska mova i literatura v shkoli (The Ukrainian Language and Literature in School)

Ukrayinska mova v shkoli (The Ukrainian Language in School)

Ukrayinsky istorychny zhurnal (The Ukrainian Historical Journal)

Voprosy filosofii (Problems of Philosophy)
Voprosy istorii (Problems of History)
Voprosy istorii KPSS (Problems of the History of the CPSU)
Voprosy yazykoznaniya (Problems of Linguistics)
Zbirnyk nakaziv ta instruktsiy ministerstva osvity Ukrayinskoyi RSR (Collection of Directives and Instructions of the Ministry of Education of the Ukrainian SSR)

6. Newspapers

Izvestia (News). Moscow
Kultura i Zhyttya (Culture and Life). Kiev
Literaturna Hazeta (Literary Gazette). Kiev
Literaturna Ukrayina (Literary Ukraine). Kiev
Literaturnaya Gazeta (Literary Gazette). Moscow
Pravda (Truth). Moscow
Pravda Ukrayiny (Truth of Ukraine). Kiev
Radyanska Kultura (Soviet Culture). Kiev
Radyanska Osvita (Soviet Education). Kiev
Radyanska Ukrayina (Soviet Ukraine). Kiev
Vechirny Kiev (Evening Kiev). Kiev
Visti (News). Kiev

INDEX

Abashidze, I.V., **29**
Academy of Pedagogical Sciences, **31, 34, 74**
Afghanistan, **179**
Armenia, **5, 29, 37, 130**
Azerbaidzhan, **5, 29, 130, 147**

Balitsky, V.A., **19, 21, 25**
Barudzin, S., **202, 203**
Bazhan, M., **32**
Belgium, **176**
Belorussia, **5, 29, 40, 72, 93, 117, 123**
Beria, L., **23**
Bilodid, I.K., **49, 51, 52, 59, 71, 137**
Bondar, Alla, **51, 52, 61, 85, 86**
Books,
    in libraries, **67-69**
    in Ukrainian, **68**
    reference, **144-147**
Brezhnev, L., **105, 156**

Canada, **179-180, 183**
Central Rada, **12**
Chauvinism, **3, 16, 166**
Chervonenko, S.V., **32**
Chornovil, V., **208**
Chubar, V.Ya., **12, 13**
Collectivization, **19**
Communist International, **16**
Czechoslovakia, **180, 182-183**

Dadenkov, Yu.M., **140, 196, 222, 224**
Declaration of the Rights of the Peoples of Russia, **3**
Demichev, P.N., **200**
Discrimination,
    against higher education in Belorussia, **117**, Moldavia, **117**, Ukraine, **111** ff.
    against secondary special education in Belorussia, **93**, Moldavia, **93**, Ukraine, **92-96**
    against Ukrainian language, **102-103, 136**
    against Ukrainian schools, **75-81, 88, 160**